RENEWALS 458-4574

DATE DUE

GAYLORD			PRINTED IN U.S.A.

Palgrave Studies in European Union Politics

Edited by: **Michelle Egan**, American University USA, **Neill Nugent**, Manchester Metropolitan University, UK, **William Paterson**, University of Birmingham, UK

Editorial Board: **Christopher Hill**, Cambridge, UK, **Simon Hix**, London School of Economics, UK, **Mark Pollack**, Temple University, USA, **Kalypso Nicolaïdis**, Oxford UK, **Morten Egeberg**, University of Oslo, Norway, **Amy Verdun**, University of Victoria, Canada, **Claudio M. Radaelli**, University of Exeter, UK, **Frank Schimmelfennig**, Swiss Federal Institute of Technology, Switzerland

Following on the sustained success of the acclaimed *European Union Series*, which essentially publishes research-based text-books, *Palgrave Studies in European Union Politics* publishes cutting edge research-driven monographs.

The remit of the series is broadly defined, both in terms of subject and academic discipline. All topics of significance concerning the nature and operation of the European Union potentially fall within the scope of the series. The series is multidisciplinary to reflect the growing importance of the EU as a political and social phenomenon. We will welcome submissions from the areas of political studies, international relations, political economy, public and social policy, economics, law and sociology.

Submissions should be sent to Amy Lankester-Owen, Politics Publisher, 'a.lankester-owen@palgrave.com'.

Titles include:

Ian Bache and Andrew Jordan (*editors*)
THE EUROPEANIZATION OF BRITISH POLITICS

Richard Balme and Brian Bridges (*editors*)
EUROPE–ASIA RELATIONS
Building Multilateralisms

Derek Beach and Colette Mazzucelli (*editors*)
LEADERSHIP IN THE BIG BANGS OF EUROPEAN INTEGRATION

Milena Büchs
NEW GOVERNANCE IN EUROPEAN SOCIAL POLICY
The Open Method of Coordination

Dario Castiglione, Justus Schönlau, Chris Longman, Emanuela Lombardo, Nieves Pérez-Solórzano Borragán and Mirim Aziz
CONSTITUTIONAL POLITICS IN THE EUROPEAN UNION
The Convention Moment and its Aftermath

Morten Egeberg (*editor*)
MULTILEVEL UNION ADMINISTRATION
The Transformation of Executive Politics in Europe

Kevin Featherstone and Dimitris Papadimitriou
THE LIMITS OF EUROPEANIZATION
Reform Capacity and Policy Conflict in Greece

Stefan Gänzle and Allen G. Sens (*editors*)
THE CHANGING POLITICS OF EUROPEAN SECURITY
Europe Alone?

Isabelle Garzon
REFORMING THE COMMON AGRICULTURAL POLICY
History of a Paradigm Change

Heather Grabbe
THE EU'S TRANSFORMATIVE POWER

Katie Verlin Laatikainen and Karen E. Smith (*editors*)
THE EUROPEAN UNION AND THE UNITED NATIONS
Intersecting Multilateralisms

Esra LaGro and Knud Erik Jørgensen (*editors*)
TURKEY AND THE EUROPEAN UNION
Prospects for a Difficult Encounter

Paul G.Lewis and Zdenka Mansfeldová (*editors*)
THE EUROPEAN UNION AND PARTY POLITICS IN CENTRAL AND
EASTERN EUROPE

Ingo Linsenmann, Christoph O. Meyer and Wolfgang T. Wessels (*editors*)
ECONOMIC GOVERNMENT OF THE EU
A Balance Sheet of New Modes of Policy Coordination

Hartmut Mayer and Henri Vogt (*editors*)
A RESPONSIBLE EUROPE?
Ethical Foundations of EU External Affairs

Lauren M. McLaren
IDENTITY, INTERESTS AND ATTITUDES TO EUROPEAN
INTEGRATION

Christoph O. Meyer, Ingo Linsenmann and Wolfgang Wessels (*editors*)
ECONOMIC GOVERNMENT OF THE EU
A Balance Sheet of New Modes of Policy Coordination

Daniel Naurin and Helen Wallace (*editors*)
UNVEILING THE COUNCIL OF THE EUROPEAN UNION
Games Governments Play in Brussels

Frank Schimmelfennig, Stefan Engert and Heiko Knobel
INTERNATIONAL SOCIALIZATION IN EUROPE
European Organizations, Political Conditionality and
Democratic Change

Justus Schönlau
DRAFTING THE EU CHARTER

Angelos Sepos
THE EUROPEANIZATION OF CYPRUS
Polity, Policies and Politics

Palgrave Studies in European Union Politics

Series Standing Order ISBN 978–1–4039–9511–7 (hardback) and
ISBN 978–1–4039–9512–4 (paperback)

You can receive future titles in this series as they are published by placing a standing order.
Please contact your bookseller or, in case of difficulty, write to us at the address below with
your name and address, the title of the series and one of the ISBNs quoted above.

Customer Services Department, Macmillan Distribution Ltd, Houndmills, Basingstoke,
Hampshire RG21 6XS, England

The Europeanization of Cyprus

Polity, Policies and Politics

Angelos Sepos

Lecturer in EU/European Politics
University of Newcastle upon Tyne, UK

First published 2008 by
PALGRAVE MACMILLAN

Palgrave Macmillan in the UK is an imprint of Macmillan
Publishers Limited, registered in England, company number
785998, of Houndmills, Basingstoke, Hampshire RG21 6XS.

Palgrave Macmillan in the US is a division of St Martin's Press LLC,
175 Fifth Avenue, New York, NY 10010.

Palgrave Macmillan is the global academic imprint of the above companies
and has companies and representatives throughout the world.

Palgrave® and Macmillan® are registered trademarks in the
United States, the United Kingdom, Europe and other countries.

ISBN-13: 978–0–230–01946–1   hardback
ISBN-10: 0–230–01946–3   hardback

This book is printed on paper suitable for recycling and made from fully
managed and sustained forest sources. Logging, pulping and manufacturing
processes are expected to conform to the environmental regulations of the
country of origin.

A catalogue record for this book is available from the British Library.

A catalog record for this book is available from the Library of Congress.

10   9   8   7   6   5   4   3   2   1
17   16   15   14   13   12   11   10   09   08

Printed and bound in Great Britain by
CPI Antony Rowe, Chippenham and Eastbourne

To Aoife,
And my parents, Gloria and Makis

Contents

List of Tables and Figures

Tables

Figures

Acknowledgements

I would like to thank the editors of the Palgrave European Union Politics Series, particularly Professor Neill Nugent for his incisive and thorough comments and suggestions throughout various stages of the book, and their team Amy Lankester-Owen, Gemma d'Arcy Hughes and Ann Marangos for the copy editing and technical support throughout.

I am also grateful to a number of scholars for their invaluable comments and insights on various chapters of the book, particularly Professor Ulrich Sedelmeier (LSE), Dr Maarten Vink (University of Maastricht), Professor Ben Tonra (University College Dublin), Professor Ian Bache (University of Sheffield) and Professor Robert Ladrech (Keele University). I would also like to thank Gianpiero Torissi for his great assistance in the analysis of economic data and the design of graphs and charts and Talya Sheinkman for her rigorous proof-reading of the manuscript.

I would also like to thank the numerous Cypriot Government officials in Nicosia and Brussels who were kind enough to provide me with the necessary official documents and data as well as share their views, time and insights on the issue.

The book has also benefited from the research and academic environment at various institutions, particularly the European University Institute, the University of Cyprus and the University of Newcastle.

Finally, I would also like to thank my family and friends in Cyprus, as well as the UK and Ireland and particularly Aoife, for her love, support, inspiration, encouragement and patience.

Angelos Sepos
Newcastle upon Tyne
24 March 2008

List of Abbreviations

AA	Association Agreement
AFIS	Automated Fingerprint Identification System
AP	Accession Partnership
AKEL	Ανορθωτικό Κόμμα Εργαζόμενου Λαού or Progressive Party of the Working People
CAP	Common Agricultural Policy
CDI	Centrist Democrat International
CEE	Central and Eastern European countries
CFSP	Common Foreign Security Policy
COREPER	Committee of Permanent Representatives
CSO	Civil Society Organization
DIKO	Δημοκρατικό Κόμμα or Democratic Party
DISY	Δημοκρατικός Συναγερμός or Democratic Rally
EAGGF	European Agricultural Guidance and Guarantee Fund
EC	European Community
ECB	European Central Bank
ECSC	European Coal & Steel Community
EDA	European Defence Agency
EDEK	Κίνημα Σοσιαλδημοκρατών or Social Democrats
EDU	European Democrat Union
EEC	European Economic Community
EMCDDA	European Monitoring Centre for Drugs and Drug Addiction
EMP	Euro-Mediterranean Partnership
EMU	European Monetary Union
ENP	European Neighbourhood Policy
EOKA	Εθνική Οργάνωση Κυπρίων Αγωνιστών or National Organization of Cypriot Fighters
EP	European Parliament
EPC	European Political Cooperation
EU	European Union
EUCD	European Union Christian Democrat Workers
EUROKO	Ευρωπαικό Κόμμα or European Party
EUSC	European Union Satellite Centre
EPP	European People's Party
ERM	Exchange Rate Mechanism

ESDC	European Security and Defence College
ESDP	European Security and Defence Policy
FYROM	Former Yugoslav Republic of Macedonia
GATT	General Agreement on Tariffs and Trade
GDP	Gross Domestic Product
GERD	Gross Domestic Expenditures on R&D
GRECO	Group of states Against Corruption
ICT	Information and Communications Technology
IDU	International Democrat Union
IGC	Inter-Governmental Conference
ISS	European Union Institute for Strategic Studies
MEP	Member of the European Parliament
MOKAS	Unit for Combating Money Laundering
MTCR	Missile Technology Control Regime
NATO	North Atlantic Treaty Organization
NFPOC	National FRONTEX Point of Contact
NGO	Non Governmental Organization
NUTS	Nomenclature of Units for Territorial Statistics
OLAF	European Fund Prevention Office
OSCE	Organization for Security and Cooperation in Europe
OECD	Organization for Economic Cooperation and Development
PASOK	Πανελλήνιο Σοσιαλιστικό Κίνημα or Panhellenic Socialist Movement
PJCCM	Police and Judicial Cooperation in Criminal Matters
QMV	Qualified Majority Voting
RoC	Republic of Cyprus
SIRENE	Supplementary Information Request at the National Entries
SIS	Schengen Information System
TAIEX	Technical Assistance Information Exchange
TMT	Tűrk Mukavemet Teşkilati or Turkish Resistance Organization
TNC	Third Country Nationals
'TRNC'	'Turkish Republic of Northern Cyprus'
UNFICYP	UN Peace-Keeping Force in Cyprus
WTO	World Trade Organization

1
Introduction: Conceptualizing and Theorizing Europeanization

The recent accession of Cyprus[1] to the European Union (EU) makes it timely to examine the impact of the latter on the *polity, policies* and *politics* of the country. What began in the early 1970s as a political strategy to strengthen the country's newly independent status subsequently had an important impact on all dimensions of life in Cyprus. The aim of this book is to provide an examination of this impact on key areas of the country, that is, its executive, legislative and judicial authorities; political parties and public opinion; economy; agricultural and regional policies; foreign policy; and justice and home affairs.

This book will draw primarily from the Europeanization agenda in order to examine this reciprocal relationship between Cyprus and the EU. Other research agendas, such as multi-level governance (Houghe, 1996; Marks *et al.*, 1996; Bache, 1998) and policy networks (Eising & Kohler-Koch, 1999; Bomberg & Peterson, 1999; Peterson, 2004), Europeanization (Radaelli, 2000a, 2004; Caporaso *et al.*, 2001; Heritier, 2001; Knill, 2001; Dyson, 2002; Olsen, 2002; Dyson & Goetz, 2003; Schimmelfennig & Sedelmeier, 2005; Goetz, 2006; Graziano & Vink, 2007) draw significantly from 'grand' and 'meso' level theories of European integration such as neo-functionalism (Haas, 1958, 1975; Lindberg, 1963), liberal intergovernmentalism (Moravcsik, 1993) and neo-institutionalism (March & Olsen, 1984; Hall & Taylor, 1996; Pierson, 1996; Pollack, 2004) as well as from social constructivist approaches (Checkel, 1999; Christiansen *et al.*, 1999; Risse, 2004) in the area. While Europeanization has been criticized for being an amalgam of these theories, its practice of borrowing insights with rationalist and constructivist roots can often be useful in explaining such case studies.

Definition of Europeanization

Since the first use of the term in the 1980s, the concept of Europeanization is becoming increasingly popular. Europeanization is not itself a theory, but a phenomenon that a range of theoretical approaches have sought to explain. Goetz (2001a: 211) has cautioned that Europeanization can easily become 'a cause [i.e. the EU] in search of an effect [at the domestic level]'. In regards to its actual definition, there are various suggestions in the literature. Ladrech (1994: 69), for example, defines it as an 'incremental process re-orienting the direction and shape of politics to the degree that EC political and economic dynamics become part of the organizational logic of national politics and policy-making. From a similar perspective, Radaelli (2000a: 4) argues that Europeanization consists of processes of (a) construction, (b) diffusion and (c) institutionalization of formal and informal rules, procedures, policy paradigms, styles, 'ways of doing things' and shared beliefs and norms that are first defined and consolidated in the EU policy process and then incorporated in the logic of domestic discourse (national and subnational), political structures and public policies. Other studies have also put emphasis on Europeanization as institutionalization (Stone Sweet *et al.*, 2001) and an interactive process (Goetz & Hix, 2000) while scholars working on the notion of *référentiel* (Muller, 1995) would argue that there is a Europeanization when the EU becomes the *referential* (i.e. the reference point) of domestic political action. From a different perspective, Caporaso *et al.* (2001: 3) define the concept 'as the emergence and development at the European level of distinct structures of governance'. Olsen (2002: 924), provides the broadest definition of Europeanization: changes in external territorial boundaries; the development of institutions of governance at the European level; the penetration of European level institutions into national and subnational systems of governance; the export of European forms of political organization and governance beyond Europe; and as a political project in support of construction of a unified and politically strong Europe. Finally, more simply, Schimmelfennig & Sedelmeier (2005: 7) define Europeanization 'as a process in which states adopt EU rules'.

It is important to note that Europeanization is not synonymous with convergence, harmonization or European integration. The latter concept belongs to the ontological stage of research, that is, the understanding of a process in which countries pool sovereignty, whereas Europeanization is post-ontological, being concerned with what happens once EU institutions are in place and produce their effects (Radaelli, 2000a: 7).

Thus, when examining Europeanization one begins from the notion that there is a process of European integration under way, and that the EU has developed its own institutions and policies over the last fifty years or so. In this sense, Europeanization is not concerned with why and how Member States produce European integration, and whether the EU is more inter-governmental or supranational – rather, it aims to bring domestic politics back into understanding European integration (Radaelli, 2004: 2–3). It is thus argued that integration theories are not well suited to understanding Europeanization as their main puzzle is the explanation of dynamics and outcomes of European integration rather than domestic effects (Börzel, 2004).

Mechanisms of Europeanization

An array of mechanisms of Europeanization have been identified that could be divided on the basis of their theoretical basis, i.e. rationalist or constructivist, and the type of the Europeanization process they induce, i.e. 'top-down' or 'bottom-up'. Rationalist mechanisms are based on the notion of 'optimality', that is, actors follow a certain policy because they believe it would reap the greatest rewards, whereas constructivist mechanisms are based on the notion of 'appropriateness' with actors following a certain policy because they perceive it to be appropriate in terms of their beliefs, ideas and norms. 'Top-down' processes of Europeanization are those that are driven by the EU whereas 'bottom-up' processes are those that are driven by society and local state actors (Table 1.1).[2] Thus, drawing on institutionalism in organizational analysis, Radaelli (2000b) presents the mechanisms of *coercion, mimetism* and *normative pressures* in EU policy diffusion.[3] Knill and Lehmkuhl (1999) distinguish between *institutional compliance* or *positive integration* where the EU prescribes a particular framework, which is imposed on Member States, *changing domestic opportunity structures* or *negative integration* which allows for a redistribution of resources between national actors and *policy framing* or *framing integration* which influences to the point of modifying the beliefs and the common understandings of domestic policy-makers.[4] Other scholars remind us of the *judicial review* as a mechanism of change (Weiler, 1991; Conant, 2001) while others emphasize the *regulatory competition* as triggering domestic change (Majone, 1996).[5] Moreover, Kohler-Koch (1996) highlights subtle – yet crucial – mechanisms that go beyond the issue of the impact of EU policy on the 'balance of power'. Other scholars (Caporaso *et al.*, 2001) have drawn attention to the so-called 'goodness of fit' (i.e. institutional and policy compatibility)

Table 1.1 Typology of mechanisms of Europeanization

	Theoretical origin of mechanism of Europeanization		Actor-induced mechanism of Europeanization	
	Rationalist	Constructivist	EU-driven ('top-down')	State-driven ('bottom-up')
Knill & Lehmkuhl (1999)	Positive Negative	Framing	Positive Negative	Framing
Radaelli (2000b)	Coercion Mimetism	Mimetism Normative pressures	Coercion Normative pressures	Mimetism
Grabbe (2001)	Gate-keeping Benchmarking & monitoring Provision of legislative and institutional templates Aid & technical assistance Advice and twinning	Aid & technical assistance Advice and twinning	Gate-keeping Benchmarking & monitoring Provision of legislative and institutional templates Aid & technical assistance	Aid & technical assistance Advice and twinning
Schimmelfennig & Sedelmeier (2005)	External incentives Lesson drawing	Social learning Lesson drawing	External incentives Social learning	Lesson-drawing

Source: author's compilation.

and 'misfit' between domestic institutions and European policy.[6] By focusing on the 'goodness of fit' these authors draw our attention to *explanatory* factors related to any mechanism of change (Knill, 1998; Knill & Lenschow, 1998; Börzel, 1999; Duina, 1999; Heritier *et al.*, 1996; Caporaso *et al.*, 2001). Furthermore, in a study focusing on the mechanisms of Europeanization used specifically on candidate states, Grabbe (2001) distinguishes five mechanisms that effect change through *conditionality*[7] and the accession process: gate-keeping; benchmarking and monitoring; provision of legislative and institutional templates; aid and technical assistance; and advice and twinning.[8] Finally, in a seminal volume on the impact of Europeanization on the candidate countries of Central and Eastern Europe, Schimmelfennig and Sedelmeier (2005) identified the following mechanisms: (a) a rationalist 'external incentives' model based on the logic of 'consequences', 'optimality', 'cost–benefit analysis', 'carrot or stick' or 'conditionality', which follows the strategy of 'reinforcement by reward'; (b) a constructivist 'social learning' model based on the notion of 'appropriateness'; and (c) a dual rationalist–constructivist 'lesson-drawing' model that can be based on both logics of 'consequences' and 'appropriateness'. More specifically, according to the 'external incentives' model, the EU sets the adoption of its rules as conditions that the Central and Eastern European (CEE) countries have to fulfil in order to receive rewards (i.e. assistance and institutional ties) from the EU. The 'social learning' model focuses on identification of CEE countries with the EU vision and mission, after a process of deliberation and persuasion by the EU of the legitimacy of its rules as key conditions for rule adoption, and where EU identities, norms and values become internalized at the domestic level. The 'lesson drawing' model, drawn from Rose (1991), is a response to domestic dissatisfaction with the *status quo* whereby policy-makers adopt EU rules not because of external incentives but because they believe that these can provide effective solutions to domestic problems and challenges. In the rationalist variant of this model, the learning process is characterized by 'simple learning' that leads to a change in the means but not the ends, whereas its constructivist variant is characterized by 'complex' learning that includes a modification of underlying goals and a change in policy paradigms.[9] The authors make a further key distinction. The 'external incentives' and 'social learning' models are exclusively EU driven, whereas the 'lesson drawing' model is exclusively candidate state driven (Schimmelfennig & Sedelmeier, 2005: 8). It is generally considered that constructivist (or cognitive) models can potentially have more profound and transformative effects than rationalist models, because domestic actors essentially change their mentality, approach, thinking, identity and ultimately long-term preferences, which can have more lasting effects than simply acting on a cost–benefit analysis which has a certain coercive element in it. At the same time, it is useful to note that these models can also be complementary and mutually reinforcing, thus a combination of both ultimately leads to greater transformation. Finally, one can argue that the 'social learning' model can in some cases also be candidate state driven, in the sense that national policy-makers and citizens voluntary adopt EU norms and beliefs because they recognize that these are of higher value to their own.

Processes of Europeanization

The literature above essentially understands Europeanization as a 'downloading' and 'cross-loading' process (Howell, 2004; Major, 2005; Wong, 2007) whereby candidate and Member States download institutions, policies and procedures from the EU, within a context of social learning and lesson-drawing where there is an exchange of ideas, norms, beliefs and traditions but also policy transfer and exchange of 'best practices' between Member States. In other words, the common denominator of those studies is that the independent variable, the cause, is the EU and the dependent variable, the effect, is the state and its institutions, politics and policies. A more neglected – though important – aspect of Europeanization – which somewhat blurs the distinction between cause and effect and independent and dependent variables – is the understanding that there is also an 'uploading' process of Europeanization, where candidate and Member States also project their own institutions, policies and procedures to the EU, thus shaping the general trajectory of European integration in ways that suit their national interests. This 'uploading' process has been identified within the broader EU literature (Wallace, 1971; Katzenstein, 1997; Jeffery & Patterson, 2003) and within the specific Europeanization agenda (Bomberg & Peterson, 2000; Bulmer & Burch, 2001b; Tonra, 2001; Olsen, 2002; Dyson & Goetz, 2003; Börzel, 2003b; Radaelli & Bulmer, 2004; Major, 2005; Wong, 2007). Most of these studies drew empirical evidence from large Member States (e.g. UK and Germany), some of them from small (e.g. Netherlands, Ireland, Denmark) while there is a scarcity of studies on candidate and third countries that focused on this dimension.

The overall understanding from these studies is that Europeanization is a downloading, uploading and cross-loading process where there is a constant, dialectical, and cyclical fueling of institutions, policies, processes,

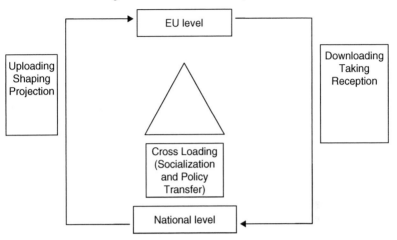

Source: Adapted from Major (2005: 182).

Figure 1.1 Europeanization as a downloading, uploading and cross-loading process

ideas, norms and beliefs between the national and EU level, and between the various national levels. In this process, states download EU institutions, policies and procedures at the domestic level, they upload their national policies, institutions and preferences at the EU level, and they cross-load, that is, learn, mimic and socialize with each other, in the broader EU arena (Figure 1.1).

Dimensions of Europeanization

Another aspect of Europeanization that has drawn attention in the literature is how the territorial and temporal dimensions of a country may affect the impact of these mechanisms and processes, and ultimately the type of its Europeanization experience. These two intervening variables arguably mediate the relationship between Europeanization and its mechanisms and processes of change. The territorial dimensions of a country include its geographical (location, size of territory and population, distance, physical barriers), political/administrative (age of democracy, type of democracy, type of government, type of electoral and party system), economic (Gross Domestic Product [GDP] per capita, openness of economy) and social/cultural/linguistic/historical attributes (including shared memories and identities). Thus, geography can influence transport and migration costs and affect communications and the flow of ideas; its political/administrative structure can influence political relations and attitudes towards integration; its economic structure can affect the types of trade relations, financial flows and patterns of labour mobility; and social/cultural/linguistic/historical attributes can influence the capacity for mutual understanding and speedy transfer of ideas and practices. Terms such as 'families of nations'[10] (Castles, 1993), 'centre and periphery'[11] (Rokkan, 1980, 1999; Meny and Wright, 1985) and 'constellation'[12] (Mouritzen & Wivel, 2005) structures, as well as 'clusters of Europeanization'[13] (Goetz, 2006) seek to encapsulate these territorial dimensions that shape a country's Europeanization experience. Thus, for example, a number of scholars point out how a country's small size[14] may accentuate its peripherality and encourage a distinct Europeanization experience (Katzenstein, 1985; Knudsen & Clesse, 1996; Svetlicic, 1997; Goetschel, 1998; Wallace, 1999; Milward, 2000; Thorhallsson, 2000; Amstrong & Read, 2002; Thorhallsson, 2006). In particular, they point to common experiences in terms of their greater dependence than large states, on market economies and supranational institutions (e.g. the Commission), weaker but also more informal and flexible public administrations, limited bargaining leverage at the EU level and a tendency to prioritize specific policy areas (e.g. agriculture, regional policy).[15] Similarly, other scholars point to how a country's southern-Mediterranean status accentuates a distinct Europeanization experience (La Spina & Sciortino, 1993; Aguilar Fernandez, 1994; Pridham & Cini, 1994; Pridman, 1996; Morlino, 1998; Taggart, 1998; Diamandouros & Gunther, 2001; Featherstone & Kazamias, 2001; Pinto & Texeira, 2002; Royo & Manuel, 2003; Falkner *et al.*, 2005; Lucarelli & Radaelli, 2005). In particular, they point out the existence of a 'Mediterranean syndrome' defined by these countries' economic development and social stratification as a consequence of late industrialization, their relatively greater importance on agriculture and services, their financial dependence on EU development aid, their weak bargaining strength and ability to shape EU institutions and policies, their weak public administrations and poor implementation records, their weak and individualistic civil societies and capital, their fragmented party-dominated policy processes, their tendency for corruption and clientelism and their relative absence of popularly based or party Euroscepticism.[16] Thus, on the basis of these insights one can indentify in Europe territorial constellations of small versus large, south versus north and core versus peripheral states.

The temporal dimensions of a country can also significantly affect a country's Europeanization experience. This dimension has four components. It consists of the country's time of accession to the EU in relation to: (a) its domestic political and economic development; and (b) the phase of European integration (cf. Pierson, 1996; Goetz, 2006). It also includes a country's 'temporal rules of governance' that is (c) the temporal rules or inner clocks of its government/administrative structure and (d) the strategic use of temporal governing devices such as calendars, timetables and road maps (Ekengren, 2002; Eder, 2004; Goetz, 2006). In regards to the first time component, accounts of the Southern Europeanization experiences routinely note the interaction between integration, post-authoritarian democratization and socioeconomic modernization in the Greek, Portuguese and Spanish cases (Featherstone & Kazamias, 2001; Pinto & Teixeira, 2002; Royo & Manuel, 2003). Similarly, in the case of the CEE countries, Europeanization and post-communist democratization are equally entangled (Dimitrova, 2004; Pridham, 2005).[17] One can argue there is also an interaction between Europeanization and post-colonial democratization in Cyprus, Malta and Ireland. Much like former authoritarian (Greece, Portugal, Spain) and communist states (CEE states),[18] post-colonial states in Europe, as well as in Africa and Asia, share a certain affinity in terms of their processes of state and nation-building, most of them being problematic and ridden with ethnic conflict, civil war, political turmoil and divisions.[19] Moreover, the political, economic and social fabric of these societies bares the specific imprint and legacy of their former colonial rulers – in the case of Cyprus, imperial Britain. The political and economic development of these countries, government institutions, political culture, identity and citizenship, all bear post-colonial characteristics and have shaped a unique Europeanization experience for these states. Thus, countries emerging from authoritarian, colonial and communist societies face greater adaptation challenges on their path towards the EU than consolidated democracies. Countries in which Europeanization, post-authoritarian, post-communist and/or post-colonial democratization and economic liberalization closely interact are also more likely to find themselves in the position of policy-takers rather than policy-shapers, not least because they lack the strong domestic institutional foundations of consolidated democracies.

Another commonality of these states is that they have been part of agrarian and predominantly catholic and orthodox Europe that was slow in reforming its traditions, as opposed to the 'fast' countries of the industrial and protestant Europe of the Northwest which were engaged in the Reformation process. These 'slow' European counties are 'laggards' and followers of integration initiatives and are reluctant to engage in differentiated integration initiatives such as multi-speed and variable geometry

Europe in order to realize their policy ambitions. They are characterized by anticipatory, adaptive and 'downloading' Europeanization, and they are generally in the fringes of EU policy-making processes. 'Slow' states are also characterized by immature liberal democracies and weak and inefficient political and economic institutions. In regards to the second time component, the time of a country's accession to the EU in relation to the nature of the Union at the time defined in terms of the prevalent EU policy-making mode also creates a distinct Europeanization experience. Thus, for example, countries that joined the EU at a time when 'integration through law' was the predominant form of EU policy-making, might find it more difficult to reorient their domestic arrangements towards new governance instruments than those that have had to confront a more diverse policy repertoire from the beginning. Similarly, countries that joined the EU during a time when the 'regulatory mode' was prevalent and where domestic costs of integration could be cushioned by large transfer payments are likely to develop different patterns of domestic mobilization than those in which early adaptational costs remained largely uncompensated. With the same logic, countries that joined at a time when the prevalent EU policy-making mode was the 'community method', 'distributional mode' or 'intensive transgovernmentalism' are likely to have different responses to Europeanization.[20] With regards to the third time component, the degree of disparity between the institutional and administrative rhythms – or 'inner clocks' – of countries, that is, the time, sequence and speed with which national institutions and administrations work, between the equivalent EU rhythms may create greater pressures of adaptation for those states. Regarding the fourth time component, the way in which domestic actors make use of temporal devices such as calendars, timetables, road maps and deadlines can speed or slow down Europeanization. For example, the use of these temporal devices can slow or speed up the opening or closing of accession chapters during accession negotiations and the transposition of EU law into domestic law. Hence, on the basis of these insights one can identify temporal constellations of new versus old, slow versus fast and imperial versus post-colonial states.

Aims and method

This book has a dual aim: (a) to indicate the impact of the EU on the polity, policies and politics of Cyprus, as well as the impact of Cyprus on the institutions, policies and procedures of the EU; and (b) to identify the *rationalist* and *constructivist* mechanisms as well as *downloading, uploading* and *cross-loading* processes of Europeanization that have effected this impact in light of the country's *territorial* and *temporal* dimensions. In this process, it will also attempt to synthesize and enhance these mechanisms, processes and dimensions of Europeanization, as well as distinguish alternative rival hypothesis of factors that induce domestic and EU change, such as globalization, democratization, and other internal dynamics and processes.[21]

More specifically, in regards to the first aim, the book identifies the impact of the EU on the executive, legislative and judicial authorities (*polity*), political parties and public opinion (*politics*), and economy, agricultural, regional, foreign and justice and home affairs policies (*policies*) of Cyprus, and vice versa the impact of Cyprus on the major institutions and policies of the EU (e.g. European Monetary Union [EMU], Common Foreign Security Policy [CFSP]/European Security and Defence Policy [ESDP], Police and Judicial Cooperation in Criminal Matters [PJCCM]). In regards to the second aim, it distinguishes empirically the significance of rationalist and constructivist incentives in effecting change in the country. One way to distinguish these different incentive mechanisms is to focus on the details in the policy-making processes and trace specific aspects of the interaction between EU institutions and domestic politics (Andonova, 2005: 139). Thus, when *rationalist* mechanisms are taking place (i.e. within a context of a logic of consequences), there should be greater emphasis on institutional mechanisms such as monitoring, strategic information-sharing, dependency of assistance on particular outcomes, and negotiations of follow-up procedures. When *constructivist* mechanisms are taking place (within the logic of appropriateness) one should notice processes of network-building, capacity-building, framework agreements, and support for transnational expert groups. Furthermore, *downloading* processes of Europeanization are distinguished in the cases of adaptation of EU institutions, policies and procedures at the national level; *uploading* in the cases of projection of policy preferences at the EU level and shaping of EU institutions, policies and procedures; and *cross-loading* in the cases of policy transfer to and from other Member States as well as in mutual exchange of norms, ideas, beliefs and traditions within the EU arena. Finally, the role of the country's *territorial* (small, southern, peripheral and distant) and *temporal* (new, slow, post-colonial) dimensions in impacting the functioning of these mechanisms and processes can be distinguished by a comparative analysis with the Europeanization experiences of countries with the exactly opposite characteristics.

In order to achieve these goals, the book follows a methodological approach that combines both quantitative and qualitative methods. Thus, the quantitative approach will be useful for instances where the impact of Europeanization can be measured on the basis of numerical data (e.g. impact on economy, agriculture, regional policy, public opinion) whereas the qualitative approach (i.e. interviews, official documents) will be useful for instances where Europeanization cannot be measured exclusively on such data (e.g. impact on government, foreign policy). The qualitative approach will also be particularly useful in identifying the various mechanisms of Europeanization that have effected change in the country, as well as these downloading, uploading and cross-loading processes. Thus, for example, in order to document the various motivations for policy change and policy outcomes, one has to examine officials' personal statements and official documents (government and parliamentary records at both the national and EU levels), while also searching for gaps or disconnects among rhetoric, stated motivation, material interests, and policy outcomes (Andonova, 2005). For example, the adoption of EU norms despite recognized failures of financial assistance or rule adoption exceeding formal EU requirements may indicate strong influence of 'social learning' and 'lesson drawing'. By contrast, evidence of little policy action in support of principles embraced rhetorically or the reversal of internationally promoted principles as a result of a change in the strategic environment or material interests will indicate a weak impact of transnational learning and norm diffusion.

Literature review

The overwhelming majority of studies on the relation between Cyprus and the EU have focused on the impact of the latter on the Cyprus problem (Nugent, 2000; Diez, 2002; Baier-Allen, 2004; Tocci, 2004; Christou, 2004; Eralp & Beriker, 2005; Richmond, 2006) while others have also touched upon this issue through their overall examination of the Cyprus conflict (Joseph, 1997; Kramer, 1997; Brewin, 2000; Theophanous, 2000; Green & Collins, 2003; Richter & Fouskas, 2003) and in comparative studies assessing the role of the EU in conflict resolution (Coppieters *et al.*, 2004; Diez *et al.*, 2006; Tocci, 2007). This important issue is not the focus of this book, although it is inevitably addressed in the historical chapters and the Europeanization of the country's foreign policy. Another volume (Stefanou, 2005) focused on the transposition of the EU *acquis* into Cypriot national law, a process commonly referred to as harmonization. Again, this is not the focus of this volume – harmonization and Europeanization are distinct terms (Radaelli, 2000a: 6). Rather, the book's distinctive contribution is that it aims to offer the first systematic examination of the impact of the EU on the polity, policies and politics of Cyprus, and vice versa, by drawing from both *rationalist* and *constructivist* mechanisms and *downloading, uploading* and *cross-loading* processes of Europeanization while also assessing how the country's *territorial* and *temporal* dimensions have mediated the impact of these mechanisms and processes. In this process, it ultimately aims to synthesize and enhance these mechanisms and processes of Europeanization and assess their applicability to other countries with particular *territorial* and *temporal* dimensions, whether inside or outside the EU.

Organization

The book is structured as follows: Chapter 2 examines the process of the creation of modern Cyprus and how various European and other imperial powers have shaped the country's political, economic and social fabric and defined the country's turmoil-ridden history. Chapter 3 examines the evolution of Cyprus' relations with the EU explaining the context under which the country gradually integrated into the European Community (EC)/EU, the strategies employed to achieve that, as well as the position of various European powers and EU institutions on the country's bid for membership. Chapter 4 examines the impact of Europeanization on the executive, legislative and judiciary authorities in Cyprus. The chapter also examines the workings and pitfalls of the country's national coordination of EU policy system involving the three levels of governance. Chapter 5 examines the impact of Europeanization on the Cypriot political parties and public opinion. It provides a historical analysis of the Cypriot party system and examines reforms in terms of the parties' policy/programmatic content, organizational structures, patterns of party competition, party-government relations and relations beyond the national party system. It also addresses the cohesive impact of the process of Europeanization on the parties and further reforms required in the institutions, practices, norms and behaviours of these political parties in order to help their constituencies meet the challenges of the new European environment. The second part examines diffuse and specific support of the Cypriot public towards the EU and its institutions and policies. Chapter 6 analyses the impact of Europeanization on the structure of state–economy relations as well as the nature of the country's economy. It provides a historical analysis of the state of the Cypriot economy and focuses on reforms in the domestic markets, state institutions, macroeconomic fiscal and monetary policy as well as changes in the country's trade patterns as a result of market liberalization. It also examines past and ongoing reforms to prepare the country for its participation in the euro and the Lisbon process. Chapter 7 examines the impact of Europeanization on the agricultural and regional policy regime of the country. The first part analyses the historical importance of the agricultural sector for the Cypriot economy as well as the structural reforms that have occurred in this sector from the adoption of the EU's Common Agricultural and Fisheries Policies. The second part analyses the territorial and institutional reforms which have taken place for the purpose of absorbing the EU's structural and cohesion funds, the impact of these funds on the economy as well as further reforms that are required to increase the absorption and management capacity of the state. Chapter 8 examines the impact of Europeanization on the foreign policy of the country. It focuses on the impact of the CFSP/ESDP on the institutions and nature of the Cypriot foreign policy, with emphasis on its relations with the principle actors of the Cyprus conflict, that is, the Turkish-Cypriot community, Turkey, Greece and the UK, as well as its relations with other major EU Member States and world powers such as the US, Russia and China, as well as states in the EU's neighbourhood. Chapter 9 examines the impact of Europeanization on the country's justice and home affairs policy. It focuses on the various reforms that have taken place as a result of the adoption of the various provisions of the Schengen *acquis*, including in the areas of external borders, immigration, organized crime and drug trafficking, terrorism, corruption, judicial cooperation in civil and criminal matters and human rights. Finally, the conclusion assesses the overall impact of Europeanization on Cyprus and examines the interrelation of these mechanisms, processes and dimensions of Europeanization while also assessing their implication to other countries, whether inside or outside the EU.

2
The Making of Modern Cyprus: An Overview

Europe and Cyprus

In order to examine the relationship of Cyprus with the EU, it is important first to provide a historical overview of the relationship of the country with Europe. The latter is a contested concept, however – partly because 'it has forever been in a process of invention and reinvention as determined by the pressure of new collective identities' (Delanty, 1995: 1). It means different things to different people in different contexts and it is thus difficult to conceptualize it. Efforts towards this goal have been to define Europe along various dimensions as: (a) an idea – linked with the pursuit of values of freedom, democracy, autonomy, unity and diversity; (b) an identity – linked with common social, cultural (including religious) and/or historical attributes (including shared memories); and (c) a reality – linked with the EU polity and its geo-political region with geographical boundaries potentially expanding up to the Ural mountains. These are again contested concepts. For example, it has been argued that the European idea has actually reinforced rather than undermined the ideology of nationality (and nationalism) and hence contributed to divisions rather than unity (Delanty, 1995: 8). Also, as early as the 5th century BC, philosophers such as Herodotus saw no fixed geographical boundaries for Europe (Pagden, 2002: 36), while the identification of the continent with Christendom became widely contested after the 15th century with the march of the Ottoman Empire towards the west. Nevertheless, the conventional wisdom is that Europeans share a Greco-Roman heritage characterized by commonalities in all forms of human governance, that is, language, politics, education, philosophy, science and the arts. Part of this heritage are notions such as reason, science and rationality, the values of individual freedoms and rights, and the associated notions of classical liberalism and democracy, which originated in Ancient Greece and were later enhanced by intellectuals of the Enlightenment Period and the French Revolution in the 18th century.

Cyprus has been part of this heritage on many levels. First, the anthropological and ethnic origin of the country descends from the Myceneans, who first settled the island in the 16th century BC spreading the Greek language and culture to the indigenous population. The island was also controlled by other European cultures such as the Romans (58 BC–AD 395), the Byzantines (395–1191), the English Crusaders (AD 1191), the French Lusignans (1192–1489) the Venetians (1489–1571) and the British Empire (1878–1960) who brought their own customs and traditions and influenced the fabric of the island's society. It was also conquered by non-European cultures such as the Assyrians and Egyptians (8th–7th century BC), Persians (6th century BC), the Arabs (AD 649–965) and the Ottoman Empire (1571–1878). The island's geo-strategic position in the Eastern part of the Mediterranean, a cross-road between Europe, Asia/Middle East and Africa, made it an attractive – and due to its small size – easy acquisition and base for military and trading purposes. Nevertheless, throughout these periods, the local population retained for the most part its Greek Christian Orthodox culture with the Church playing a decisive role in maintaining the cohesiveness of this identity. At the same time, these foreign controls also brought settlements from other ethnic cultures such as the Maronites, Latins and Armenians and mainly Muslims descendants of the Ottoman Empire.[1]

Ottoman and British rule in Cyprus (1571–1959)

These foreign powers left their imprint on the country's political, economic and social characteristics. Thus, for example, as a result of the Ottoman Rule, the island did not participate in the liberalization and modernization process that took place in Western Europe and which resulted from the Enlightenment and the French revolution in the 18th century. The aforementioned notions of reason, science and rationality, the values of individual freedoms and rights, and the associated notions of classical liberalism and democracy belatedly reached the island. Also, the Ottoman *millet* system which allowed religious authorities to govern their non-Muslim populations, significantly strengthened the political and economic[2] role of the Orthodox Church in Cypriot society, making its Archbishop the *Ethnarch* (Εθνάρχης) or leader of the Greek-Cypriot population. Thus, a century later, Archbishop Makarios was not only the leader of the de-colonization struggle but also the first

President of the Republic upon its independence in 1960. And today the Church is one of the most powerful economic institutions in the country with significant involvement in national and state affairs, influencing government appointments, having a strong voice on 'national issues' (εθνικά θέματα) and even suggesting the endorsement of presidential candidates.[3] Moreover, the dominant clientelistic structures in Cypriot society can also be traced in this era. The Ottoman *muchtar* system allowed the elected village headman (or *muchtar*) to serve as the leader and patron of the local Christian population – as well as an actor of Ottoman repression in case of disobedience – thus defining a patron-client structure which persisted and spread horizontally and vertically in society and politics in the post-Ottoman era.[4]

British rule had a significant impact on these dimensions of the country.[5] The early British policies between 1878 and 1931 significantly reformed the administration, institutions, laws and economy of the island. While many of these reforms were positive (e.g. a reliable administrative system, stable currency, improvements in health and education), many were in direct opposition to local customs and traditions, and antagonized the traditional authority and legitimacy of the church[6] as well as the wider strata of the population, namely the peasants and the emerging urban middle class. This inevitably created strains among the local population that provided for the dynamic growth of an anti-British movement (Markides, 1977: 6). In particular, major issues of contention up until 1930 regarded the composition and decision-making practices of the British-established Legislative Council whereby British officials and Turkish-Cypriot representatives could outvote the Greek-Cypriot majority on any measure, curbing the traditional powers of the Greek Orthodox Church, as well as the widely unpopular Tribute that employed a double tax on the Cypriots and that was used to service a debt previously incurred by the British in the days of the Ottoman rule.[7]

These antagonisms found their voice in the *Enosis* (*Ενωσης*) or Unification movement which called for the union of the island with the Greek mother-land. The movement originated as early as 1821–29 when Greek-Cypriot bishops and clergy-men voiced their support for the Greek independence movement and called for the unification of the island with the mother-land only to be crushed by the Ottoman rulers. The notion of *Enosis* was also in sync with the Greek nationalistic notion of *Megali Idea* (*Μεγάλη Ιδέα*) or Great Idea developed in the 1880s and which called for the unification of all Greek-Orthodox territories in the region. These calls for unification resurfaced in October 1931 from the Bishop of Kition – which subsequently led to mass riots against the

British Government House in Nicosia. Riding the tide of decolonization trends, the Greek-Cypriots reactivated their struggle in the late 1940s. In 1948, the Greek Orthodox Church rejected the British Constitutional Plan proposing limited self-government through a Consultative Assembly; and in 1950, backed by the communist party Progressive Party of the Working People (AKEL), it called a plebiscite on the question of *Enosis*, whereby 96 per cent of the exclusive Greek-Cypriot turnout voted in favour. During this time, Greece supported the cause and brought the case of Cypriot self-determination to the UN in August 1954 (Stefanidis, 1999: 66). It was perceived at that time by Greek diplomatic circles that such a demand would have been more acceptable by the international community rather than that of *Enosis*, though the latter remained the ultimate goal. It was perceived by Greek-Cypriot leaders that once self-determination was achieved, the goal of *Enosis* could have been engineered through a nation-wide referendum. In June 1958, British Prime Minister Harold Macmillan presented a 'partnership' plan for Cyprus that essentially entailed the sharing of administration of the island – a system of 'triple condominium' – by Greece, Turkey and the UK.[8] The plan was quickly rejected by Makarios and the Greek government and, critically, those developments also urged him to shift his policy of *Enosis* via self-determination, to that of an independent state, as he perceived the Macmillan plan as an 'Anglo-Turkish collusion' for the 'de facto' division of the island (Stephens, 1966: 150–66).

During the earlier years of British rule, there was no evidence of inter-communal conflict between the Greek and Turkish-Cypriot communities. Indeed, there was an underlying tension between the two communities stemming from differences in terms of religion, language and culture but that tension was never manifested into a political or ethnic conflict. This occurred when the Greek-Cypriot desire for *Enosis* became more pronounced throughout the years combined with the opposite determination of the Turkish-Cypriot community to avoid such a scenario. However, the British policy of non-relinquishment of Cyprus[9] coupled with its universal colonial policy of 'divide and rule' (also applied in other countries such as India) which pitted the two communities against each other and then assumed the role of the arbitrator, clearly exacerbated and spurred these tensions. Indeed, until the mid-1940s, Turkey and the Turkish-Cypriots remained largely oblivious to Greek and Greek-Cypriot objectives (Tocci, 2004: 45). The British, who saw the *Enosis* movement threatening their presence in the island strongly encouraged Turkey and the Turkish-Cypriot community to counter-mobilize in order to prevent Greek and Greek-Cypriot objectives.

Indeed, the British clearly played the Turkish and Turkish-Cypriot card in their favour (Attalides, 1979; Ertekún, 1981; Tocci, 2004). The British presence in the island was thus legitimized in the eyes of the local popula-tion and the international community as being necessary to ensure that the equal rights between the two ethnic groups were preserved. In reality, however, British elites favoured a tense and conflictual bi-ethnic rela-tionship, as it would justify their presence as an arbitrator in the island. Indeed, the British throughout the years 'ruled the island through the Greek, Turkish and other communities, rather than Cypriots' (Horton-Kelling, 1990: 7). This would ensure the persistence of a weak Cypriot identity that would undermine any possible decolonization movement.

That movement, however, did come into existence with the creation of the Greek-Cypriot nationalist organization *EOKA* (*Εθνική Οργάνωση Κυπρίων Αγωνιστών*) or National Organization of Cypriot Fighters in the early 1950s, whose political wing was headed by Archbishop Makarios and military wing by Georgios Grivas – a Cyprus born colonel of the Greek army.[10] Its main aim was the expulsion of British troops from the island and union with Greece. On the opposite side, there was the establishment in 1958 of the Turkish-Cypriot paramilitary organization TMT (Túrk Mukavemet Teşkilati) or Turkish Resistance Organization – led by former 'President' of the 'TRNT' Rauf Dentkas – which on the one hand, cooperated closely with the British forces to suppress the *Enosis* movement, and on the other, articulated its own counter-position of *Taksim* or partition of the island into Greek-Cypriot and Turkish-Cypriot zones.[11] During the struggle the British intensified their 'divide and rule' policies within the broader civilian Cypriot population adding to further polarization of the two communities. Thus, Greek-Cypriot labour employed in the bases were replaced by Turkish-Cypriot labour, and special and ethnically segregated police units were created (Panayiotopoulos, 1999: 40).[12]

After a five year (1955–59) EOKA guerilla warfare campaign, Britain, Greece and Turkey and the leaders of the Greek-Cypriot and Turkish–Cypriot communities, Archbishop Makarios and Fazil Kutchuk respec-tively, signed the Zurich–London Agreements in February 1959. The Agreements led to three associated treaties: The Treaty of Establishment, the Treaty of Alliance and the Treaty of Guarantee. The first provided for the establishment of an independent state (on 16 August 1960) with consociational characteristics aimed to accommodate the ethnic diver-sity of the island,[13] as well as two British sovereign bases in the island;[14] the second provided for security cooperation among Cyprus, Greece and Turkey, including the stationing of military forces from the latter two, in order to preserve the peace in the island; and the third, more controversially, provided for a guaranteeship from Britain, Greece and Turkey for the continuation and maintenance of the constitution and the independence and territorial integrity of the island. This latter Treaty effectively provided the right to these powers to militarily intervene in order to restore a disruption of the constitutional order.

It is important to indicate that the Cyprus' decolonization struggle shared significant similarities – but also differences – with other such movements in Europe (e.g. Ireland), Africa (e.g. Nigeria, Sierra Leone, Uganda), and Asia (e.g. India/Pakistan). All of these post-colonial states were ridden with ethnic conflict, civil war, political turmoil and divisions and generally problematic processes of state-formation and nation-building following their decolonization struggles.[15] In particular, Cyprus shared considerable similarities with the former British colonies of Ireland and India, both of which were partitioned at the end of colonization. In all three cases, there was a triangular relationship between the nationalist majority (i.e. Catholics in Ireland, Hindu in India, Greek-Cypriots in Cyprus), who cherished the theory of one nation and sought to restore or establish its independence as a unit; the minority (i.e. Protestants in Ireland, Muslims in India, Turkish-Cypriots in Cyprus), which when faced with the prospect of rule by the majority community, formulates a two-nation theory, or its near-equivalent; and the imperial power (i.e. Britain) predisposed to holding the balance, but only for so long as that might be to its own advantage, within the limits of its resources and consistent with its image of its world role (Mansergh, 1997: 34–5). Also, as evident in the cooperation between the Turkish-Cypriot and British forces, in this triangular pre-transfer of power situation, there was 'a tendency for the second and third parties, the minority and the outgoing imperial power, to be drawn together in resistance to the demands of the first, the majority nationalist party' (Mansergh, 1997: 48). But there was an important difference between the Cyprus struggle and that of India and Ireland. Unlike those movements, the desire for freedom in Cyprus was not articulated as a demand for independence but for *Enosis* or unification with the mother-land, Greece. This was a unique situation in that the nationalist majority of the colony (i.e. Greek-Cypriots) shared the same ethnicity with another country (Greece) and was encouraged – on the basis of the notion of *Megali Idea* – to depend on its support for the success of the movement. In that sense, the *Enosis* movement owed a significant debt to nineteenth century European irredentism (Stefanidis, 1999: 230) as well as to the anti-colonialism movement in the mid-twentieth century. This articulation of the goal of

Enosis meant that the movement acquired an exclusively Greek-Cypriot characteristic making no recognition of Turkish-Cypriot national aspirations and indeed implied their suppression (Panayiotopoulos, 1999: 40). This lack of unity that characterized the Cypriot movement – though manifested differently as indicated above – was very much a common feature in the Irish and Indian struggles characterized by inherent tensions between the different ethnic groups in these countries. Indeed, as Masnergh (1997: 36) points out referring to the Irish case, 'the pursuit of autonomy without prejudice to unity was not, and is not, psychologically an easy assignment as many others in Europe, Asia and Africa were also to learn'. This structural inability of the two Cypriot communities to rally together, stemming from their inherent tensions linked to difference in ethnicity, language and religion, and exacerbated by the British 'divide and rule' policies, ultimately weakened the movement resulting in the subsequent division of the island and the maintenance of British bases and influence in the island. Overall, one can argue that both Ottoman and British colonialism, not only left its imprint in the country's institutions, political culture, economy, social character and demographics but also defined the nature of relations between the existing ethnic groups with all the subsequent consequences for the future of the country.

Post-independence Cyprus (1960–)

The post-independence period of Cyprus was also shaped by these legacies. There was significant tension and disagreements between the two communities over the establishment of these agreements. Much of the Greek-Cypriot population, particularly those who actively took part in the EOKA struggle, saw the Zurich-London Agreements as a betrayal of the cause of *Enosis* and 'the lesser of two evils', that is, the partition of the island into two separate ethnic zones. There was also the outcry that the Cypriot constitution violated the self-determination of the Cypriot people as it did not emanate from them, having not been ratified in a referendum or the Parliament (Tornaritis, 1979: 32; Constantinou, 2006: 298). Others, however, point out that while the process of self-determination and independence may not have been the usual one (i.e. by a plebiscite), the very process of factual devolution of sovereignty from the colonial power to the new Cypriot state should be considered as an exercise of this right – an identical process that took place in other decolonized states as well (Crawford, 1979: 101; Chrysostomides, 2000: 58–9).

This ambiguity in the 1960 constitution on the conception and perception of Cypriot citizenship and identity further complicated an already conflicted Cypriot identity that aimed to reconcile the uneasy relationships between the two communities and their respective motherlands, as well as between themselves. The conflicting Cypriot identity rested in the ambivalence within the Greek-Cypriot and Turkish-Cypriot psyches between, on the one hand, the strong identification with Greek and Turkish nationalisms and the respective goals of unification with the motherlands (i.e. 'the primordial attachment'), and on the other, the reluctant identification with Cypriotness and the ensuing reality of independence.[16] These ambiguous and conflicting perceptions of Cypriot identity later had important implications for both communities in regards to its relation and response to European identity and citizenship.[17] Once the new state began functioning, grievances soon emerged in the Greek-Cypriot population over the consociational polity. In particular, the Greek-Cypriots resented the constitutional provision of the 7:3 ratio accorded to the two communities in the executive and public administration arguing that it did not reflect the demographic realities of the island, unfairly over-representing the Turkish-Cypriots. Also, there was frustration over continuous deadlocks in decision-making emanating from separate legislative majorities and presidential veto rights, as well as over general inefficiency stemming from the costly duplication of positions and functions in the legislature and the executive (Kyriakides, 1968: 143). Finally, there was an underlying suspicion from the Greek-Cypriots that Turkish-Cypriot officials were purposefully sabotaging the functioning of the polity in order to provide Turkey with an excuse to intervene.

In November 1963, Archbishop Makarios sought to address these grievances by proposing to amend the Constitution on thirteen points, including presidential vetoes, separate legislative majorities, the separate municipalities and the distinctions based on ethnicity made in courts. He also proposed the re-scaling of ethnic ratios in the civil service, the police and military according to population ratios. His efforts were motivated partly from addressing real problems in the functioning of the new consociational polity (i.e. decision-making deadlocks, inefficiencies) as well as appeasing his domestic opponents who accused him of capitulating on the issue of *Enosis* and minority rights for the Turkish-Cypriots (Clerides, 1989: 130). In retrospect, in spite of Makarios' well documented failings, one has to acknowledge that he was confronted with an extremely difficult, if not impossible, task and responsibility of reconciling two divided communities with conflicting interests, building a bi-ethnic nation and consolidating independence, while at the same time negotiating and dealing with the interests and power-struggles between the UK, Greece, Turkey as well as the US and USSR. In any event, his proposals spurred a wave of protests from the Turkish-Cypriots who perceived these amendments as a reduction of their political equality guarantees, and a progression towards the creation of a unitary state with minority rights for their community. The revelation at the time of the existence of a secret 'Akritas Plan', formulated by Minister of Interior Polycarpos Yorgadjis, aiming to forcefully suppress Turkish-Cypriot resistance to these amendments, though never implemented, further exacerbated insecurities within the Turkish-Cypriot community. The constitutional crisis led to an outbreak of violence between 1963 and 1967 with mutual attacks, atrocities and many casualties from both communities, with former EOKA and Turkish Resistant Organization (TMT) members driving the conflict, and with Greek and Turkish forces actively participating in the violence.[18] Bi-communal contacts at this point ceased to exist with the Turkish-Cypriots withdrawing from the government in 1963 setting up their own Provisional Turkish Cypriot Administration in 1967 in order to govern their community confined in various enclaves throughout the island.[19] In December 1963, a Turkish-Cypriot crowd clashed with Yorgadjis plainclothes agents and almost immediately Greek-Cypriot paramilitaries attacked the Turkish-Cypriot Omorphita suburb of Nicosia. In March 1964, the first UN peace-keeping force in Cyprus (UNFICYP) was introduced – it still remains today – but that failed to stop the violence.[20] And in August 1964, Grivas – who returned from Greece and took control of Greek forces in the island, including much of the Cypriot National Guard – attacked the Turkish-Cypriot enclave of Kokkina, a major pathway for the deployment of arms from mainland Turkey. Turkey responded with heavy fighter jet bombings of Greek positions in Tyllyria. In 1965 there was a failed attempt to find a political solution through the report of Galo Plaza Lasso, a special UN mediator appointed by UN Secretary General U Thant, who approached the problem in bi-communal rather than international terms (Ker-Lindsay, 2005: 12), criticizing both Greek-Cypriot *Enosis* and Turkish-Cypriot *Taksim*, and proposing a centralized and independent Cyprus with the protection of both majority and minority rights and demilitarization of the island.[21] The proposal was received positively from the Greek-Cypriots but negatively from Turkey and the Turkish-Cypriots who by now strongly supported a federal bi-communal polity. Then in November 1967, Grivas forces attacked the Turkish-Cypriot enclaves of Kophinou and Ayios Theodhoros bringing Turkey and Greece to the brink of war, which was only avoided with US intervention. Turkey responded with an ultimatum to Greece which, persuaded by the US, scaled down its military presence and ensured Grivas' departure from the island in 1968 (Crawshaw, 1986: 6–7; Christou, 2004: 50). At that point, Makarios sought to consolidate his position by reducing the number of National Guard troops (most of them loyal to Grivas) and established his own paramilitary force loyal to the independence cause. Grivas, however, eventually returned for the second time to the island in 1971 and officially formed the right-wing split-off paramilitary organization EOKA B which aimed to pressure Makarios to move away from the independence agenda once and for all and return to the original EOKA idea of *Enosis* – EOKA B eventually played a key role in the events of 1974.

An important factor that exacerbated tensions on the island and further propelled Cyprus towards a permanent division was the ascendancy – by *coup d'état* – in power in April 1967 of the US-backed right-wing military junta in Greece. The Greek colonels pursued a fierce policy of *Enosis* with Cyprus by all available means, including violence towards Greek-Cypriots and Archbishop Makarios who was the subject of several assassination attempts. The Cyprus National Guard, which was made up of Greek officers from the mainland and EOKA extremists, was to play a crucial role under the leadership of Grivas and guidance by the junta in undermining the authority of Makarios, through portraying him as a communist and a traitor to the cause of *Enosis*.

The post-independence period also saw an increased involvement and interest of the US and the USSR in the island's affairs, with the latter becoming part of the Cold War dispute. Following Greece and Turkey's admittance to the North Atlantic Treaty Organization (NATO) in February 1952, the US increasingly saw Cyprus as a potential candidate for membership in the organization, particularly during the peak of the Cold War in the mid-1960s and 1970s. Potentially, it was also a way to pacify the island by giving its two members, Greece and Turkey, a key role in running the transantlantic base in the island. Cyprus was also important to the US in the context of the latter's support for Israel, as an extra western flank to defend Israel in the event of a large-scale attack (Mallinson, 2005: 100) – hence the 1997 triangular US–Turkey–Israel military and defence agreement.[22] Such proposals met with the fierce resistance of Archbishop Makarios, who was eager to preserve the independence and sovereignty of the island and to steer its foreign affairs away from the Cold War rivalry and any foreign involvement. His efforts towards that goal included founding and taking a leading role in the Non-Alliance Movement in the early 1950s, involving the United Nations as much as possible in any dispute, as well as officially keeping a neutral stance towards the two superpowers. In reality, however, Makarios was keen in involving the USSR in the island's affairs, which proclaimed its support for the Republics' self-determination, and which could potentially counterbalance the Anglo-American factor which was perceived as serving the interests of Turkey. Makarios' flirtations with the USSR,[23] his toying with the East–West divide, and the relative strength of the communist AKEL party that supported him, alarmed the US, who saw him as a nuisance in the region and even characterized him as the 'Castro of the Mediterranean' (Mallinson, 2005: 45). Thus, in the summer of 1964, during the height of inter-communal violence, US State Secretary Dean Acheson stepped in and undermined Makarios' vision of independence by proposing the notion of *double Enosis*, that is, the unification of a significant Greek-Cypriot territory with Greece, and concessions to Turkey in the form of military bases and autonomous Turkish-Cypriot enclaves in the north (Tocci, 2004: 54).

The relationship between Makarios and the military dictatorship in Athens reached a breaking point when the Greek-junta organized a military coup against him in 15 July 1974, in close coordination with EOKA B personnel led by Nikos Sampson who was installed by the junta as a *de facto* President of Cyprus.[24] Following the coup, Turkey landed 40,000 Turkish troops near the northern city of Kyrenia on 20 July 1974 capturing a small strip of land around the city with little resistance from the Cypriot National Guard.[25] Turkey invoked Article 4 of the Treaty of Guarantee which allowed a guarantee power to intervene in order to restore the constitutional order in the island. A ceasefire was achieved by the UN on 22 July 1974 and leaders from all parties (i.e. three guarantee powers and two communities) met on 14 August 1974 to discuss a political resolution to conflict.[26] Meanwhile, Sampson resigned and Glafkos Clerides was appointed as acting President of the Republic of Cyprus. Also, following these events and under pressure from Greek public opinion, the Greek military junta collapsed on 23 July 1974 and Constantinos Karamanlis restored democracy in the country. In Geneva, Turkey and the Turkish-Cypriots demanded, non-negotiably, the creation of a bi-zonal federal system with 34 per cent of territory under Turkish-Cypriot control. When President Clerides asked for an adjournment of 36–48 hours for consultations, Turkey – within a few hours – attacked for a second time and occupied 37 per cent of the island.[27] In reality, Turkey, following the constitutional crisis and conflictual events of the previous decade, had no intention of reaching a political solution in Geneva. It did not intend to restore the constitutional order on the basis of the 1960 agreements, but essentially aimed to permanently separate – by further force – the two communities. Hence, its claim to invoke Article 4 of the Treaty of Guarantee was never taken seriously by the United Nations – and the international community – whose numerous Security Council Resolutions condemned the military intervention (353/1974), the maintenance of Turkish forces in the island (353/1974; 367/1975) and the subsequent establishment of the 'TRNC (541/1983)'.[28]

It is also important to indicate the role of the US and Britain during those critical events in 1974. Thus, according to Greek junta colonel Patakos, it was US Foreign Secretary Kissinger who encouraged the regime to organize the *coup d'état* and dispose of Makarios (Hitchens, 1997; Venizelos & Ignatiou, 2002: 431). It has also been revealed that neither of these countries prevented Turkey from attacking the island during both phases of the military operations. Britain's then foreign secretary and soon to be prime minister James Callaghan later disclosed that Kissinger 'vetoed' at least one proposed British military action to pre-empt the Turkish landing. After those events, Callaghan admitted that Britain had had a legal obligation to take action (O'Malley & Craig, 1999: 159). In reality, however, Britain was content to merely express public disaproval and more importantly to ensure that the sovereignty of its military bases was preserved during those events. And the US, preoccupied with the Watergate scandal domestically and Vietnam externally was content to allow its close ally to enforce a *de facto* division on the troubled island. Later on, an unapologetic Kissinger infamously stated that the Cyprus problem was solved in 1974 (O'Malley & Craig, 1999). In the summer of 1974, American Ambassador Davies was assassinated in Nicosia by Greek-Cypriot activists in protest of the perceived American betrayal.[29]

With regards to the European Community (EC), and in light of Cyprus' Association Agreement (AA)[30] in 1972, the French Presidency convened a meeting of the nine Member States at the time in 1974, within the framework of the newly formed European Political Cooperation, and issued démarches and communiqués to Athens and Ankara calling for a ceasefire, on the basis of UN Security Council Resolution 353, and supporting the short-lived Geneva negotiations. As indicated by Nuttall (1992: 119) the 'French Presidency of the EPC took immediate and forcefull action to coordinate the action of the nine' with 'the policy lead given to the UK, happy to secure multilateral support for its efforts in dealing with an intractable problem'. The problem with this strategy, however, was that Britain was not a neutral actor in the conflict, given its role as guarantee power with its own strategic interests in the island and policies broadly aligned with the US, which took a passive, if not encouraging approach towards Turkey's military's intervention. This raised concerns among the Greek-Cypriot side about the neutrality of the EC/British led initiative. Nuttall (1992: 120) indicates that newly democratic Greece's immediate intention to seek membership of the Community and its application being welcomed by a number of Member States led by France, undermined the EC's 'even-handed approach' towards Athens and Ankara and made its initiatives 'less credible to the Turks'. In reality, however, the EC could have never been a neutral actor in the process as long as the policy initiative was surrended to the UK which had its own interest agenda in the confict. Also, the EC could have never been an effective arbitrator given the degree of US influence on the Community's foreign policy. Nuttall indicates (1992: 121) that the EC-9, after failling action on their own, simply resorted to supporting UN mediation and were even attracted in the autumn of 1976 by a 'vague' offer from Henri Kissinger to engage in a coordinated US–EPC initiative, a possibility discussed for some time until the arrival of the Carter administation, only to insist in the end that 'Cyprus should maintain the right to determine freely its foreign policy'. The EC had the option of freezing Cyprus' Association Agreement but that could have been constructive only at the *coup d'état* stages to penalize the Sampson government – once the constitutional order was restored with the Clerides government and following Turkey's military intervention it made no sense to follow that course of action since the perpetrator of international law at that time was Turkey not the Greek-Cypriot government. Indeed, Nuttall (1992: 122) indicates when the Political Committee of the EC met in March 1977 to discuss the status of Cyprus' Association Agreement they pointed out that freezing negotiations for the AA 'would be to administer an unnecessary rebuff to the government of Cyprus' and the only action taken was to ensure that both communities would benefit from the agreement following the *de facto* division of the island. In retrospect, the response of the EC to the 1974 crisis in Cyprus was one of the many other examples at the time of a reactive, toothless and incoherent EC foreign policy during that era, where mediation was left to the US and the UN. It is nonetheless one of the first examples of where the dynamics of the conflict slowly began to penetrate and play out at the EU level.

The political, economic and social consequences on the island as a result of the events of 1974 were grave. Military intervention not only cemented political and physical division between the two communities but also had important consequences on the economy and social fabric of the island. Loss of human life and displacement of population was significant. There were 5000 Greek-Cypriot casualties (of whom 1,619 were reported missing[31]), 160,000–200,000 Greek-Cypriots refugees and 50,000–60,000 Turkish-Cypriots were transferred to the north in an agreed exchange of populations. The economy of the island suffered significantly with the GDP dropping by 17.9 per cent, investment by 29.9 per cent, consumption by 15.2 per cent, imports by 21.3 per cent and exports by 25.2 per cent.[32] Among the consequences of this, was the creation of an underlying class and identity cleavage *within* the two communities, that is, between the dispossessed refugees and those who retained their homes and possessions. More vividly, the division further reinforced the ethnic, religious, linguistic and cultural cleavage between the two communities. Perceptions of 'self' and the 'other' were strengthened and the colonial notion that the two communities are unable to peacefully co-exist without an arbitrator or a dividing line between them became more salient. The division also meant that Europeanization had uneven political, economic and social effects in the two parts of the island, with the south and its legitimate government benefiting from strong and formal institutional contacts with the EU, economic ties and trade with Member States and EU socialization processes as opposed to the north part which did not effectively participate in this process and where EU legislation and the *acquis* is suspended in that part of the island.[33]

Overall, the trauma of war in 1974, as well as the conflictual events that preceded it, created a permanent sense of insecurity of another possible conflict, particularly among the Greek-Cypriot population, which has penetrated and has been reflected in all aspects of life of Cypriot people, and has accentuated the conflictual relationship and deep-rooted divisions between the two communities with, some speculate, irreversible effect. The *status quo* of the *de facto* partition of the island has remained an anathema to those in both communities, as well as the international community, who have sought to find a solution to this intractable problem. Accession to the European Union was one of the means to catalyze the process of political settlement, alleviate this insecurity, mend the relations between the two communities and achieve prosperity for both.

Post-war Cyprus (1974–)

The post-war period was marked by numerous initiatives to find a political solution to the conflict acceptable to both communities, as well as efforts for economic recovery from the war. In regards to the latter, there was remarkable success for the Greek-Cypriot community which, within less than a decade, despite losing the most resource-rich part of the territory, not only recovered but superseded the 1974 growth levels though tourism, construction and sound micro and macro-economic policies, and benefiting by being the only internationally recognized legal entity on the island. In contrast, the Turkish-Cypriot reliance on Turkish aid and its fluctuating economy as well as shaky economic policies, caused the community to suffer economic stagnation and low growth, despite inheriting the resource-rich part of the island. In addition, the Turkish Cypriots were not a recognized political entity, and suffered economic isolation and embargo from both the Greek-Cypriot and international communities. Eventually, many indigenous Turkish-Cypriots emigrated and were replaced by settlers from mainland Turkey.[34] Regarding efforts for a political settlement, initiatives were short lived and unsuccessful in providing a comprehensive solution to the problem, but they did provide the basis upon which current inter-communal discussions are now framed. The 1977 and 1979 High Level Agreements between Archbishop Makarios[35] and Rauf Denktash, and President Kyprianou and Rauf Denktash respectively, were particularly important because 'for the first time, the two communities agreed to seek a settlement on the basis of a bizonal, bicommunal federal Republic' and since then have been perceived as 'an acceptable framework and a basis for the search of a peaceful and lasting political settlement in Cyprus' (Joseph, 1997: 135–6). These agreements also expanded on issues such as respect for human rights, fundamental freedoms for all citizens, the demilitarization of the island and adequate guarantees for the independence, sovereignty and territorial integrity of the Republic. In 1986, UN Secretary General Javier Pérez de Cuéllar presented President Spyros Kyprianou and Rauf Denktas with a Draft Framework Agreement outlining proposals for communal representations in the executive and legislature as well as territorial exchanges. In 1992–93, UN Secretary General Boutros Boutros Ghali presented President Clerides and Rauf Denktash with a 'Set of Ideas' as well as 'Confidence Building Measures' aimed to build on previous executive, legislative and territorial issues within the framework of a bi-communal, bi-zonal polity but also reduce restrictions of contacts between the populations of both communities. Subsequent talks within the UN framework in Troutbeck, New York in July 1997 and Glion-sur-Montreux, Switzerland in August 1997 also failed to produce any comprehensive settlement as the necessary political will for compromise from both sides was lacking. Then in August 1998, the Turkish-Cypriot leader moved away from the notion of a bi-zonal, bi-communal federal polity and proposed a 'confederal' solution and a form of 'partnership' settlement that would recognize the special relationship between Greek-Cypriots and Greece and between Turkish-Cypriots and Turkey. Rauf Denktas' decision was driven by Turkey (Ugur, 2000: 236) but also influenced by the acceptance of Cyprus' candidacy for EU membership (in June 1993) and the beginning of accession negotiations in March 1998, without Turkish-Cypriot representation despite invitations from both the EU and the Greek-Cypriot side. It also stemmed from the fundamental belief within the Turkish-Cypriot community that there are two sovereign people in the island and that any settlement will need to recognize the existence of two states. This was quickly rejected by the Greek-Cypriot leadership – which was further away from its vision of a centralized state – and for a few years negotiations stalled only to be resumed in 2002 with initiatives from the new UN Secretary General Kofi Annan aimed to bring the two communities closer together culminating in his presentation in 11 November 2002 to President Clerides (subsequently replaced by Tassos Papadopoulos after presidential elections in February 2003) and Rauf Denktas of a comprehensive plan for the settlement of the Cyprus conflict. The aim was that a settlement would be reached before affirmation of Cyprus' accession at the Copenhagen European Council in December 2002.[36] The plan was subsequently revised three times[37] until its fifth and final version was presented on 31 March 2004 in Burgenstock, Switzerland. The final version of the Plan foresaw the evolution of the Cyprus Republic into the United Republic of Cyprus, with a different name, flag and national anthem. Borrowing heavily from the Swiss and Belgian federal models, it proposed the construction of a common state with a single sovereignty, consisting of Greek-Cypriot and Turkish-Cypriot component states, with their own legislative and executive powers. The plan foresaw a single Cypriot citizenship, but at the same time it provided the citizen the right to have a citizenship status of one of the two component states (federated states). The common state (federal government) would have competencies on matters such as foreign affairs (including conclusions of international treaties and defence policy), relations with the EU, the functions of the Central Bank, economic (budget, indirect tax-customs) and trade policy, natural resources, communications, federal police, justice and home affairs and antiquities. The component states would be equal between them and *vis-à-vis* the common state. They would have competencies on issues such as education, environment, tourism, health, energy policy, public works and transport, their own police, and the right to sign agreements with other states on cultural and economic issues provided that those do not undermine the authority of the common state. The executive authority would be vested in a Presidential Council consisting of four Greek-Cypriots and two Turkish-Cypriot members, who would elect President and Vice-President among them, one from each community, and on the approval of the Parliament, and who would alternate in their functions every 20 months during the council's five-year term of office.[38] The legislative authority would involve the creation of two chambers, that is, the Upper House (Senate) consisting of an equal number of legislators (24) from each community and the Lower House (Chamber of Deputies) consisting of 48 seats allocated proportionately to the population, with at least one-third of the seats allocated to each component state – for legislation to pass it would require the approval of both chambers. The judiciary would entail a Supreme Court with an equal number of judges from each community (3) and an additional three foreign judges appointed by the Presidential Council (not nationals of the three guarantee powers). In case of decision-making deadlocks in the executive authority, these 9 judges would settle the dispute. On the issue of security, the three guarantee powers, that is, Greece, Turkey and Britain were retained and an equal number of Greek and Turkish soldiers (less then 6000 each) would be based in the island, with provisions for a gradual reduction of those forces in 2018 conditioned on Turkey's accession to the EU. The UNFICYP as well as the sovereign territory of the British bases would also be maintained. In regards to territorial issues, the plan foresaw with two maps a reconfiguration of the territorial authority of the two component states, with the first map providing the Turkish-Cypriot state 28.5 per cent of the island and the second map 28.6 per cent – as opposed to its *de facto* 37 per cent territory. The territorial issue was linked with the reinstatement into possession, whereby limited percentages of refugees would regain possession of their properties. Finally, a Reconciliation Commission would be established, aiming 'to promote understanding, tolerance and mutual respect' between the two communities.[39]

A referendum was held on 24 April 2004 for both communities whereby Greek-Cypriots rejected it with an overwhelming 75.8 per cent majority and Turkish-Cypriots approved it with a 64.9 per cent majority.[40] From the position of the Attorney General of the Republic Alekos Markides on the first draft of the Plan,[41] as well as from a population survey conducted during the time,[42] it is revealed that the Greek-Cypriot 'No' was strongly influenced by the plan's perceived inadequacies on the aspects of security[43] and withdrawal of Turkish forces,[44] property,[45] settlers,[46] power-sharing[47] and arbitration mechanisms,[48] residency and return of refugees,[49] territory[50] and potential negative economic consequences[51] – particularly on the lower social classes – resulting from re-unification. Also, while the Attorney-General stressed that the Plan foresaw the evolution and not the dissolution of the Cyprus Republic – a key concern of the Greek-Cypriot community as the latter implies the coming together of two sovereign states and thus the legitimacy of the 1974 military intervention and partition – its reference to 'a new state of affairs' and the symbolic significance of the new name, flag and national anthem raised anxieties among the population and reinforced the opposite perception. These concerns were manifested in the lack of support from President Papadopoulos and his ruling party centre-right Democratic Party (DIKO) as well as other parties of the governing coalition, left-wing AKEL[52] and the Social Democrats (EDEK), a strong majority of the population, including most of the 1974 refugees. The right-wing Democratic Rally (DISY) and its historical leader former President Glafkos Clerides supported the plan – though the majority of its constituency ended up voting against it – while the small centre-left United Democrats party headed by former President George Vassiliou was the only party whose leadership and constituency both supported it. In contrast, the Turkish-Cypriot 'Yes' was influenced by the prospect of EU membership through reunification and perceived political and economic benefits for the community, the strong acceptability of the plan's power-sharing provisions and security guarantees with the involvement of Turkey. In particular, accession via acceptance of the plan would provide the Turkish-Cypriot community an equal standing in the representative institutions of the Union and help stabilize its fluctuating economy with the EU's fiscal and monetary instruments, structural and cohesion funds and access to the European and international markets. Also, in regards to power-sharing the Plan satisfied a key concern of the Turkish-Cypriot community, that of political equality and the right to veto executive decisions of the federal government, thus easing fears of potential political domination from the Greek-Cypriot majority. The provision of the prolonged maintenance of Turkish forces and their conditional withdraw depending on Turkey's accession to the EU also provided the community a security guarantee in case there was a constitutional breakdown in the new polity, and also promoted the strategic interests and European aspirations of the Turkish motherland. Also, the reference in the Plan to the creation of 'a new state of affairs' and the symbolic significance of a new flag, national anthem and name of the emerging polity provided the Turkish-Cypriot community a significant sense of disassociation from the Republic of Cyprus (RoC) – perceived by the Turkish-Cypriots as having ceased to exist in 1963 when they departed from the government and being associated with the atrocities of 1963–74 (Tocci, 2004: 58). While the historical leader of the community, Rauf Denktash and his centre-right ruling party the National Unity Party, consistently opposed the plan, other major parties such as the left-wing Republican Turkish Party led by Mehmet Ali Talat, as well as the majority of the Turkish-Cyprus population supported it. In regards to the guarantee powers, Greece, through its Prime Minister Costas Karamanlis, cautiously supported the plan 'whose positives out-weigh the negatives' though he emphasized that Greece would respect any decision by the Greek-Cypriot people in accordance with the principle 'Cyprus decides and Greece supports'.[53] Turkish Prime Minister Recep Tayyip Erdogan actively supported the Plan urging the Turkish-Cypriots to vote in favour, while the UK was also strongly in favour of it being one of the key constructors of the plan. The 2004 referendums marked the first time that the Greek-Cypriot side rejected a proposed UN initiative and the Turkish-Cypriot side agreed to it – since 1974 the Turkish-Cypriot side was viewed as the primary obstacle to a solution (Tocci, 2007: 38).[54] Following the referendum and the accession of Cyprus to the EU in May 2004, there have been few initiatives to re-ignite negotiations, the most important being an agreement on 8 July 2006 by President Papadopoulos and new 'President' of the 'Turkish Republic of Northern Cyprus' ('TRNC') Mehmet Ali Talat to engage in a process that would create the conditions for the commencement of substantive negotiations for the solution of the Cyprus problem within the UN framework.

This chapter has mostly dealt with non-EU issues but it is imperative to provide an understanding of both the internal and external forces that shaped the political, economic and social fabric of modern Cyprus, and which ultimately defined the country's *territorial* and *temporal* dimensions. The way in which the country responded to and influenced the process of Europeanization has been conditioned by those particular dimensions.

3
The Evolution of Cyprus' Relations with the EU

Association Agreement and Custom's Union (1972–88)

The first efforts of Cyprus to develop relations with the European Economic Community (EEC) began in December 1962 when the newly independent Republic of Cyprus submitted its application for an Association Agreement (AA). This decision was influenced by the UK's application for membership in 1961. As a member of the Commonwealth, Cyprus was seriously concerned about the implications of Britain's potential membership on its trade exports. On the other hand, the British Government encouraged Cyprus to negotiate an AA with the EEC, as the only way to preserve the privileged trading rights in the British market that the island enjoyed within the framework of its Commonwealth status. However, the island's application for an AA was abandoned in 1963 when Charles De Gaulle vetoed Britain's application for membership. The Cypriot Government renewed its efforts with a new application in August 1970 – a year after the British Government's application to join the EC was re-activated – and which eventually led to the signing of the AA in 19 December 1972.[1]

The AA provided for the gradual reduction of tariffs on industrial goods and agricultural products, ultimately aiming for a realization of a Custom's Union between the RoC and the EEC within a period of ten years. The Agreement was divided into two stages – the first stage would be completed in June 1977 and the second stage in December 1982. Yet, given the dramatic events on the island in 1974 – the Greek-led coup and the subsequent Turkish military intervention – and the inevitable catastrophic consequences on the island's economy, the implementation of the AA was delayed. In fact, there were even deliberations about a possible suspension altogether, but eventually the EC decided against that.[2]

34

After several extensions of the first stage of the AA, an Additional Protocol was signed on 22 May 1987 for the implementation of the second stage which would pave the way towards the progressive realization of a Custom's Union.[3]

There were important economic and political reasons for the island to initiate integration with the EC. As a former British colony, Cyprus enjoyed special trading rights within the British market and the island adjusted its (mainly agricultural) exports on the basis of that market. Thus, in 1970, Britain absorbed 60.3 per cent of the island's total agricultural exports and 56.3 per cent in 1971 (Tsardanidis & Ifestos, 1991: 28). With the accession of Britain to the EEC, however, and the application of the community's external customs rules and the provisions of the Common Agricultural Policy (CAP) the island's privileged rights would have to be terminated. The AA was a way to maintain that favourable access to the British market. Other reasons for the application for an AA were: to maintain the competitiveness of Cypriot products with other Mediterranean countries (e.g. Morocco, Tunisia, Israel) which had concluded similar privileged trading agreements with the EEC; to bring about a stimulus to its agricultural and industrial modernization and growth through the influence of a large and demanding market and the transfer of capital, technology and management skills; and to achieve closer political ties with the EC, a rising civil power in international affairs and a balancing force in the Mediterranean theatre of conflict in the Cold War era.

The latter factor touches upon the political reasons for initiating the AA. In the 1960s the relationship between the two main communities of the island – the Greek-Cypriot majority and the Turkish-Cypriot minority – severely deteriorated, with deadly clashes between the two communities in 1963 and 1967 and with the Turkish-Cypriots eventually withdrawing from the government. The embattled Greek-Cypriot President Archbishop Makarios saw in the AA a way to ensure the government's international and legal status as well as improve security on the island. It was also a way to induce Turkey to pressure the Turkish-Cypriots to return to the government so as to enjoy the full benefits of the AA.

In regards to the positions of political parties on the AA, the four largest parties in the 1970s (i.e. the Centre-Right Unity Party; the Progressive Front, AKEL, and EDEK) had differing positions. The first two were in favour of the AA whereas the latter two were against it. The Unity Party and the Progressive Front, while expressing their concerns on some economic issues, argued that the AA satisfied in the best possible manner the interests of Cyprus. In contrast, the left-wing AKEL and EDEK parties argued against the AA and in favour rather of a preferential trade agreement, 'since the latter offered more flexibility, and tariffs would also be lower'.[4] However, behind these economic reservations there were mostly political concerns. The two left-wing parties feared that the AA would undermine the non-aligned character of Cypriot foreign policy and lead towards a more Western orientation (Tsardanidis, 1991: 44). Yet within a climate of anti-governmental paramilitary activity from EOKA B, and in light of the fact that, the two left-wing parties were otherwise firm supporters of Makarios' Presidency – who also reiterated his commitment to maintaining the island's non-aligned policy – these parties choose not to pressure Makarios any further on this issue.

The Turkish-Cypriots perceived the AA as beneficial to their community. The Turkish-Cypriot representative, Mr Orak, argued that the AA would increase the exports of the main agricultural products' and given the fact that 30 per cent of the total agricultural land was owned by Turkish-Cypriots and 66 per cent of the population of the Turkish-Cypriot community was occupied with agriculture, the AA was endorsed. At the same time, he stressed that measures should be taken to ensure that both communities benefit from the AA.[5]

Turkey tried to establish a direct channel of communication between the Turkish-Cypriot community and the EEC, something that was rejected by the latter which stated that the only recognized authority was the RoC.[6] The EEC regarded that Article 5 of the AA was sufficient to ensure the protection of the Turkish-Cypriot community.[7] At the same time, the EEC stressed that both communities should benefit from the AA. On the basis of this, the RoC formed a consultation committee with the participation of leaders of the Turkish-Cypriot community, including the President of the Turkish Trade and Industrial Chamber (Tsardanidis, 1988: 65–6).

Similarly, before the signing of the Additional Protocol in 1987, there were disagreements between Greek-Cypriot political parties. On the domestic front, AKEL expressed its concerns regarding certain terms of the Protocol, arguing that the existing terms would hurt the interests of certain sectors (e.g. livestock-breeders, nut producers) while there were also concerns from traditional pro-Europe Democratic Rally (DISY), mainly because of lobbying from strong interest groups such as the Federation of Employers and Industrialists as well as the Cyprus Trade and Industrial Chamber. Many of these concerns had their roots in the impending 1988 Presidential Elections where President Spyros Kyprianou would be running against the candidates of these two parties, but eventually lose to AKEL-backed George Vassiliou.

Turkish-Cypriots, through their new leader Rauf Denktash and 'President of the TRNC', expressed their strong objections to the signing of the Additional Protocol in 1987. Denktash threatened that the Turkish-Cypriot community would withdraw from the ongoing bi-communal negotiations if the Protocol was signed. Despite the accepted notion that the weak Turkish-Cypriot economy would also benefit from agricultural exports from the north – via the south – as well as from the creation of incentives for economic reforms in the Turkish-Cypriot legislation (e.g. the adjustment of the Turkish-Cypriot tariff system with that of the south), the main concern was that the agreement would reinforce the notion of non recognition of the newly formed 'TRNC'. Thus, during technical level meetings between Commission officials with the northern authorities on 17 January 1986, Turkish-Cypriot officials requested, on the basis of the non-discrimination Article 5 of the AA, that economic aid be provided directly to the 'TRNC' – and not through the Republic of Cyprus as provided by the AA[8] – a request that was rejected by the EEC.

The AA proved to be beneficial for the country with the signing of three Financial Protocols in this period and the preservation of the special trading relations with the important British market. Others, however, point out that despite the reductions in tariffs, Cypriot agricultural products were better off under the Commonwealth regime (Vassiliou, 1976, 2004). Similarly, others point out that the Community's reductions in tariffs in the agricultural and industrial sector were so small that it did not substantially benefit these sectors of the island (Yannopoulos, 1977: 194). At the same time, it is generally accepted that the signing of the AA paved the way for the development of the political relationship between Cyprus and the EEC and laid the foundations for a more dynamic and competitive Cypriot economy.

Application for membership (1990)

On 3 July 1990, during the Italian Presidency of the European Council, the RoC submitted its application for membership in the EU. This possibility had been discussed two years earlier when the Greek Government suggested to the Greek-Cypriot leadership that the application be submitted during the second half of 1988 when Greece held the Presidency of the European Council. The argument was that the Greek Presidency would ensure the speedy reference of the application to the European Commission, as well as provide the Greek-Cypriot leadership with additional negotiating power in the bi-communal dialogue which had just began in August 1988. The Cypriot Government, headed by newly elected President George Vassiliou – who had the backing of left-wing AKEL and EDEK- did not find these arguments convincing, and in fact, perceived them as serving the interest of the opposition parties – particularly right-wing DIKO – which had close ties with the right-wing Greek Government (Vassiliou, 2004:35). President Vassiliou was also discouraged by some European circles to do so in light of the imminent rejection of Turkey's application for membership (Vassiliou, 2004: 37). Some circles later criticized the Cypriot Government's refusal as a missed opportunity to include the island in the Scandinavian wave of enlargement.

There were important political, economic and other incentives for Cyprus to achieve EU membership. From a strategic point of view, the Greek-Cypriots viewed membership serving four main objectives: (a) to strengthen the sovereignty, unity and security of the Republic; (b) to function as a 'catalyst' for the efforts to solve the Cyprus problem; (c) to strengthen democracy and social justice; and (d) to increase economic development, potentially for both communities.

Conflict and insecurity had long been the dominant element in Cypriot history. In the second half of the twentieth century, the people of Cyprus had been through the bloody decolonization struggle (1955–59) conducted by EOKA against the British Empire, armed clashes between the two communities in the aftermath of the independence (1963–67), a civil strife within the Greek-Cypriot community with political persecutions and assassinations between supporters of President Makarios and EOKA B personnel (1967–73), and the bloody events in July 1974, with the Greek-junta instigated coup by EOKA B and the subsequent military intervention of Turkey which divided the island. By the mid-1970s, peace and security was the main demand from both communities, yet past conflict between them had severely damaged their relations, as evident from the continued division of the island and the accession of only the Greek-Cypriot-led Republic of Cyprus.[9] Within the EU, it was hoped that security would increase significantly for both communities, but especially for the Greek-Cypriots who viewed the EU framework as a guarantee against any future military action by Turkey.

Moreover, as a Member State, the Greek-Cypriot community would be able to participate in the institutions and decision-making process of the EU, voice its positions, enhance its status in international affairs, create new coalitions and alliances with European and other states, and promote its national cause from the platform of Europe. From the point of view of Greek-Cypriots, it was hoped that the 'EU strategy' would be the decisive addition to the other existing strategies (i.e. inter-communal talks, internationalization, special relationship with Greece, American mediation[10], a deterrent strategy) (Tsardanidis & Nicolau, 1999) that would help break the deadlock with a view towards achieving the unification of the island. The Cyprus Government's effort to complement (or substitute entirely) these strategies by involving the EU factor rested on two pillars: a) to show to the European and international community that the Greek-Cypriots were determined and committed to a solution of the problem and to bi-communal negotiations leading to this goal; b) to initiate closer ties with the EU through the signing of the AA, the conclusion of the Custom's Union and the launch of accession negotiations leading to membership (Vassiliou, 2004).

Membership would also strengthen democracy, ensure the human rights of all citizens, including minorities, and the efficient and democratic functioning of the institutions of governance. It would also contribute to social justice, helping to achieve equality of sexes and races, meritocracy, health and security in the working place, aid to individuals with special needs, including old people, the increase of pensions and social welfare.

Substantial economic incentives would also derive from membership. Following the destructive effects on the economy of the island by the events in 1974, the Greek-Cypriot economy managed to recover in the early 1980s and in fact, achieve admirable levels of economic performance considering the circumstances.[11] Yet EU membership was a significant incentive to the Cypriot economy. Already, in 1986, 48.3 per cent of total exports were directed towards the EC market, including 70 per cent of agricultural exports and 36 per cent of industrial exports. In the same year, total exports to the EC surpassed the traditional Arab market and considering that exports to the US, Central and Eastern Europe and the Scandinavian countries was low, the main incentive was to secure and enhance the access of Cyprus to the European market. And in 1986, imports from the EC amounted to 60 per cent of total imports, signifying the increasing importance of this market. Under these circumstances, there were particular incentives for Cyprus to secure and further enhance its economic relationship with the EU. More particularly, EU membership would help modernize and restructure the – primarily family-based – industrial sector, increase the sector's low productivity and competitiveness and ensure access to high-quality European industrial products. The agricultural sector would also benefit from the participation in the EU's CAP by increasing productivity with the promotion of technical progress and the utilization of factors of production (e.g. labour) and increasing individual earnings of citizens occupied in this sector. Membership would also attract significant direct foreign investment from Europe, where the relatively cheap and highly skilled labour force could help Cyprus become a base for production and exports of goods in the region. Cyprus would also benefit significantly with the acquisition of structural and cohesion funds as well as from other forms of technical and financial aid within the framework of the pre-accession strategy. Finally, in a globalized economy, where small states are more vulnerable to competition than large states, within the EU they can benefit from its various protectionist policies (e.g. anti-dumping measures) and at the same time share its growth and development.

The European Commission issued its Opinion on the application of Cyprus on 30 June 1993 which was later endorsed by the European Council on 4 October 1993. In its opinion, the Commission confirmed that Cyprus satisfied the Copenhagen criteria for membership and was suitable to become a member of the Community.[12] In addition, it cited the European character and vocation of the island:

> Cyprus's geographical position, the deep-lying bonds which, for two thousand years, have located the island at the very fount of European culture and civilization, the intensity of the European influence apparent in the values shared by the people of Cyprus and in the conduct of the cultural, political, economic and social life of its citizens, the wealth of its contacts of every kind with the Community, all these confer on Cyprus, beyond all doubt, its European identity and character and confirm its vocation to belong to the Community (Opinion of the European Commission, Paragraph 44).

It is important to indicate that the Cypriot Government submitted the application on behalf of the whole population of the island. The Turkish-Cypriot community opposed the application and rejected the right of the Cypriot Government 'to commit the whole population of the island in this decision'. In addition, the Turkish-Cypriots argued that under the founding constitution of 1960, they had the right to veto any decisions concerning issues of the island's foreign policy, as well as that Cyprus was not allowed to accede an international organization that Greece and Turkey (two of the guarantee powers) were not members. However, the EC rejected this argument and stated its firm position 'on the legitimacy of the RoC, which is in accord with UN Resolutions, and of the non-recognition of the Turkish Republic of Northern Cyprus' (Opinion of the European Commission, Paragraph 8).

Furthermore, regarding the Cyprus problem, the Commission stated:

> A political settlement of the Cyprus question would serve only to reinforce this vocation and strengthen the ties which link Cyprus to Europe. At the same time, a settlement would open the way to the full restoration of human rights and fundamental freedoms throughout the island and encourage the development of pluralist democracy (Opinion of the European Commission, Paragraph 45).

Also:

> The Commission is convinced that the result of Cyprus's accession to the Community would be increased security and prosperity and that it would help bring the two communities on the island closer together (Paragraph 46).

And:

> Cyprus' integration with the Community implies a peaceful, balanced and lasting settlement of the Cyprus question – a settlement which will make it possible for the two communities to be reconciled, for confidence to be reestablished and for their respective leaders to work together (Opinion of the European Commission, Paragraph 47).

The Commission pointed to some problems stemming from the *de facto* division of the island:

> As a result of the *de facto* division of the island into two strictly separated parts, the fundamental freedoms laid down by the Treaty, and in particular, freedom of movement of goods, people, services and capital, right of establishment and the universally recognized political, economic, social and cultural rights could not today be exercised over the entirety of the island's territory. These freedoms and rights would have to be guaranteed as part of a comprehensive settlement restoring constitutional arrangements covering the whole of the Republic of Cyprus (Paragraph 10).

Finally, on Cyprus' economic performance, the European Commission stated that:

> the adoption of the *acquis communautaire* by Cyprus will pose no insurmountable problems. The Commission is not underestimating the problems that the economic transition poses. However, the economy

of the southern part of the island has demonstrated an ability to adapt and seems ready to face the challenge of integration provided that the work already started on reforms and on opening up to the outside world is maintained, notably in the context of the customs union. This opinion has also shown that there will be a greater chance of narrowing the development gap between north and south in event of Cyprus's integration with the Community (Paragraph 46).

On 4 October 1993, the European Council endorsed the Commission's approach 'to propose, without awaiting a peaceful, balanced and lasting solution to the Cyprus problem' and invited the Commission 'to open substantive discussions with the Government of Cyprus' to help it prepare for the accession negotiations' (European Council Conclusions). In November 1993, substantive discussions began between the RoC and the EC and were successfully completed in February 1995. The primary objective of these discussions, which covered a broad range of subjects, was to enable Cypriot officials to familiarize themselves with the *acquis communautaire* and to identify the areas in which Cypriot legislation needs to be harmonized with the *acquis*. The June 1994 European Council in Corfu concluded that 'an essential stage in Cyprus' preparations for accession could be regarded as completed' and that 'the next wave of EU enlargement will include Cyprus and Malta'. Prior to this, Greece threatened to veto both the CEE enlargement process, as well as Turkey's Custom's Union, unless Cyprus was included in the next wave of enlargement (Nugent, 2000: 134). The Corfu decision was subsequently confirmed at the European Council meetings in Essen (December 1994), Cannes (June 1995), Madrid (December 1995) and Florence (June 1996). On 6 March 1995, with the conclusion of Turkey's Custom's Union, it was also agreed – in the General Affairs Council – that the negotiations with the RoC would be launched, on the basis of the Commission's proposals, six months after the successful completion of the 1996 Inter-Governmental Conference (IGC). On the basis of this decision, the 16th Association Council meeting between Cyprus and the EU held on 12 June 1995 agreed on a pre-accession strategy in order to prepare Cyprus' accession to the EU. This strategy included the establishment of a 'structured dialogue', which consisted of meetings of Ministers and experts on issues such as social policy, justice and home affairs and financial and monetary affairs. Between 1995 and 1997, several such meetings took place; these provided the opportunity for Cyprus officials to have a regular and in depth exchange of views and ideas with Union officials. The structured dialogue served as a useful instrument in helping Cyprus harmonize its legislation, policies and practices with the *acquis communautaire*, and prepare itself for a smooth and rapid transition to membership. In addition, the pre-accession strategy provided for the participation of Cyprus in various European programmes in fields such as education and training (e.g. Socrates, Leonardo and Youth for Europe), audiovisual media (e.g. Media II), scientific research and technological development (e.g. Fourth Framework Programme), cultural cooperation (e.g. Ariane, Kaleidoscope, Raphael programmes) and energy (e.g. Save II). It also provided the possibility of funding Cyprus under the Euro-Mediterranean Partnership's regional component.[13] In a sense, the pre-accession strategy and its structured dialogue was a response to Cyprus' demands for clear instructions for its membership negotiations. However, it was not about the import of ready-made EU models; rather, it sought to encourage the Cypriot Government to devise national institutional solutions to cope with the *acquis*.

Moreover, the Technical Assistance Information Exchange (TAIEX) office of the EU provided Cypriot civil servants, members of the House of Representatives and professional and commercial associations with technical assistance services (e.g. experts advice, study visits, seminars and workshops, training etc) in the field of approximation, application and enforcement of legislation. There was also participation in certain targeted projects, aimed at boosting judicial and administrative capacity and projects in the area of justice and home affairs especially relating to external border control, law enforcement issues and the setting up of support and technical structures such as computerized databases compatible with European technical infrastructures.[14]

Furthermore, as a means of preparing its first opinion on Cyprus' application for membership, the Commission asked for information on twenty-three areas of the country's political, economic and social life. To collect information from the individual ministries, central offices and agencies, Cyprus had to decide on a key responsible institution and develop structures and procedures for cooperation and coordination. From the second to the third stage, that is, in the run-up to negotiations, Cyprus tried to strengthen its strategic policy planning capacities. All of this happened in the context of the successive stages of consolidation and modernization of its public administration.

Moreover, during the June 1995 meeting, the Fourth Financial Protocol (totalling 74 million ECU) was signed and covered the period up to 31 December 1998. The protocol had a pre-accession character and aimed to promote the development of the Cypriot economy and facilitate its transition with a view to EU accession. Finally, the European Parliament also expressed its support for Cyprus' application for membership in July 1995 highlighting 'the European vocation' of the island and stating that 'Cyprus' accession is important to all Member States'.[15]

In July 1997, the EC published 'Agenda 2000', its report on the challenges, impact and strategies for the next wave of enlargement, where it confirmed once again, on the basis of its previous positive recommendations, that accession negotiations should begin with Cyprus, along with Poland, Hungary, the Czech Republic, Estonia and Slovenia, six months after the end of the 1996–97 IGC in Luxembourg.[16] The Luxembourg European Council, in December 1997, confirmed again that accession negotiations of this group of countries would begin in March 1998, adding that accession would benefit all communities in Cyprus and help to bring about civil peace and reconciliation.[17]

Membership negotiations (1998–2002)

Accession negotiations began on 30 March 1998 and their conclusion was confirmed at the Copenhagen European Council in December 2002. Again, the Turkish-Cypriot leadership was invited by both the Greek-Cypriots and the EU to participate in the negotiations but declined citing the same arguments outlined during the application of the Republic for membership. The aim of the negotiations was to prepare the country to adopt and implement the *acquis communautaire*.[18] The EC monitored the progress of Cyprus towards meeting the criteria and implementing the *acquis* through its yearly Regular Reports.[19] Within this period, there were important developments.

In a landmark decision at the Helsinki European Council in December 1999, the EU stated that the solution of the Cyprus problem was not a prerequisite for the island's accession to the Union.[20] Prior to this, Greece consented to the EU's decision to grant Turkey a candidate status only when the Council made it clear that 'a political settlement to the Cyprus problem would not be a precondition to the island's accession to the EU'.[21] Also, on 13 March 2000, the European Council established an Accession Partnership (AP) between Cyprus and the EU with a view towards enhancing the pre-accession strategy of the island. The purpose of the AP was to set out in a single framework the priority areas for further work identified in the Commission's Regular Reports on the progress made by Cyprus towards membership of the EU, the financial means available to help Cyprus implement these priorities and the conditions which would apply to that assistance. The AP provided the basis for a number of policy instruments which were used to help the candidate states in their preparations for membership.[22] These included *inter alia* the updated National Programme for the Adoption of the *acquis* prepared by Cyprus, the pre-accession fiscal surveillance procedure, the Pre-accession Economic Programme, the Pre-accession pact on organized crime, a national employment strategy in line with the European Employment Strategy, and sectoral plans necessary for the participation in the Structural Funds after membership.

In December 2002, the European Council in Copenhagen declared the end of Cyprus' accession negotiations and also added that in the absence of a settlement, the application of the *acquis* to the non government controlled areas would be suspended, until the Council decided unanimously otherwise, on the basis of a proposal by the Commission. As evident from personal accounts of then Cypriot Foreign Minister Ioannis Kasoulides, particularly during the period leading up to the European Council, the government had to appease concerns and sometimes strong objections from key Member States such as France, the Netherlands and Italy, particularly as they related to the possibility of the EU 'inheriting' a divided island in the EU, and the implications of this on key policies such as the CFSP/ESDP, as well as deal with the particular 'special interests' of Britain in the island as they related to its role as a guarantee power, its Atlantic relationship with Turkey, and the British bases on the island (Kasoulides, 2007). Meanwhile, the Council invited the Commission, in consultation with the government of Cyprus, to consider ways of promoting economic development of the northern part of Cyprus and bringing it closer to the Union. The programme was launched in June 2003.[23]

Accession (2003–)

Finally, on 16 April 2003 the Accession Treaty was signed at the Athens European Council, paving the way for Cyprus to become a Member State of the EU as of 1 May 2004.[24] The Accession Treaty included Protocol 10 which established that Cyprus entered the EU as a whole but that the *acquis* was suspended in the northern part of the island ('areas not under effective control of the Government of the Republic of Cyprus').[25] In May 2005, Cyprus was admitted to the Exchange Rate Mechanism (ERM II) and in 1 January 2008 it joined the eurozone.

This chapter has examined the historical relationship of Cyprus with the EU since the early 1960s beginning with the country's AA and

Custom's Union, application for membership and accession negotiations, full membership and the post-accession period. It provides an understanding of the internal and external dynamics that contributed to the country seeking integration with the EC/EU and the various strategies employed to achieve that, as well as the positions of various EU states and institutions on the country's accession process. The country's Europeanization process both before and after membership was significantly shaped by these dynamics, strategies and positions.

4
Government: Executive, Legislative and Judicial Authorities

Introduction

The scholarly literature on the impact of Europe on the executive, legislative and judicial authorities of the Member States is particularly widespread. Increasing attention has been placed on the impact of the EU on national administrations and structures of Member States (Lequesne, 1993; Jeffery, 1996; Meny *et al.*, 1996; Wessels & Rometsch, 1996; Hanf & Soetendorp, 1998; Goetz, 2000; Kassim *et al.*, 2000; Bulmer & Burch, 2001a; Heritier, 2001; Knill, 2001; Laffan, 2001; Closa & Heywood, 2004; Goetz & Meyer-Sahling, 2007). The literature on the impact on the governments of candidate and new Member States, is less extensive but it is gradually increasing (Janblonski, 2000; Goetz, 2001b; Lippert *et al.*, 2001; Laffan, 2003; Fink-Hafner, 2005; Lippert & Umbach, 2005; Sepos, 2005b; Zubek, 2005; Dimitrova & Toshkov, 2007).

The impact of the EU on national governments as actors is strongly contested, with intergovernmentalists arguing that governments both control and are strengthened by European integration (Hoffmann, 1966; Moravcsik, 1993; Milward, 2000), neofunctionalists (Haas, 1958; Stone Sweet & Sandholz, 1998), neo-institutionalists (Pierson, 1996; Pollack, 1997) and multi-level governance theorists (Marks *et al.*, 1996) recognizing the importance of national governments but also recognizing the constraints that the EU imposes on them. The EU's effects on governments as administrators are less hotly disputed, although there are differences concerning its relative importance as a source of administrative change. One view holds that the EU impact has been minimal, when compared to other sources of change such as new public management reform and privatization (Wallace, 1996; Goetz, 2000; Page, 2003). Another view holds that integration may not have brought about a fundamental transformation, but has nevertheless led to important changes at the administrative level (Knill, 2001; Kassim *et al.*, 2001). As far as national parliaments, the consensus in the literature is that European integration is at least one of the factors that have contributed to a shift of power from the legislatures to the executives (Wessels & Rometsch, 1996; Maurer & Wessels, 2001). Their ability to influence governments in regards to EU policy varies mostly due to pre-existing constitutional arrangements, but their role is increasingly becoming more important (Pappas, 1995; Norton, 1996) particularly in exercising parliamentary scrutiny[1] regarding EU affairs (Holzhacker, 2007: 144). Still there is a need to know more about the constitutional bases, institutional arrangements and the functioning of parliamentary EU affairs committees (152). With respect to national courts, Conant (2001) revealed substantial cross national and subnational divergence in the extent to which national courts participate in the European legal system (2001: 97). And Chalmers (2000), focusing on Britain, discussed the effects of Europeanization upon judicial hierarchy, interaction between parliament and judicial system, and the frequency of the use of EC law in judicial decision-making. Nyikos (2007: 193) reveals that national courts have engaged, at varying degrees, in the European policy process for various reasons: judicial empowerment, outsourcing, efficiency, pressure on the part of litigants, increasing levels of transnational trade and general political awareness. They have accepted supremacy and direct effect, but to varying degrees, in narrow areas, or with reservations. At the same time, it is pointed out that little is known about the effects of Europeanization on court composition, appointment processes, or alterations to judicial proceedings (192).

The impact of Europeanization on the Government of Cyprus

Europeanization had a significant impact on the country's executive, legislative and judicial authorities. In regards to the executive, there was the establishment of joint EU–Cyprus institutions within the framework of the AA in 1972 such as the Association Council, consisting of Foreign Ministers of the EU Member States, government representatives from Cyprus and the EU Commissioner for External Relations; the Association Committee with its sub-committees, consisting of senior civil servants of the Council, the Cyprus government and the Commission. As a central focus of cooperation and coordination, these institutions would assist the implementation of the AA and serve as a discussion forum between the EU and Cyprus. As the central decision-making body, the Association Council would deal with broad political aspects and take binding decisions in areas provided by the AA. The Association Committee was put in charge of the preparation and coordination of the work of the Association Council and could be compared to the Committee of Permanent Representatives (COREPER) in the Council. A range of working groups were also created that mirrored the chapters and obligations of the AA and covered national preparations. These joint Cyprus–EU institutions were also replicated with the advent of the Custom's Union (1987) such as the Custom's Union Council and the Joint Custom's Union Committee and others were created after the advent of the Accession Partnership (2000) such as the Joint Consultative Committee between the Committee of the Regions and the Cypriot Liaison Committee for Cooperation with the Committee of the Regions, established in December 2001.[2] Moreover, there was also the establishment of new institutions as a result of the broader obligations stemming from EU membership such as the Ministerial Committee for EU Affairs (1991),[3] the Cyprus Academy of Public Administration (1991),[4] the Office of the Ombudsman (1991),[5] the European Institute of Cyprus (1996),[6] the Office of the Chief Negotiator (1998)[7] and its successor institution the Office of the Coordinator for Harmonization of Cyprus to the EU (2003)[8] and the Diplomatic Office (2003)[9] within the Presidential Palace. There was also the re-organization and upgrading of existing institutions with the establishment of European Union Affairs Directorates within the Ministry of Foreign Affairs and Finance, the Planning Bureau and the Law Office of the Republic[10] and the establishment in all ministries of small EU units consisting of 2–3 officials responsible for the harmonization process.[11] Many of these institutions were 'borrowed' from states with similar legal and institutional traditions such as the UK and Ireland.[12] Another example involves the borrowing of institutional mechanisms (e.g. Conference Centre for the Presidency) from Slovenia, the first small and new Member State that holds the EU's Presidency. There was also the establishment of implementing agencies for taking on the *acquis* as well as other institutions for example, for the management of external assistance schemes (i.e. the International Office of the Planning Bureau).

Furthermore, reforms have also taken place in the representative institutions of the state at the European level, that is, the state's Permanent Representation to the EU. The Cyprus government established a representative institution in the EU since 1972.[13] That delegation handled both the country's bilateral relations with Belgium and its relations with the EU. In 2000, and in an effort to prepare the country for accession, the delegation was divided into two bodies: the Permanent Representation of Cyprus to the EU, and the Cypriot Embassy in Belgium. The Permanent Representation constitutes the formal link between the national capital and Brussels and is the key institution as far as the conduct of the state's EU policy at the European level. Headed by an Ambassador, who invariably hails from the diplomatic corps, the Permanent Representation is serviced, in the main, by national officials on secondment. The expanding scope of EU activity has led to a corresponding increase in the size and variety of such officials. Initially dominated by diplomats and Finance and Agricultural Ministry officials, the Cypriot Permanent Representation has acquired specialists to shadow the increasing number of policy sectors.[14] 'Upstream', the broad mission of the Permanent Representation is to defend the interests of Cyprus. Such functions include providing a Brussels base for national negotiators; coordinating policy and procedures with the European institutions; providing an official point of contact between the government and EU institutions and other Member States; conducting negotiations at working group and COREPER level; gathering information and acting as an antennae; influencing the EU policy agenda (Wright, 1996); and maintaining contact with private interests. Its 'downstream' functions include reporting back to the appropriate national bodies; advising the capital; and participating in domestic coordination (Hayes-Renshaw *et al.*, 1989; Wright, 1996; Spence, 1999; Kassim *et al.*, 2001).

In regards to the legislative authority, there was the establishment of joint EU–Cyprus institutions within the framework of the AA such as the Association Parliamentary Committee (or Joint Parliamentary Committee) comprising members of the Cypriot Parliament and the European Parliament (*EP*). The Joint Parliamentary Committee was established in order to foster closer links and political contacts between the Cypriot House of Representatives and the EP.[15] Also, during accession negotiations, the House of Representatives established a special Committee for European Affairs (2001) which examined proposed EU legislation, whereby, by its approval, the House could apply a fast track procedure to adopt them in the plenary.[16]

Since 2005, the fast track procedure has been terminated and EU legislation is examined by all parliamentary committees whose competences are affected by the particular EU legislation. The House has also established a European Union Directorate consisting of legal officers who have received specialized training in European law, in order to assist the members of the European Affairs Committee in their tasks. While the House of Representatives has no binding power on the executive, it influences the

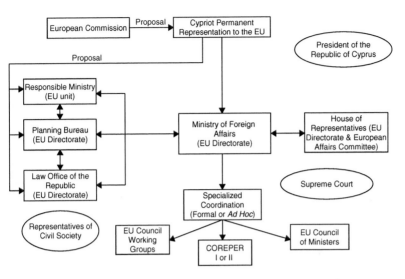

Figure 4.1 The national coordination of EU policy in the Republic of Cyprus

process though its political statements in the plenary but also through parliamentary scrutiny with the invitation of government officials to the regular meetings of its committees with the aim of reporting on the EU issues that are on the agenda at the Council of Ministers level.[17]

In regards to the judicial authority, there was an increase in the role of the Court in the conduct of Cyprus' EU policy. While there was little observable change in the structure, rules of procedure, practice and workload of the Courts as a result of EU accession, they have nevertheless been forced to engage more actively in the European judicial process, primarily as a result of the guiding EU legal principles of direct effect and supremacy but also as a result of other secondary legislation. Thus, there were a number of constitutional changes on issues such as the supremacy of EU law in relation to the national constitution,[18] the preliminary ruling procedure and the European Arrest Warrant, the latter dealing with the sensitive issue of the requirement of surrender of Cypriot nationals to the authorities of other EU states.

The resulting process for the national coordination of EU policy in Cyprus, as it involves the three levels of government, is as follows (Figure 4.1). Drafts of the Commission's proposal are communicated from the Cypriot Permanent Representation to the EU Directorates of the Ministry of Foreign Affairs, Planning Bureau and the Law Office of the Republic as well as the responsible line ministries. The EU Directorate of the Ministry of Foreign Affairs which, since the neutralization of the Office of the Chief Negotiator, acts as the *de facto* – but not official – central coordination authority of the state on EU affairs[19] organizes and chairs special coordination meetings with the purposes of preparing the country's common position at all three levels of decision-making, that is, working-group, COREPER and Council Ministers. Those meetings are attended by officials of the responsible line ministry, the Planning Bureau, the Law Office of the Republic and representatives of civil society. Most of the times these meetings take place in the Foreign Office but they can also take place in the other aforementioned institutions depending on the issue. Coordination of these meetings can be both formal and *ad hoc* – the former involves greater costs and thus occurs only when an issue becomes politicized. Throughout this process, EU legislation is also examined by the European Affairs Committee, as well as other competent parliamentary committees, and the EU Directorate of the House of Representatives which aim to shape the executive's position on the given EU issues, through forwarding legislation to be debated in the plenary but also through parliamentary scrutiny of the executive's positions on the higher levels of EU decision-making. The Supreme Court, as well as the other lower courts, also monitors EU legislation so that it conforms to the constitution of the Republic and recommends changes when necessary. The President is informed about the whole process, though more particularly when issues become politicized, through his Diplomatic Office and a small circle of officials consisting primarily of the Ministers of Foreign Affairs and Finance, the Permanent Representative of Cyprus to the EU, the Permanent Secretary of the Planning Bureau, the Attorney-General, as well as the relevant minister to the given EU issue, and other political advisors who are not necessarily members of the government.[20] When a common position is reached within the specialized coordination process it is communicated by the Foreign Ministry to the Cypriot Permanent Representative as well as the responsible line minister who will represent Cyprus in the EU Council of Ministers. When the proposal is adopted at the EU level, its implementation at the domestic level is monitored by the Ministry of Foreign Affairs, the Planning Bureau, the Office of the Coordinator for Harmonization of Cyprus to the EU and other competent line ministries.[21]

The whole process is not without its deficiencies. For example, Cypriot officials in Brussels have stated that the fact that the Foreign Ministry has not been officially designated as the central coordination authority of the state on EU affairs – with the Planning Bureau sometimes alternating in that role – often creates confusion whereby officials in Brussels do not distinguish the lead voice in the capital when it comes to dealing with EU issues, and 'they address their concerns to individual line ministries' instead.[22] Hence, the fact that, as opposed to other Member States, the Cypriot Permanent Representation sends the drafts of the Commission's proposals not only to the Ministry of Foreign Affairs but also to all concerned ministries and other authorities. Moreover, inter-ministerial coordination is limited, negative coordination exists, while there is a lack of an arbitration mechanism to settle inter-ministerial divergences in positions, all contributing to weakening the overall governmental strategy of the country and the coherence of its common position at the EU level.[23] The designation of a clear central coordination authority may increase coordination efficiency at the domestic horizontal and vertical level as the examples of the UK (i.e. European Secretariat) and France (i.e. Secrétariat Géneral du Comité Interminstériel) indicate.[24] Also, while human resources within the Permanent Representation have steadily expanded over the years (Table 4.1) more needs to be done as far as increasing the quantity and quality of the diplomats.[25] The particular territorial dimension of the country, that is, its peripheral and distant status creates an added incentive to allocate greater human resources to compensate for this lack of proximity to day-to-day policy-making in Brussels.[26] Furthermore, certain line ministries need to further strengthen their EU divisions as well as adjust their personnel policies to support for example, the 'recycling' of officials through Brussels, look to recruit officials with appropriate language skills, and introduce special training programmes. With respect to the latter, the budgeting for personnel and training to departments has not been conducive to the even development of European expertise across the Cyprus government. Figures indicate that some ministries, such as that of Finance, Agriculture and Justice and Public Order absorb the vast majority of funds allocated for these activities.[27] This need for strengthening EU expertise in public administration is also emphasized by high-ranking Cypriot officials.[28] In addition, serious consideration should be given to the notion of revising the constitution in order to allow the establishment of a junior Minister for European Affairs.[29] Such a post, which has been created in most Member States,[30] can complement the wide role of the Minister of Foreign Affairs, providing expertise on EU affairs, as well as act as an early warning system to the Commission's proposals. Consideration should also been given to the establishment of a special unit/secretariat of EU affairs within the Presidential Palace of Cyprus. As mentioned earlier, the President is supported in his/her role of providing the general guidelines of a state's EU policy through his Diplomatic Office and a small circle

Table 4.1   Composition of the Cyprus Permanent Representation to the EU

	No. of Staff*						
	2001	*2002*	*2003*	*2004*	*2005*	*2006*	*2007*
Ministry of Foreign Affairs**	6	8	11	11	11	14	16
Ministry of Finance	1	1	2	2	6	5	6
Ministry of the Interior	0	1	1	1	2	2	4
Ministry of Labour and Social Insurance	0	0	1	1	1	1	2
Ministry of Defence	1	1	1	1	2	3	3
Ministry of Justice and Public Order	0	0	0	0	1	2	3
Ministry of Education and Culture	0	0	0	0	1	1	1
Ministry of Commerce, Industry and Tourism	1	1	2	2	4	4	4
Ministry of Health	0	0	0	0	1	2	2
Ministry of Communications and Works	1	1	1	1	2	2	2
Ministry of Agriculture, Natural Resources and Environment	1	1	3	3	4	3	4
The Planning Bureau	0	1	1	1	1	1	2
The Legal Service (or Law Office)	0	0	1	1	2	2	2
TOTAL	11	15	24	24	38	42	51

Notes: *Excluding clerical and ancillary personnel;
**Including the ambassador and his deputy.
Source: Data compiled from the Cyprus Permanent Representation to the EU (2001–2007).

of high ranking ministerial and government officials, as well as political advisors. However, the whole process of EU policy-making within the Presidential Palace is *ad hoc* and the President is only informed about EU issues once they become politicized. In addition, the Diplomatic Office is under-staffed and under-specialized in EU issues with most resources and expertise devoted to the Cyprus problem.[31] In light of the demands of EU membership and the increasing need for the President to engage in a more routinized role in EU decision-making, for example, assembling regularly for meetings of the European Council and taking the lead in Inter-Governmental Conferences, as well as meeting the demands of sharing the EU's Presidency, there will be a need to either strengthen the EU dimension of the Diplomatic Office or establish a new EU unit within the Presidential Palace which would regularly brief, inform and involve the President in this more day-to-day processes of EU policy-making, including the Council of Ministers meetings, and act as an early warning system to prevent issues from becoming politicized, as well as dealing with them effectively once they do. The establishment of the Diplomatic Office in Cyprus was based on similar mechanisms in other Member States such as Germany (Chancellor's Office) and Britain (Prime Minister's Office) though these institutions are more specialized in EU affairs (e.g. through sub-EU units) and routinely involved in the state's day-to-day EU policy-making (Kassim *et al.*, 2001: 67).

Furthermore, there is a need for the state to devote more resources and attention to those early stages of EU decision-making (i.e. Council working groups and COREPER) where reportedly 90 per cent of EU legislation is decided at those stages (Soetendorp & Hosli, 2000). The earlier a common position is decided at the domestic level and instructions are sent at the Cypriot Permanent Representation, the more likely that there would be time for lobbying EU institutions and other Member States to shape those crucial early stages of EU decision-making. This again depends on having an effective central coordination mechanism which would ensure that all domestic interests are taken into account early at the domestic level and there is no delay in communicating the common position to Brussels. It also depends on enhancing the quantity and quality of Cypriot officials who participate in those early stages.

Moreover, the House of Representatives and its European Affairs Committee needs to get involved more effectively in the country's EU policy-making. This would necessitate an increase in the Committee's meetings per presidency and its participation in shaping domestic policy for all stages of EU decision-making, including working group and COREPER level.[32] This would involve a more effective coordination between the executive and legislative authority, with the former informing the latter earlier and more comprehensively and the latter claiming more pro-actively its right to participate in the EU policy-making process – the designation of a central coordination mechanism may positively contribute to this.

Finally, in regards to implementation of EU directives and regulations there is significant room for improvement as the Cypriot state needs to devote its attention to ensuring that formal implementation is actually accompanied with 'street implementation', that is, the effective and full transposition of EU legislation 'on the ground'. Although Cyprus' formal implementation record is comparatively good within the EU context,[33] those estimates actually tell half of the story since a large number of these directives and regulations are not correctly applied 'in the field', prompting the Commission to resort to infringement proceedings to remedy that.[34] Also, more needs to be done with regards to ensuring that various actors (e.g. local government in regional policy) take – as they should – a lead role in the implementation process and by the same token, are held accountable for any discrepancies in the process.

Overall, the impact of European integration on Cyprus' national executive, legislative and judicial authorities has been evident in the following domains: (a) There has been the establishment of new mechanisms, or the adaptation of existing structures or procedures, to manage EU policy coordination; (b) government departments working in areas with an EU dimension have reorganized their internal operation and structures, and introduced new procedures; (c) there has been the creation of new national bodies or the strengthening of existing ones at the national level in order to provide the President with the institutional support necessary to meet these demands; (d) the national parliament has increased its role in the policy-making process but its real impact is still limited compared to the executive; (e) the Court has increased its participation in the policy-making process; (f) the centrality of the ministry of foreign affairs in EU policy-making has been reinforced although other bodies, such as the Planning Bureau, also play an important role in the process; and (g) within this process, the role of the Permanent Representation is increasingly becoming more important, performing important 'upstream functions' and 'downstream' functions. At the same time, there is a further need for strengthening and upgrading the domestic EU machinery in the state, with institutions and practices established throughout Europe.

Identification of mechanisms, processes and dimensions of Europeanization

Regarding the models of Europeanization identified by Schimmelfennig & Sedelmeier (2005), a *rationalist* external incentives mechanism was evident in the various government reforms in the executive, legislative and judicial authorities as prescribed by the Association Agreement, the Accession Partnership and the Commission's Regular Reports, and in light of the strong incentives of pre-accession aid (the four Financial Protocols) and institutional ties (Association, Custom's Union, candidacy and membership). These reforms were evident, for example, in the creation of joint Cyprus–EU institutions (e.g. Association and Custom's Union Committees, Joint Parliamentary Committees), the Office of the Ombudsman and the International Office of the Planning Bureau. The *constructivist* social learning mechanism was evident in the context of Cyprus' Structured Dialogue whereby 'soft money' and a process of deliberation and persuasion contributed to capacity-building (e.g. TAIEX), policy-networking of Cypriot officials (e.g. working committees) exchange of information and institutional building. In the post-accession period it is also evident in the participation of Cypriot officials at various stages of EU policy-making (i.e. working groups, COREPER, Council of the EU). The *dual rationalist–constructivist* lesson-drawing mechanism was evident in the establishment and upgrading of EU directorates and committees within various government departments despite not being requested by the Commission in its Regular Reports. Many of these reforms were a result of the existence of the 'Structured Dialogue' and EU centred epistemic communities whereby national officials sought to copy, emulate and adopt elements of programs and institutions that they learned through their professional contacts with EU and other Member State officials. For example, there was borrowing from the UK, Ireland and Slovenia institutional mechanisms for the reorganization of ministerial departments and authorities (i.e. EU Directorates and Units) for the purposes of EU policy-making as well as for meeting the demands of the EU Presidency (e.g. Conference Centre for the Presidency and Diplomatic Office). Here, the country's *territorial* and *temporal* dimensions such as its small (i.e. Ireland and Slovenia), new (i.e. Slovenia) and post-colonial (i.e. UK and Ireland) status determined the source of lesson-drawing. At the same time, the limits of the dual rationalist-constructivist lesson-drawing mechanism are also evident in that many EU established 'best practices' such as the clear designation of a central coordination mechanism, the post of Junior Minister of European Affairs, and an EU Directorate within the Head of State institution, have yet to be adopted in Cyprus despite evidence of domestic coordination inefficiencies. Also, there is still room for improvement in staffing more efficiently and effectively (in quantity and quality) EU units within ministries and the Cypriot Permanent Representation to the EU, as well as improving the implementation record of the country. Here again, *territorial* and *temporal* dimensions of the country such as its small, southern and post-colonial status have mediated many of these deficiencies. In particular, the lack of staffing resources for the Cypriot Permanent Representation and the EU directorates are related to the small size of the country and its mediocre record in implementation follows the southern pattern across Europe. The institution of the Junior Minister – not only in EU affairs but in all policy areas – is in conflict with the 1960 constitution, a vestige of colonial times.

While there is much evidence of the *downloading* process of Europeanization with the establishment of joint Cyprus–EU institutions and other prescribed institutions such as the Office of the Ombudsman and the International Office of the Planning Bureau, there was little evidence of an *uploading* process in regards to government structures. Due to its small size and political clout, both as a candidate and Member State, Cyprus had little influence in uploading its institutional structures at the EU level. In regards to the *cross-loading* process, Cyprus officials were involved in the socialization process through the various EU networks, and there was also evidence of policy transfer on EU coordination mechanisms from countries with similar territorial and temporal dimensions such as UK, Ireland and Slovenia.

This chapter has examined the impact of Europeanization on the country's government focusing on the executive, legislative and judicial authorities. It has also examined future possible institutional adaptations that would facilitate the effective participation of the country in the EU policy-making process. It has indicated that *rationalist, constructivist* and *dual-rationalist–constructivist* mechanisms, as well as *downloading* and *cross-loading* processes were at work in effecting change in these areas – in contrast, there was little evidence of an *uploading* process. It has also indicated how the *territorial* and *temporal* dimensions of the country such as its small, southern and post-colonial status have mediated the impact of these mechanisms and processes.

5
Political Parties and Public Opinion

Introduction

The extent to which Europeanization has impacted on national political parties, in the same way as other areas of the state, has been an issue of debate. Mair (2000: 4) observes that Europeanization has a limited impact on national party systems. He argues that 'of the many areas of domestic politics which may have experienced an impact from Europe, it is party systems in particular that have perhaps proved to be most impervious to change'. This may have to do with the fact that while national political parties have incentives and motivations to change and adapt to the new environment, they are constrained in a number of ways. 'Unlike government bureaucracies, individual politicians, and interest groups, national political parties do not have the ability or opportunity to develop privileged or intimate relationships with authoritative EU actors' (Ladrech, 2001: 5). Unlike these actors, political parties are constrained by the fact that the Treaties forbid the transfer of EU funds to national parties (Article 191, Treaty of Nice), and in this sense they have little if anything else to gain from EU resources. Also, national parties do not have an extra national space to operate within, since their representative institution, that is, the European Parliament, does not have the mandate or composition to intervene in national circumstances (Ladrech, 2001: 5).[1]

At the same time, both Mair (2000, 2007) and Ladrech (2001, 2007) as well as other scholars (Poguntke *et al.*, 2007) observe that European integration does impact on political parties, either in a direct or indirect way. For Duverger (1994), the EU pushes political parties of the Member States to undertake a 'genuine revolution' which is as important 'as that which transformed clubs of notables into mass organizations at the turn of the century' (Duvurger, 1994: 162). Others indicate that political parties are forced to deal with Europeanization as something that constitutes a fundamental change to their operational context (Marks & Wilson: 2000; Ladrech, 2001; Binnema, 2002; Luther & Muller-Rommel, 2002). In particular, Ladrech (2001) identified five areas of parties' activities influenced by Europeanization: (a) policy/programmatic content; (b) organizational structures; (c) patterns of party competition; (d) party–government relations; and (e) relations beyond the national party system (Ladrech, 2001: 8). Poguntke *et al.* (2007) argued that European integration effects change on the parties': (a) formal structure; (b) presence; (c) personnel resources; (d) material resources; (e) information resources; and (f) the process of internal party politics. Luther and Muller-Rommel (2002: 7–11) presented six clusters of change faced by political parties due to the process of European integration: socioeconomic change (growth of population, occupational structures, etc.), alterations to political values and national political culture (e.g. weakening social basis of left–right conflicts, emergence of new social movements), radical transformation in the structure of political communication (e.g. internet, increased costs), change in the political issues and policy agendas that shape the political discourse (e.g. inclined attention to defence and security issues), the economic problems posed by the growing interdependence between European states and from globalization and the reforms in their constitutional systems undertaken (e.g. decentralization of authority). Moreover, Mair (2000: 48–9) highlights the indirect impact observing that European integration increasingly operates to constrain the freedom of movement of national governments, and hence encourages a hollowing out of competition among those parties with a governing aspiration. As such, it promotes a degree of consensus across the mainstream and an inevitable reduction in the range of policy alternatives available to voters'. Also, Mokre and Pollak (2001: 3) observe that the power of parties to act as distributive agents according to their vision of a societal model and preferences is weakened by the monetary and stability oriented prerogatives of the EU: the obligation to comply with the Maastricht criteria puts remarkable strain on national budgets and consequently has important effects on the capacity of political parties to design national tax, wage and labour market policies.

Finally, Marks and Wilson (2000: 437) also observe that the dual character of European integration – economic and political – creates tensions for parties that compete on the *class cleavage*. For social democratic parties, economic integration, on the one hand, threatens social democratic achievements at the national level by intensifying international economic competition and undermining Keynesian responses to it, while it also increases the substitutability of labour across countries, fosters economic inequality and pressures employers to demand labour flexibility. On the other hand, political integration promises a partial solution for remedying these problems by recreating a capacity for authoritative regulation at the European level. For parties on the right, economic integration is beneficial because it constrains the economic intervention of national governments since it lowers the costs of shifting investment between various countries and impels national governments to compete in attracting capital to their country thus discouraging market regulation, social policy and taxation. Conversely, political integration threatens to create a supranational government for the EU as a whole that can regulate markets while negating regime competition among individual states in the integration European economy (Marks and Wilson, 2000: 438).

On the basis of these insights, one can observe significant reforms in various dimensions of the domestic party system in Cyprus. Yet before doing so, it is worth providing a short overview of the history of the Cypriot political system and its parties.

History of Cypriot political parties

The political system between the 1950s and late 1970s was dominated by the charismatic figure of Archbishop and first President of the Republic Makarios (1960–74) (Markides, 1977). The 1981 parliamentary elections marked a new era in Cypriot party politics (Hadjikyriakos & Christophorou, 1996) whereby the creation of new parties sought to provide new perspectives and aimed to fill the power vacuum left with the death of Makarios in 1977. Also, the electoral system for parliamentary elections changed in 1981 from the initial plurality block vote to a reinforced proportional distribution of seats, with a threshold of 8 per cent and compulsory voting.[2] Political development continued throughout the 1980s and 1990s with the institutionalization of municipal elections (1986) and the creation of new independent and non- or semi-governmental authorities and institutions (Ierodiakonou, 2003). Elections became more substantial and the number of seats in the House of Representatives increased from 35 to 56, while over 2,650 local authority posts became elected offices in 1985. The electoral competition rules further changed in 1995, with the adoption of a system of proportional representation and the threshold set at one 56th of the vote (for the 56-member chamber). The voting age in all elections was changed from 21 to 18 in 1997 (Christophorou, 2006: 515).

AKEL (Ανορθωτικό Κόμμα Εργαζόμενου Λαού) was constituted in 1941, succeeding the Communist Party formed in 1924.[3] It was founded under British colonial rule and conditions of political vacuum; through impressive early electoral successes the party gained legitimacy and established its authority as a major political force, which remains today. AKEL was excluded from the handling of the Cyprus issue and the anti-colonial struggle, and faced legitimacy problems in the transitional period to independence. After testing its influence by opposing Makarios in the first parliamentary elections (December 1959), the party offered him unconditional support. Later, it offered support to presidential candidates without participating in government. It received in return ministerial portfolios for prominent individuals enjoying its confidence. Under the plurality system, AKEL was content with a limited number of seats in the House of Representatives.

The years of perestroika and the collapse of the communist world coincided with the death of Ezekias Papaioannou, AKEL Secretary-General for 39 years, and internal crisis, which erupted in 1988, created ideological differences, personal rivalries and persisting problems from the party's heavy losses in the 1985 Parliamentary Elections. The crisis, which continued after the election of the current Secretary-General, Demetris Christofias, ended in 1990.

The party has consistently sustained its image as a Marxist–Leninist party deeply committed to communist ideals – though without launching itself into ideological debates or revolutionary positions – and views itself as the sole representative of the working class and the left progressive forces. In the last Parliamentary Elections the party received the largest number of votes (Table 5.1) and its Secretary-General was elected in 2001 as the President of the House of Representatives (*Vouli*). It is also, notably, the largest communist party in Europe (Christophorou, 2003; Dunphy & Bale, 2007).[4] AKEL works for a fully independent, sovereign, non-aligned, demilitarized, democratic, federal Cyprus and for socialism. It places particular emphasis on rapprochement with the Turkish-Cypriots having organized since 2000 a number of common forums with Turkish-Cypriot left-wing parties Republican Turkish Party[5] and the New Cyprus Party[6] (formerly Patriotic Unity Movement).[7]

AKEL's view of EU association and membership has historically been negative on the basis of their ideological origins, that is, anti-western and anti-capitalist. In particular, AKEL warned that the AA 'would put the Cyprus economy in an unfavourable competitive position *vis-à-vis* the economic EEC giants, would result in the shrinking of the industry and agriculture in the island ... and lead to unemployment and

Table 5.1 Cypriot political parties and their European parliament political group affiliations

European political group	Cypriot political parties	Cypriot parliamentary elections, 21 May 2006, % of vote and no. of seats (+/−2001)
Confederal Group of the European United Left/Nordic Green Left (EUL/NGL)	AKEL (Progressive Party of the Working People)	31.1%, 18 seats (−3.6%, −2 seats)
Group of European People's Party and European Democrats (EPP-ED)	DISY (Democratic Rally)	30.3%, 18 seats (−3.6%, −1 seat)
Alliance of Democrats and Liberals in Europe (ALBE)	DIKO (Democratic Party)	17.9% , 11 seats (+3.1%, +2 seats)
European Socialists (PES)	EDEK (Socialist Party)	8.9%, 5 seats (+2.4%, +1 seat)
European Democratic Party (EPD)	EUROKO (European Party)	5.7%, 3 seats (+0.6, +1 seat)
Group of the Greens	OIKOLOGOI (Greens)	1.9%, 1 seat (−)
European Liberal Democrat and Reform (ELDR)	EDI (United Democrats)	1.5%, / (−1.0%, −1 seat)
–	KEP (Movement of Free Citizens)	1.2% – (//)
–	EURODI (European Democracy)	0.4% – (//)

Source: author's compilation.

underemployment'. The party also viewed the AA as being 'in conflict with the non-aligned character of Cypriot foreign policy', and 'the EEC, apart from the economic union, the political extension of NATO in Europe'. It thus argued against the AA and in favour of a preferential trade agreement, 'since the latter offered more flexibility, and tariffs would also be lower'.[8] AKEL was also opposed to the application for membership in 1990. The party was in favour of the creation of a 'common European home' where Cyprus could take part, but did 'not equate the ideas of the common European home with the EEC'.[9] The views of AKEL in regards to the EU officially changed in 1995. While still regarding the EU 'as an advanced form of capitalist and political integration', in light of the 'new realities with the dissolution of the USSR and the serious weakness of the non-aligned movement' and on the prospect of membership contributing to the resolution of the Cyprus problem and reunification of the island, the party supported the launch of accession negotiations with the EU. At the same time, it expressed its serious reservations on the 'conservative nature of the *acquis communautaire* especially regarding the economic and social fields. Thus, at that time AKEL was prepared to speak in favour of Cyprus' membership 'but only on the pre-condition that the EU would help the correct resolution of the Cyprus problem, that the whole of Cyprus would accede to the EU, and that important social and economic achievements of the people would be safeguarded'.[10] Since then, AKEL's rhetoric and discourse has been more supportive of EU membership, although it has not refrained from criticizing the EU's 'conservative nature', a 'form of 'capitalist and political integration' while also being cautious in regards to the 'catalytic effect' of the Union in regards to the efforts to solve Cyprus problem.[11] The official party position was against the 2003 UN-sponsored Annan Plan for the reunification of Cyprus.[12]

EDEK (Κίνημα Σοσιαλδημοκρατών) was founded in 1969 by Vassos Lyssarides (Archbishop Makarios' physician) and is now led by Giannakis Omirou. In 1972, it objected to the AA stressing the non-aligned foreign policy of the country, the association of the EC to NATO, and the negative impact of the AA on the industry and agricultural sector. Historically, the party favoured a national health care system and the nationalization of banks and foreign owned mines. It also favoured an intensification of trade with the Arab world as an alternative to the AA. Its positions softened in the 1980s and have gradually turned into consistent support for EU membership, as a means to increase economic growth and to ignite the efforts to solve the Cyprus problem. The party was a staunch opponent of the Annan Plan.

At the other end of the political spectrum, the DISY (Δημοκρατικόσ Συναγερμόσ) created in 1976 by Glafkos Clerides (President of the Republic, 1993–2003) and cadres from the former Unified Party and the Progressive Front, which collapsed following support by some of their officials for the coup against Makarios in summer 1974. The party faced exclusion and systematic denigration from pro-Makarios forces as it was held responsible for offering shelter to perpetrators of the coup and the extreme right. It is indicative that its road to parliament was barred in 1976 despite its 27 per cent of the popular vote. In time, however, DISY emerged as a reliable political force, an alternative to the failing pro-Makarios alliance. DISY's electoral successes in the parliamentary elections of 1981 and, in particular, of 1985, when it became the largest party, gradually opened the road to full legitimacy.

The party is led by Nikos Anastasiades (since 1997) and received the second largest number of votes in the last parliamentary elections, though the same number of seats as AKEL (Table 5.1). It adheres to the western ideals of democracy, freedom and justice and its ideology is based on right-wing, Christian Democratic values. The party, founded on pro-Western and pro-NATO principles, has always been a staunch supporter of Cyprus' EU membership. It was the first Cypriot political party to participate in like-minded European and international organizations such as the European Democratic Union (EDU) and the European Union of Christian Democrat Workers (EUCD) (1979), the Centrist Democrat International (CDI) (1982), the International Democrat Union (IDU) (1983) and the European People's Party (EPP) (1994). It has always supported the need for stronger links with the European Union, the Council of Europe and all other European Institutions, as a means for economic development and security as well as a vehicle to help the resolution of the Cyprus problem. The official party position was to support the Annan Plan.[13]

DIKO, (Δημοκρατικό Κόμμα) formed in 1976 by the successor of Makarios, President Spyros Kyprianou (1977–88) is located on the left of centre of the political spectrum and aims to offer citizens an alternative to left-wing AKEL and right-wing DISY. President of the Republic Tassos Papadopoulos succeeded Kyprianou in 2000 and led the party until his successor Marios Karogian took over in 2006. DIKO has also held a favourable position towards the EU, 'under the condition that European integration would be based on the implementation of principles of justice, human rights and the European *acquis*'.[14] DIKO has also been an advocate of a 'European solution' for the Cyprus problem, that is, a formula that would be operational, viable and compatible with the European acquis'. The party was a staunch opponent of the Annan Plan referendum.

The rest of the political parties, with a constituency of less than 5 per cent, are the newly formed European Party (Ευρωπαικό Κόμμα)[15] and European Democracy (Ευρωπαική Δημοκρατία),[16] both nationalist parties with a right-wing ideology, the United Democrats (Ενωμένοι Δημοκράτες),[17] a centre party formed by President George Vassiliou (1988-93) as well as the Green Party (Κίνημα Οικολόγων Περιβαλλοντιστών). All of these parties have a pro-EU agenda.

In this sense, all political parties accept and support Cyprus' accession to the EU, although they have different views on the potential ramifications and implications of accession, on both the political and economic front. Nevertheless, it would be hard to categorize any of these parties as Euro-sceptical, in the narrow sense of the term.

The impact of Europeanization on Cypriot political parties

Europeanization has impacted significantly on political parties on the basis of Ladrech's (2001) five dimensions of change. In regards to the parties' policy/programmatic content, there were significant changes. The right-wing DISY has adopted a new ideological platform called 'Eurodemocracy' and the left-wing AKEL has adopted a more pro-EU stance compared to its pre-1990 position as evident in its manifesto and rhetoric and discourse, while all parties have addressed issues that are important for the EU, such as the environment – the creation of the Cypriot Green Party in 1996 is partly a result of European environmental norms.[18] This pro-European agenda is partly explained by the southern *territorial* character of the country and the general absence of popular and party-based euro-scepticism in such countries (Taggart, 1998) and partly with the fact that Cypriot political parties recognized the important role that the EU can play in the resolution of the Cyprus problem and were appealing to a European audience. In other words, there was an 'ideological convergence' between all parties concerning the principle of using the EU as a catalyst for solving the problem. Indeed, there were and still are differences between these parties in regards to the approach and method of using the EU factor, but there is a strong agreement about the utility, value and benefit of this national strategy.[19] In that sense, all Cypriot political parties have been consistently promoting and projecting national preferences at the EU level through their political group affiliations in the European Parliament, in parliamentary committees and plenary sessions. Cypriot Members of the European Parliament (MEPs) have also been using their EU credentials, often with the support of their European colleagues, in order to highlight the continuing division of the island, the refusal of Turkey to recognize the Republic as well as the maintenance of British Bases on the island.[20]

In regards to their organizational structures, there were changes concerning their practices, procedures and power relations. In order to fill the shortage of expertise in EU affairs, parties reached out to notables from various interest groups, social sectors (e.g. the public service) and the academic field. Some parties (e.g. EDEK) created think tanks, while all parties established units and secretariats on EU affairs. In that regard, EU specialists have increased their membership in key national party bodies such as executive committee, national executive, party council and party congress. In regards to party competition, there has been a professionalization in the design and organization of the parties' campaign strategies and execution, as for example, the hiring of image and political consultants, the raising of single issue campaigns (e.g. environment, education), the use of logos and symbols used by European parties as a means to promote their European identity (e.g. EDEK uses the red rose emblem of the Party of European Socialists), and an increased participation of European MPs during party campaigning. There were also reforms to party–government relations and relations beyond the national party system, for example, cooperation with transnational institutions, such as party federation and EU institutions, as well as affiliations with their respective party groups at the EU level (Katsourides, 2003: 2–10).

Finally, there has been a small but steady increase in the participation of women in the legislature at the national and local level in the last three rounds of elections (1996–2006),[21] which has traditionally been low,[22] and a change in political party attitudes in regards to utilizing their influence in the constituencies. This shift in attitude has translated into the adoption of statutory provisions from some political parties in regards to the proportionate representation of women in the party ranks (for example, a 30 per cent threshold has been set by DISY on this matter) as well as an increased promotion of women as notable candidacies from all parties. Overall, however, the total representation of women in Cypriot politics, that is, in executive and legislative positions at the national and local level, remains relatively low, around 16 per cent,[23] lower than the EU average (24 per cent) and particularly lower when compared to north western Europe – figures that reflect the broader role of women in Cypriot society.[24]

Moreover, European integration has also functioned as a cohesive force for parties in Cyprus. As opposed to other Member States (Aylott, 2002), the EU has been a force of unity in regards to the Cyprus problem, where all parties see the Union as a factor that could promote the reunification of the island and ensure security in the island. The fact that Cypriot parties had to appeal to a European audience regarding this issue, has also contributed to them adopting a 'pro-European' agenda in their programmatic contents. Finally, Mokre and Pollak (2002: 12) also point out to the educative and training role of parties, that is, educating citizens about European issues as well as training political elites something that is also evident in the case of the Cypriot political parties.

Furthermore, in line with Marks and Wilson (2000: 435) perception of the dual character of European integration process (political and economic), for parties on the left of the ideology axis such as AKEL and EDEK the process of political integration presented them with a chance to regulate aspects of economic integration, especially issues

relating to workers' rights and social subsidies. Kreppel (1999: 18) empha-
sizes the importance of workers rights and conditions in the workplace
for the left wing parties in forming coalitions in the European Parliament, while Marks and Wilson (2000: 435) note the need to regulate
them because of the pressures of employers for labour flexibility and economic inequality fostered by economic integration. AKEL has declared
emphatically that the harmonization process with the *acquis communautaire* has been one sided and stressed the importance of coming
to terms with all of its dimensions. Special reference is made to the
social subsidies field and the workers rights both at work and in crisis
situations (e.g. unemployment and dismissals). Through this indirect
process left wing parties find the chance of regulating the markets effectively by enhancing this capacity through the EU. The same logic in
reverse applies for DISY. For right-wing parties' economic integration is
beneficial because it constrains the economic intervention of national
governments. Thus, DISY hides behind the harmonization obligation
to pursue its own goals, liberalization and privatization, for which it
could carry a significant political cost. Nevertheless the Europeanization
process is seen by DISY as a confirmation of its visionary policy since its
foundation in 1976 and especially to issues relating to the modernization
of public service and the liberalization of private initiative (Katsourides,
2003).

Moreover, the impact of Europeanization on parties' programmatic or
ideological dimensions is also pointed out by Luther and Muller-Rommel
(2002: 15). They refer to four key dimensions of political parties that concern empirical political science. One of them is their desire to exercise
political power through office seeking in order to realize their policy preferences. This is evident in most municipal elections where candidates
were mostly selected through parties' procedures and very few chose to
defy party leadership. Also, given the locals' aspiration and the parties'
need to penetrate the local communities by acquiring a local form of
power (Luther & Muller-Rommel, 2002: 11) the selection was based primarily on the ability to attract voters through local notables regardless of
education, age, and ability to place the community in this changing environment caused by the European integration process. The result is that
many of the candidates and in return many of the elected community
officials are people of a certain age whose only benefit and ability were
the local networks they established in villages and small communities
over the years. The picture is slightly different in the big municipalities
where attributes such as education and networks on a higher level play
a more prominent role.

In spite of the modernizing and generally positive impact of Europe on Cypriot political parties, further reforms are required, more particularly in dissolving the patron–client structures between parties and their voters and the way in which these parties exercise power, particularly in regards to the selection of candidates. In a challenging European environment where local communities and regions need to establish links and partners at the EU level and create channels in order to access and shape EU-decision-making, the primary criteria for selection should be qualifications, experience, expertise and character and the competence of the candidate to integrate his/her community at the European level. For example, to consider one aspect, the absorption of EU funds from these communities will depend exactly on the ability and expertise of these local officials to mobilize the community, provide the locals with the necessary information regarding these projects, and apply for and manage these funds. Indicative of the general opinion of citizens on political parties, only 19 per cent of citizens 'trusts political parties' stating that more needs to be done to ensure accountability.[25] For example, in last parliamentary elections (May 2006), 16.6 per cent of the population (or 80,000 voters) did not vote for any party, a 3 per cent increase from 2001. The participation of women in Cypriot politics also needs to increase and the statutory provisions adopted in some parties will need to be replicated by the total spectrum of the political system.

Finally, one can argue that the increasing bi-communal contacts between Greek-Cypriot and Turkish-Cypriot parties has also been fueled by the Europeanization process which generally contributes to a moderation of positions between conflicting parties and increased socialization and economic integration (such as opening of the Green Line borders). However, one should also take into account that much of this rapprochement process is also a result of the democratization processes throughout the island and other internal reconciliation processes.

Identification of mechanisms, processes and dimensions of Europeanization

Overall, more *constructivist* than *rationalist* mechanisms have contributed to reforms in the Cypriot parties' policy/programmatic content, organizational structures; patterns of party competition, party-government relations and relations beyond the national party system. In particular, the *constructivist* social learning mechanism and the *dual rationalist–constructivist* lesson-drawing mechanism were at work in inducing change in the parties policy/programmatic content (e.g. more pro-European programmes; emphasis on European issues and agendas such as environment and gender equality), organizational structures (e.g. creation of EU units and think tanks), patterns of party competition (e.g. adoption of European campaign methods), and party–government relations (e.g. EU party affiliations, participation in European party federations). While these changes had a rationalist logic, that is, to attract more domestic voters, they were mainly induced by socialization processes of party officials at the EU level with their European counterparts, the adoption of European norms and beliefs, as well lesson-drawing in regards to successful methods and practices from other European parties. In other words, the EU and the European Parliament did not prescribe a specific model that Cypriot parties needed to adopt in the country's accession process – any changes were driven by the parties themselves with socialization and lesson-drawing processes mutually reinforcing this change. Finally, the limitations of these mechanisms were also evident in the lack of the effective dismantling of patron–client structures in the relationship between parties and their voters, the way in which these parties exercise power – practices which are in opposition to the European norms of democracy and meritocracy -and the persistent gender gap in regards to the participation in Cypriot politics. Here, *territorial* factors such as the small and southern status of the country and *temporal* factors such as its post-colonial status mediated this limited impact. In particular, the patron-client structures are vestiges of colonial Ottoman times and are particularly evident in small and southern countries (e.g. Malta, Greece) while the continuing gender gap in the participation in Cypriot politics is a pattern which is evident in most Southern Mediterranean countries.

There were little evidence of the *downloading* process of Europeanization as the European Parliament does not prescribe any specific institutional models and policies for national parties. There was, however, evidence of *cross-loading* processes where socialization and lesson-drawing processes contributed to a change in the parties policy/programmatic content, organizational structures, patterns of party competition and party-government relations. There were also evidence of *uploading* processes where political parties and their Cypriot MEP sought to project the national interests of the Republic on the Cyprus problem and its relations with Britain at the EU level.

Cypriot public opinion on the EU

In regards to public opinion in the EU, most studies have focused on how the EU is transforming national identities (Laitin, 2002;

Triandafyllidou & Spohn, 2002; McLaren, 2005; Luedtke, 2005), citizenship (Meehan, 2000; Vink, 2001; Dell'Olio, 2004) and public opinion (Gabel, 1998; Porta & Caiani, 2006; De Vreese & Boomgaarden, 2006; Rohrschneider & Whitefield, 2006) in candidate and Member States. One thing these studies have in common is the understanding of how citizens, political parties, institutional actors, interest groups and social movement organizations respond to European integration is a result of political, economic, socio-cultural, institutional and historical characteristics of the country. These actors are not merely adapting to European integration but also bear specific visions of 'what' Europe is and should be, and they do so on the basis of the aforementioned characteristics. In regards to candidate states, evidence indicates that citizens are often quite supportive of a new and unknown order, both in the context of markets (Dutch, 1993) and in political contexts (Evans & Whitefield, 2001). However, as is evident in the CEE countries, when markets and democracies are implemented, the rough and tumble of these institutions may create a harsh reality that could lead to a decline in mass support for them (Rohrschneider & Whitefield, 2006: 144). Finally, support for integration is often stimulated by the need to consolidate national independence (Rohrscheinder & Whitefield, 2006: 151).

The theoretical work of scholars (Easton, 1965; Lindberg & Scheingold, 1970) on the distinction between specific and diffuse political support for systems, whether institutions, governments or international organizations, is useful when interpreting public opinion data in the EU. Accordingly, specific or utilitarian support derives mainly from the evaluation of system outcomes (in the case of the EU, its particular policies) while diffuse or affective support refers to a reserve of attitudes (in the case of the EU how connected or attached one feels to the Union) that is independent of specific outcomes (Easton, 1965: 343–4).[26] This distinction is particularly important as diffuse support is cultivated and shaped by constructivist mechanisms such as social learning through the power of socialization and norm diffusion whereas specific support is cultivated and shaped by rationalist mechanisms through external incentives and rewards. Most Eurobarometer questions address attitudes that can be related to these two different forms of support. Thus, a diffuse or affective support is expressed in response to questions such as 'Do you tend to trust the EU and its institutions' (dubbed 'net trust').[27] A specific or utilitarian support is expressed in response to questions such as 'Do you think that your country's membership is a good thing?' (dubbed 'net evaluation') and 'Do you think that your country will or has benefited from EU membership?' (dubbed 'net benefit'). Following Niedemayer

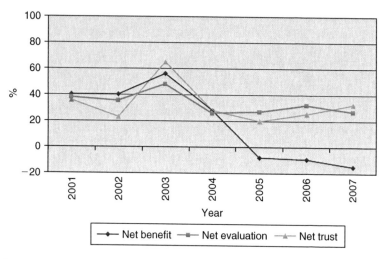

Source: Data compiled from Eurobarometer (2001–2007).
Figure 5.1   Indices of net trust, net evaluation and net benefits for Cyprus' EU membership (2001–2007)

(1995) and Closa and Heywood (2004), an index can be constructed that shows the difference between positive and negative responses. For example, in 2001, 62 per cent of Cypriots stated that they tended to trust the EU as opposed to 26 per cent who stated that they tended not to trust the EU resulting in a 'net trust' positive of 36 per cent. Similarly, in 2001, 51 per cent of Cypriots stated that EU membership was a good thing as opposed to 13 per cent who said that it was a bad thing, resulting in a 'net evaluation' positive level of 38 per cent. And in 2001, 63 per cent of Cypriots stated that their country would benefit from EU membership as opposed to 23 per cent who stated that they would not, resulting in a 'net benefit' positive level of 40 per cent. Three indices have been constructed from the above questions and are shown in Figures 5.1, 5.2, 5.3 and 5.4.[28]

Of the three indices it is diffuse support (i.e. net trust) that has the highest value (Figure 5.1) and which is consistently above the EU average (Figure 5.2) while specific support (i.e. 'net evaluation' and 'net benefit') revealed different outcomes in the pre- and post-accession period. For example, diffuse support for the EU was high throughout the accession and post-accession period reaching a peak in 2003 of positive net trust of 65 per cent compared to 6 per cent of EU average (Figure 5.2). This meant that 78 per cent of Cypriots stated that they tended to trust

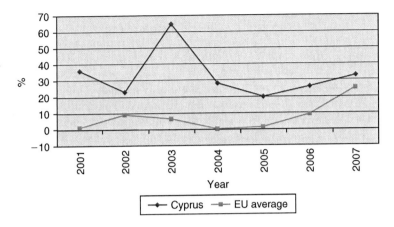

Source: Data compiled from Eurobarometer (2001–2007).
Figure 5.2   Net trust in the EU (Cyprus and EU average, 2001–2007)

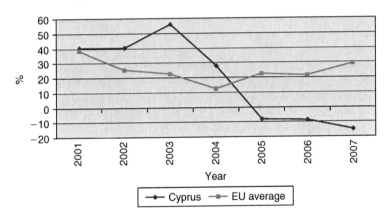

Source: Data compiled from Eurobarometer (2001–2007).
Figure 5.3   Net benefit of membership (Cyprus and EU average, 2001–2007)

the EU as opposed to 13 per cent who tended not to. Specific support was high only during accession negotiations reaching its peak in 2003, with positive net benefit being 56 per cent compared to 22 per cent EU average, meaning that 71 per cent of Cypriots stated the country could benefit from membership as opposed to 15 per cent who stated that it could not (Figure 5.3); and positive net evaluation being 48 per cent compared to 33 per cent EU average, meaning that 59 per cent of Cypriots

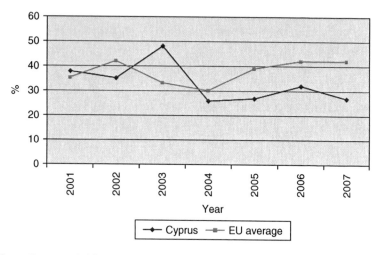

Source: Data compiled from Eurobarometer (2001–2007).
Figure 5.4 Net evaluation of membership (Cyprus and EU average, 2001–2007)

stated that membership was a good thing as opposed to 11 per cent who stated that it was a bad thing (Figure 5.4).[29] In the post-accession period, diffuse support maintained its high levels with positive net trust in 2005 being 20 per cent compared to the EU average of 1 per cent, meaning that 54 per cent of Cypriots stated that they tended to trust the EU as opposed to 34 per cent who stated that they tended not to[30] (Figure 5.3).[31] In stark contrast, specific support dramatically declined in 2005 and continued to do so for the next two years (2006, 2007) recording one of the lowest rankings in the EU in both net evaluation and net benefits. For example, in 2005 net benefits was a negative 8 per cent compared to 22 per cent EU average, the lowest recording in the EU-27. This meant that 49 per cent of Cypriots stated that the country has not benefited from accession as opposed to 41 per cent who stated that it had benefited (Figure 5.3).[32] Similarly, in the same year, net evaluation was 27 per cent compared to the EU average of 39 per cent, the 19th lowest recording in the EU-27 (Figure 5.4). This meant that 43 per cent of Cypriots stated that membership was a 'good thing' as opposed to 16 per cent who stated that it was a 'bad thing'.[33]

The results indicate that in 2005, there was a dramatic shift in Cypriot public opinion towards specific support of the EU while diffuse support retained its high levels. Negative developments with regard to the Cyprus problem, primarily, as well as economy, significantly determined the perception of Cypriot citizens regarding the perceived utilitarian benefits of EU membership. When high expectations about the catalytic effect of the EU for the resolution of the Cyprus problem were not realized, with the failure to agree on the UN sponsored Annan Plan in 2004, there was a significant decline in support for EU membership the next year.[34] Also, while in 2006 and 2007 Cypriot citizens recognized that accession has been beneficial to the economy in general (47 per cent), services (63 per cent), the exporting sector (52 per cent) and the standard of living (49 per cent), accession is also seen as having a negative impact on agricultural (58 per cent), industrial (52 per cent) sectors as well as on employment conditions (59 per cent), increased inflation (28 per cent) while 47 per cent of citizens disagree as to whether the EU has increased economic stability in the country (43 per cent agreed). This relative negative opinion on the country's economic situation in the post-accession period has also shaped the attitudes of Cypriots towards the European Monetary Union. In 1007, half of the Cypriot population was in favour of the EMU and its euro currency (7 per cent increase since 2006), yet these evaluations are significantly lower than the EU-27 average (63 per cent) with the country being in the bottom five of EU-27 Member States (Slovenia being on top and the UK being on the bottom). In general Cypriots are fearful of the negative consequences of the euro on the economy. In 2006, 60 per cent indicated that the economic situation of the country would deteriorate in the next 12 months and that employment conditions would worsen – these citizen's evaluations were one of the most pessimistic in the EU (EU-25 being 39 per cent)

Moreover, as in other Member States, perceptions of the EU are largely mediated by the domestic state of affairs and national priorities. Thus, in 2007 Cypriot citizens believed that the major socioeconomic problems that Cyprus faces are crime rate (51 per cent, the highest in the EU-27), inflation (28 per cent), the financial situation in general (16 per cent), unemployment (16 per cent) and immigration (8 per cent). Subsequently, the percentage of Cypriots who believed that the EU was contributing positively to these issues are one of the lowest in the EU, as for example in the fight against crime (36 per cent, 7th lowest in EU-27), the economy (27 per cent, lowest in EU-27) and immigration (21 per cent, 3rd lowest in the EU). And thus Cypriot citizens believed that the EU should give its highest emphasis to solidarity with poorer regions (40 per cent), the fight against crime (34 per cent), as well as the environment (38 per cent) – the latter being an exception in this rule. Also, in light of the fact that the Cyprus problem and security are *de facto* the most important issues for Cypriot citizens, and given the lack of progress on this issue despite the high expectations from the EU's involvement, it is not surprising that Cypriot citizens who believed that the EU had contributed positively to foreign and security issues are the third lowest in the EU-27 (33 per cent) and also that foreign and security issues should be one of the highest priorities of the EU (26 per cent).[35]

Finally, the role of Cypriot and European media (e.g. Euronews) has been important in shaping diffuse and specific support for the EU with the Cypriot public. In 2007, most Cypriot citizens (45 per cent) believed that EU issues were not adequately presented by the Cypriot media such as television and radio, while only 28 per cent believed that they were. Any poll indicators should be viewed in the light of these attitudes.

Identification of mechanisms, processes and dimensions of Europeanization

One can observe that the effects of *rationalist* external incentives mechanisms in creating specific support for the EU has varied through the years, with these mechanisms being more effective in the pre-accession than post-accession stage. In particular, the perceived peace, security and economic benefits of membership drove the Cypriot public to support the EU in the pre-accession stage, as evidenced by the high recordings of net benefit and net evaluation, but that support dramatically declined after accession, and particularly after the failure of the Annan Plan in 2004 and with the advent of the negative effects of market integration, with the net evaluation and net benefit (particularly) indicators showing a considerable decrease. *Constructivist* social learning mechanisms, on the other hand, were equally effective throughout the period examined (2001–2007), including after the 2004 setback and despite economic woes, with diffuse support remaining high as evident from the high values of the net trust indicator. This indicates the more constant effect of *constructivist* social learning mechanisms in shaping a favourable Cypriot public opinion towards the EU, resulting essentially from the socialization of Cypriot citizens, public officials and professionals within the EU arena and the internalization of the Union's norms, beliefs and ideas. At the same time, the *territorial* and *temporal* dimensions of the country such as its small, southern, post-colonial and new status shaped Cypriot public opinion on the EU. In particular, the public perception on the weak impact of the EU's catalytic effect on the Cyprus problem, which is linked to the country's small, southern and post-colonial status, mediated the deficiencies of these mechanisms in sustaining specific support for the EU in the post-accession period. Also, small and uncompetitive economies experience the negative and often inevitable effects of market integration (e.g. increasing prices; negative impact on vulnerable sectors and groups) to a greater degree than large states resulting in public dissatisfaction. And new Member States have all experienced a decline in mass support for the EU after high expectations for membership were not realized in the post-accession period.

There was limited evidence of *downloading* processes as the EU does not prescribe any models for states to shape specific support for the EU. However, there was evidence of *cross-loading* processes where the socialization of Cypriot citizens in the EU arena may have contributed to shaping diffuse support. *Uploading* processes were difficult to identify as Cypriot media outlets have limited access to the European public.

This chapter has examined the impact of Europeanization on the country's political parties and public opinion. In regards to political parties, it focused on reforms in the parties' policy/programmatic content; organizational structures; patterns of party competition; party-government relations; and relations beyond the national party system. It has indicated that *constructivist* and *dual rationalist–constructivist* mechanisms, as well as cross-loading processes, were at work in effecting change in these areas – in contrast, there was little evidence of the work of *rationalist* mechanisms and *downloading* processes. It has also indicated how the *territorial* and *temporal* dimensions of the country such as its small, southern, new and post-colonial status have mediated the impact of these mechanisms and processes. In regards to public opinion, it has examined specific and diffuse support of Cypriots towards the EU and its institutions and policies. It has indicated that *constructivist* mechanisms and *cross-loading* processes were more evident and consistent than *rationalist* mechanisms, while there was little evidence of *downloading* processes. This chapter has also indicated how the *territorial* and *temporal* dimensions of the country such as its small, southern, post-colonial and new status mediated the impact of these mechanisms and processes.

6
Economy

Introduction

The scholarly literature on and interest in the impact of Europeaniza-tion, and particularly the EMU, on domestic policies is in its early stages (Dyson, 2002, 2007; Beetsma *et al.*, 2003; Martin & Ross, 2004). This interest has focused primarily in monetary, exchange rate and fiscal poli-cies that affected the broad parameters of interest rates and price stability, competitiveness and trade, taxation, fiscal deficits and debt, and employ-ment. Studies have also focused on how Member States have impacted the EMU, as for example, the export of economic models and institutions such those of Germany and France (Jeffery & Patterson, 2003; Wolf & Zangl, 1996; Moravscik, 1998; Heisenberg, 1999) and how small Mem-ber States such as Belgium and the Netherlands (Maes & Verdun, 2005) have influenced the process.

Cyprus's accession process, driven primarily by the achievement of a settlement of the problem, had a profound effect in transforming its economy. The latter became more liberalized, capitalized and com-petitive, while there was also an important macroeconomic impact, with changes in patterns of production and consumption as a result of participation in the single market. The EU also energized com-petition, transmitted its prevailing economic paradigm and provided the institutional framework and external legitimization for national macroeconomic policy.

Characteristics of a small and peripheral economy

Cyprus' economy faces particular challenges as a result of its small size, peripheral and distant island status. First, its economy is highly dependent on exports: in light of the fact the domestic market is very small, a relatively high proportion of the country's output of goods and services must be sold on the export market. Secondly, it lacks natural resources: this means that local manufacturers depend heavily on imports of industrial supplies and raw material, which in turn affects their competitiveness both on the domestic and export market. Thirdly, as a distant island, this means that its local manufacturers endure higher per unit costs of transport (by sea or air) which raises the costs of production, and leads to time delays and additional costs such as warehousing.[1] Fourthly, as the quantity of domestic production and exports are negligible in relation to world trade, this leaves local producers unable to influence world markets – they are simply price-takers – and hence vulnerable to any fluctuations that may occur. The EU's protectionist policies will help alleviate this problem in terms of the world market, but it would create a new one from the liberalized European market. Fifthly, in small states infrastructural development is costly – due to the problem of indivisibility – something which undermines competitiveness by discouraging foreign direct investment (Briguglio, 1995; Buttigieg, 2004). Finally, in integrating a micro and peripheral economy into a gigantic block such as the EU – a process identified as 'asymmetric integration' (Armstrong & Read, 2002: 41) – can accentuate problems such as policy autonomy (particularly with respect to trade), trade tax revenue effects and spatial agglomeration which are associated with economic integration in general. The EU's structural and cohesion funds could have compensated for such deficiencies but the small and peripheral status of the country was not taken into account in the economic indicators and figures of the Commission's Directorate-General Regional Policy despite efforts of the country's accession negotiation team.[2] Overall, it is perceived that the EU offers significant benefits from small states' economies as it provides them access to European and world markets, increases internal competition, diversity and efficiency in the economy, as well as help them achieve macro-economic stability which increases their resilience to external shocks.

Historical context

The Cypriot economy during Ottoman rule relied heavily on farming, stock-breeding and the export of agricultural products (e.g. wheat, barley, wine, cotton, olive oil) (Rizopoulou-Egoumenidou, 1996: 196). During this period, there were few attempts made by Ottoman rulers to exploit the island's rich natural resources such as salt, forests and mines (i.e.

copper, iron pyrite, gypsum and asbestos). The island was also plagued by a series of natural disasters (i.e. drought, locusts, earthquakes, plague and famine) that depleted the population and had serious effects on both the population and the economy. Overall, this period was characterized by 'provincialism and decay, shrinking trade and hypotonic governance' (Luke, 1969: 2). Also, patron-client structures based on the *muchtar* system promoted corruption and had a negative impact on the economy.[3] The only local entity which was economically empowered by Ottoman rule – a wider result of the *millet* system[4] – was the Orthodox Church which saw an impressive rise in its land holdings (Rizopoulou-Egoumenidou, 1996: 196).

British rule did not bring an economic renaissance but significantly improved certain areas of the economy such as the mining activity which began to develop in the mid-1920s (24 per cent of GDP) as well as manufacturing (15 per cent of GDP) and construction (3 per cent of GDP) in the early 1950s. External trade of minerals (i.e. copper, iron pyrite) and agricultural products (i.e. wheat, barley, wine, citrus, potatoes) began to expand, particularly with the UK as well as Italy and Germany though the bulk of trade remained with countries such as Greece, Egypt, Palestine and Syria. Also, during this period 25 per cent of imports came from the UK (Angelides, 1996: 218). This period is also credited with the first signs of development of financial institutions in the early 1920s (e.g. Agricultural, Cooperative and Barclays Bank), tourism in the mid-1950s, as well as the organization of trade unions (Angelides, 1996; Brey, 2006). The British also made efforts to dismantle patron–client structures in the wider society, including the economy, with some positive results (Faustmann, 1998; Richter, 2003) though these proved more resilient through the years.[5] Still, the economy remained largely based on the agricultural sector, which accounted for 50 per cent of the GDP in the 1930s and 27 per cent in the 1950s (Angelides, 1996: 224).

With the end of British rule, and during the period 1960–73 the manufacturing and tourism industry began to thrive and drive the economy. Within this period, and with the exception of a recession in 1964 caused by inter-communal strife, the economy showed remarkable growth in GDP averaging 7.4 per cent,[6] investment 11 per cent, consumption 7.3 per cent, imports 10.4 per cent and exports 10.2 per cent. The first oil crisis in 1973, but more importantly, the events in 1974 that led to the division of the island were decisive in changing the nature and structure of the economy.

The war in 1974 inflicted severe economic and social dislocation on the country. It was a serious blow to all dimensions of the economy given the fact that the 37 per cent of the island's territory now under the 'TRNC' was the economic engine of the pre-1974 Republic of Cyprus. Thus, the Cypriot Government controlled part of the island in the south effectively lost 76 per cent of its agricultural resources; 49 per cent of its manufacturing sector; 40 per cent of its construction sector; 56 per cent of its mining and quarrying sector; and 87 per cent of tourist construction and investments. The loss of the port of Famagusta, which handled 83 per cent of the general cargo and 50 per cent of sea passenger traffic, and the closure of the Nicosia International Airport, currently within the buffer zone, were additional blows (Christodoulou, 1992: xlv; Hadjispyrou & Pashardes, 2003: 79). Also, GDP dropped by 17.9 per cent, investment by 29.9 per cent, consumption by 15.2 per cent, imports by 21.3 per cent and exports by 25.2 per cent. Furthermore, as a result of the influx of 200,000 Greek-Cypriot refugees (a third of the community)[7] from the Turkish controlled part, unemployment increased to 15.2 per cent (from around 3 per cent) whereas public spending increased by 11 per cent, reflecting the expansionary policy followed by the government as part of a general reconstruction policy (Hadjispyrou & Pashardes, 2003: 74–5).[8]

The reconstruction policy essentially consisted of four Economic Emergency Action Plans spanning the period 1975–86. The First Emergency Economic Action Plan (1975–76) aimed to provide basic help to Greek-Cypriot refugees, such as employment and living resources as well as laying the foundations for the rebuilding of the *de facto* territory of the country. More specifically, the plan focused on increasing production and raising investment; economizing and increasing foreign exchange reserves; providing maximum employment; and distributing more equitably the new burdens to ensure an acceptable general standard of living. The Action Plan managed to utilize the available resources, particularly displaced labour and available raw materials, re-build the infrastructure (for example, it opened a new airport in Larnaca) and oriented production to external markets. By 1976, the GDP was nearly four-fifths of that in 1973 and unemployment was reduced to a low 8.2 per cent (Christodoulou, 1992: xxxiv).

The Second Emergency Action Plan (1977–78) aimed to accelerate and broaden economic recovery from the war, and at the same time, creating conditions for sustainable development. There was emphasis on privatization and addressing the structural disadvantages of the economy such as its small size, shortage of domestic raw materials, low technological production, and labour oriented production. There was also emphasis on increasing exports and attracting direct foreign investment, particularly from Europe. The plan had its successes in increasing the country's

GDP to an average annual growth of 11.6 per cent and achieving levels of production comparable to the pre-war period (Hadjispyrou & Pashardes, 2003: 75). The economy was boosted by export manufacturing, construction for meeting the housing needs of refugees as well as for tourism infrastructure. Unemployment fell by 2 per cent and fixed capital formation was 20.5 per cent of GDP in 1978, compared to 13.9 per cent in 1976.

The Third Emergency Economic Action Plan (1979–81), aimed to consolidate these achievements and further address the structural weaknesses of the economy. Incentives and facilities were created for the adoption of technology, for training and for the use of domestic raw materials. Attention was paid to accessing overseas markets and improving fiscal and monetary soundness. Remarkably, boosted by exports and tourism, real GDP over the period 1976–81 exceeded its 1973 pre-war level, reaching a high of 12 per cent in economic growth (Hadjispyrou & Pashardes, 2003: 75). At the same time, the economy had to face high oil prices and a significant budget deficit. And inflation reached a high 13.5 per cent in 1980, with a high number of days of strike in 1981.

The Fourth Emergency Economic Action Plan (1982–86) recognized the reduced demand from the Arab markets and the need to improve access to West European markets, primarily creating closer relationships with the European Economic Community. Emphasis was also given to advancing technology in production and improving marketing. In this period, GDP increased by 5.6 per cent annually – mainly as a result of growth in tourism and services – employment was high and inflation was 1.2 per cent in 1986, down from 10.8 per cent in 1981. However, the competitiveness in domestic production remained problematic, as did the budget deficit. Investment was maintained primarily as a result of the public sector's contribution, but the annual rate of increase in fixed capital investment turned out to average about half of what had been planned, namely only 0.7 per cent. That amounted to 23.8 per cent of GDP in 1986, compared to 31 per cent in 1981. Investment in new products and high technology was particularly low and consumption rose faster than the growth of the economy. External public debt amounted to £449.1 million in 1986, that is, 39.2 per cent of GNP. Domestic savings rose by 15.2 per cent annually and were 20 per cent of GDP in 1986 (Christodoulou, 1992: xxxvi).

The Fifth Emergency Economic Action Plan (1987–91) was specifically designed to deal with the pressures of Europeanization. The signing of the Additional Protocol in 1987, envisioning the gradual completion of a Custom's Union between Cyprus and the EU, highlighted the need and acted as a significant external incentive in order to restructure and modernize the economy, improve competitiveness and transfer technology. Midway through it was revised by the new President-elect George Vassiliou, styling it the Five Year Development Plan (1989–93). The Plan aimed for an annual average growth of 5 per cent 'which would emanate from external demand and will be mainly the result of improved productivity'.[9] Unemployment and inflation would be kept at low levels and priority would be given to balancing 'fiscal magnitudes' to make the social and development programmes feasible. The target set for fiscal deficit was 1.5 per cent of GDP in 1992 (from 3.9 in 1989). The plan considered the increased dependence on tourism at the expense of primary and secondary sectors to be undesirable. It aimed for flexible specialization in manufacturing to overcome weaknesses in this sector, while it also encouraged the development of small-size enterprises.

Bearing in mind the social and economic dislocation from the 1974 catastrophe, the extent of the economic recovery in the mid-1970s and 1980s was remarkable and was rightly characterized as an 'economic miracle' (or *Wirtschaftswunder* by the German press) (cited in Christodoulou, 1992: xxi).[10] It was an achievement that was arguably a result of sheer determination, fortitude and ingenuity of a people in the face of disaster. In the post 1974 period, the Cypriot economy was transformed into a relatively modern economy by using dynamic services, industrial and agricultural sectors, infrastructure and highly educated human capital despite the overwhelming loss of resources to the north part of the island.

In 2007, the Republic of Cyprus ranked among the high-income countries in the EU, with a per capita income of CY£12383 or €21600 (EU-27, €25200). It had the highest standard of living of the new Member States and higher than some old Member States (i.e. Spain, Greece, Portugal), ranking 14th in the EU-27 (85 per cent of EU average) and 25th worldwide. The average GDP growth in the past three years was 3.8 per cent (well above the EU average of 2.0)[11] while inflation stood at 2.5 per cent and unemployment at 3.7 per cent over that period. Its economy was still dominated by the service sector, including tourism, which accounts for 77.6 per cent of the GDP and employs 72.1 per cent of the labour force – with tourism accounting for approximately a quarter of those figures. Industry and construction contribute 19.2 per cent of the GDP and employ 20.8 per cent of the labour, while agriculture makes up only 3.2 per cent of GDP and employs 7.1 per cent of the labour force. This significant dependence on tourism renders the economy vulnerable to exogenous economic and geopolitical shocks. Moreover, the island's location means that the maritime services industry (i.e. revenues from registry and taxes) is significant. In particular, Cyprus has the third largest merchant ship fleet within the EU, with 16 per cent of the total fleet of EU-27 registered under Cyprus flag. It also has the ninth merchant ship fleet within the world.[12] These ships registered in Cyprus are attracted by relatively light regulatory conditions. In consequence, Cyprus is not a natural supporter of the Commission's preferences for stronger regulation of such aspects of marine transportation as environmental damage liability and safety standards. Overall, Cypriot policy preferences tend to vary according to the service area in question, and contain a mixture of liberalizing, protectionist, and non-interference stances (Nugent, 2006: 65).

The impact of Europeanization on Cyprus' economy

The impact of Europeanization on the economic institutions and policies of the country has been significant. The tremendous incentive of participating in the common market meant that the Cypriot government had to implement significant and often drastic reforms in its economic policy regime. The Commission's Regular Reports clearly indicated the areas that needed to be addressed, and the European Central Bank provided the government with specific guidelines and directives for reform of the country's economic policy regime. Within a time span of five years, the Cypriot government implemented reforms that aimed at the dispersion of power among financial institutions and the liberalization of important sectors of the economy such as the telecoms and air transport; the provision of commercial freedom to banks in their lending policies and the revision of terms in private borrowing (e.g. eliminating the 9 per cent interest rate ceiling); the increase of the fiscal discipline on the government by ending its ability to rely on the Cyprus Central Bank and other financial institutions to cover its public deficits; and the enhancement of the Cyprus Central Bank's supervisory function over a more open and competitive domestic financial market.[13] There was also borrowing of economic policies and institutions from countries such as Greece, Slovenia and Ireland, in particular the establishment of EU Directorates within the Ministry of Finance and the Central Bank, macro-economic and fiscal policies with regards to the adaptation of the euro and even campaign strategies for the promotion of the common currency.[14] Also, with the signing of the AA in 1972, the RoC received €210 million in the form of four Financial Protocols within the period 1978–99. These funds were made available in the form of loans (€152 million), grants (€51 million), and risk capital (€7 million) with the main target sectors being small and medium-size enterprises, environment, energy and transport.

Liberalization was a political objective for the ruling centre and right-wing parties in the 1990s (i.e. DISY and DIKO) and it has continued, albeit less enthusiastically with the ruling left-wing AKEL, now in coalition with DIKO. Liberalization did not mean solely or even primarily that private enterprise had to adapt to tougher competition. Apart from the elimination of tariffs, EU regulations affected the structure of the Cypriot industry in terms of both ownership and competition. State ownership played a key role in transport, utilities, communications, energy, tourism and even banking. In the early 1980s, state-owned companies accounted for a significant percentage of both value added and employee remuneration. The extent and role of state ownership was progressively redefined. First, publicly owned industries now have less access to funding, since EU regulations placed a limit on injections of public money. Secondly, the Cypriot government had a reputation for intervening heavily in the economy – a tendency which was highlighted on various occasions – whereas this activity has now decreased. Liberalization has occurred in important sectors of the economy such as telecoms and air transport, whereas in the National Convergence Plan (2005–2009), the government recognized the need for the liberalization of the energy sector and the postal services as well as transforming cooperative societies into banks, since liberalization is expected to leave the cooperatives in a vulnerable position.

Furthermore, Europeanization has also affected the trade patterns of the country. Globalization and Europeanization have had a positive impact by bringing about a marked growth in the 'openness' of the Cypriot economy. Increasing internationalization and, in particular, the growth and diversification of exports from agricultural to manufacturing products, helped reduce what has been seen as traditional curbs in economic growth: the absence of an external dimension combined with a chronic trade deficit for as long as 50 years. Having signed up to the General Agreement on Tariffs and Trade (GATT) in the 1960s, Cyprus is a founding member of the World Trade Organization (WTO). With much of its industry dependent on imports of raw materials, including many foodstuffs, it has consistently sought to develop liberal trading relations. With the advent of the AA in the 1970s and the signing of additional protocols in the 1980s, the Cypriot economy became more open with an increase in both exports and imports (Figure 6.1). The Community's various trade agreements with non-EU countries have also facilitated the market penetration of Cypriot products in these markets.

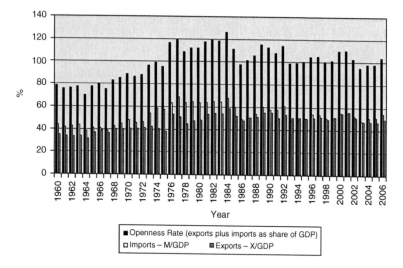

Source: Data compiled from Statistical Service (1960–2006), Cyprus.
Figure 6.1   Openness of the Cypriot economy, (1960–2006): exports and imports of goods and services (% of GDP at market prices)

Some scholars argue, however, that the improvement has only been relative as Cyprus' trade in merchandize as a percentage of GDP has remained one of the lowest in the EU. Ayres (1999: 55), for example, indicates that while the EU and its Association Agreements contributed positively to export diversification into manufacturing, overall export performance with the EU was relatively poor and this was reflected in the continuing importance of the markets in the Middle East (e.g. Egypt, Israel, Lebanon and Syria) and the growing prominence of the re-export trade. Similarly, Tsoukalas & Loizides (1999: 145) indicate that total exports to the EU increased moderately by 21 per cent during 1988–94 – despite the Custom's Union agreement – while exports to the Arab countries also increased by 20 per cent while those to Bulgaria, Romania and Russia almost trebled during the same period.

More recent data, however, indicate otherwise, that liberalization has indeed resulted in a significant shift in the quality and geographical orientation of Cypriot trade. The process of accession and membership has meant that EU states have become the main trading partners of Cypriot companies – indicative is the fact that both exports and imports towards EU countries have increased relative to non-EU countries (Figures 6.2 and 6.3).

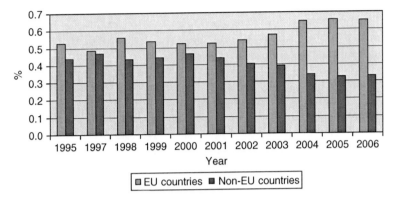

Source: Data compiled from Statistical Service (1995–2006), Cyprus.
Figure 6.2 Cyprus imports from EU and non-EU countries

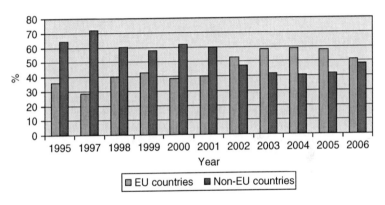

Source: Data compiled from Statistical Service (1995–2006), Cyprus.
Figure 6.3 Cyprus exports to EU and non-EU countries

This trend is clearly evident in Figure 6.4. The percentage of total Cypriot foreign trade with the EU-15(25) has increased since 1985 relatively to Middle Eastern countries (ME), Asian countries (AS) and the United States (US). For example, in 1985, Cypriot trade with EU-15 amounted to 57 per cent of total trade, whereas in 2006, with the addition of the Central and Eastern European countries, trade with EU-25 amounted to 70 per cent. In contrast, trade with Middle Eastern countries has diminished from 23 per cent of total trade in 1986 to 17 per cent in 2006; trade with Asian countries has also diminished from 16 per cent of total trade in 1986 to 9 per cent in 2006; trade with the US remained

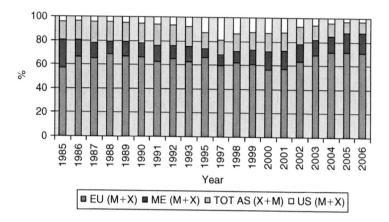

Source: Data compiled from Statistical Service (1985–2006), Cyprus.
Figure 6.4   Total Cypriot foreign trade (1985–2006 with selected countries)

low around 4 per cent of total trade throughout the years, with a short-lived increase in the late 1990s (a few years before accession) amounting to 19 per cent of total trade. That surge of trade increase with the US in 1997 was partly a result of the Cypriot government's decision to revise its policy on foreign direct investment, allowing 100 per cent of foreign ownership in certain cases. During that time, around 40 US owned firms were established in Cyprus, about half operating exclusively on an off-shore basis. By 2006, however, European firms gradually re-established their presence in the island and superseded their share of Cypriot trade.

In regards to the Middle East, total Cypriot trade towards these countries has diminished but nonetheless, this region is still the second trading partner of the island, with Lebanon, Syria, Egypt, the United Arab Emirates and Israel being the main partners.[15] With regards to the EU, the main trading partner of Cyprus has consistently been the United Kingdom, followed by Greece, Italy, Germany and France. Cyprus also maintains significant trade with Russia and an increasing trade with China (which is not included in the Asian countries). In August 2006, Cyprus signed a bi-lateral economic cooperation with China on issues such as trade, research, science and technology. Trade relations between the two countries have witnessed rapid developments over the years, with trade volumes reaching 300 million USD in 2005, up 52 per cent of the previous years.[16]

Europeanization had less of a positive impact on the competitiveness[17] of the country's economy. Competitiveness is of great importance to small states because of their particular vulnerabilities and handicaps (Briguglio & Cordina, 2004). For example, in small states infrastructural development is costly – due to the problem of indivisibility – something which undermines competitiveness by discouraging foreign direct investment (Briguglio, 1995; Buttigieg, 2004). Also, given the lack of natural resources, local manufacturers depend heavily on imports of industrial supplies and raw material, which in turn affects their competitiveness both on the domestic and export market. Thus, improving this indicator became a major objective for successive Cypriot Governments. EMU guidelines in regards to fiscal, monetary and exchange rate policies, Lisbon Process guidelines in regards to micro-economic and employment reforms partly aimed at addressing the issue of low competitiveness in the island's economy. Yet the state still has significant weaknesses in this area with global reports on competitiveness published by the World Economic Forum, ranking Cyprus as one of the least competitive countries in the EU, ranking 23rd among the EU-27 (46th worldwide), with Greece, Poland, Romania and Bulgaria being less competitive. There are various factors for this. Firstly, many of the EMU institutional and policy guidelines have not been fully understood and absorbed by the government and particularly the business environment.[18] Factors such as a continuing high public debt, goods market inefficiencies (i.e. high agricultural policy costs, significant foreign ownership restrictions), labour market inefficiencies (i.e. inflexible wages, stringent hiring and firing practices, favoritism in promotions based on family and friends relations), and weak innovation (i.e. low R & D, little collaboration between companies and universities in research, and moderate/weak scientific research institutions) have kept competitiveness indicators low. Also, demographic factors associated with the small size of the country, such as low fertility, aging population and significant emigration also undermine competitiveness. Successive Cypriot governments have shared the aim of remedying these problems, although distinct ruling party coalitions have differed over the best means to achieve this, not only because of ideological preferences but also because of political constraints on their actions and the prevailing economic paradigm.

Moreover, Europeanization had a significant effect on the macroeconomic fiscal and monetary policy of the country. The two main objectives of these two policies were to meet the Maastricht convergence criteria[19] that would enable the country to enter the eurozone as well as the Lisbon Process criteria set out to make the EU 'the most competitive and dynamic knowledge-driven economy by 2010'.

In regards to acceding the eurozone, by mid 2007 Cyprus met all but one of the Maastricht criteria, that is, it needed to lower its public debt to 60 per cent of GDP, being 69.2 per cent in May 2007.[20] Its inflation rates (2.2 per cent), long term interest rates (3.1 per cent), annual budget deficit (2.5 per cent of GDP) were within the required EU criteria, while Cyprus was admitted to the Exchange Rate Mechanism (ERM II)[21] in May 2005 towards stabilizing its national currency.[22] By November 2007, Cyprus lowered its public deficit to 60 per cent and was admitted to the eurozone on 1 January 2008.

Regarding the Lisbon League Table, Cyprus ranks 19th (2007 figures). The country has the most expensive electricity prices for industrial users in the EU-27, and it also ranks among the Member States that pay the highest level of subsidies. Cyprus, along with Spain, has recorded the fastest growth in female employment, and the island boasts the second fastest growth rate in employment in the EU (69.2 per cent) – in touching distance of the 70 per cent Lisbon target. Cyprus has thus made significant advancements in terms of bringing people into the workforce.[23] Yet, Cyprus is in the second to last position in regards to the R&D sector, which accounted for only 0.5 per cent of the GDP, far below the Lisbon goal of 3 per cent of GDP for Gross Domestic Expenditures on R&D (GERD) and having minimal contribution from the private industry (19.8 per cent of total).[24] And it still records one of the highest disparities of incomes between men and women in Europe.[25]

In its Broad Economic Policy Guidelines in 2004, the European Commission identified two main challenges for the Cyprus economy: (a) to ensure a reduction of the general government deficit on a sustainable basis; (b) to increase the diversification of the economy towards higher value added activities. In order to meet the first challenge the Commission recommended that the Cypriot Government reduce the general government deficit in a credible and sustainable way within a multi-annual framework in line with the decisions to be taken by the Council in the context of the forthcoming budgetary surveillance exercise. In order to meet the second challenge, the Commission recommended that the Cypriot Government steps up its efforts to increase the adequacy of skilled human capital, promote R&D and innovation, in particular in the business sector, and improve conditions to facilitate Information and Communications Technology (ICT) diffusion; and finally, continue to simplify the business and taxation environment.

In its yearly country reports (2006), the Commission gave specific guidelines for Cyprus in order to meet the euro target: the government will need to continue its medium term fiscal consolidation strategy, with the authorities ensuring budgetary discipline and effective financial supervision. Continued vigilance will be needed to ensure that wage developments remain in line with productivity growth. Further structural reform efforts aimed at enhancing the economy's flexibility and adaptability, including progress with the de-indexation of wage mechanisms, will also be needed in order to strengthen domestic adjustment mechanisms and support the overall competitiveness of the economy.[26] Finally, in view of the level of public debt and the projected increase in age-related spending, Cyprus is invited to control public pension expenditure and implement further reforms in the areas of pensions and health care in order to improve the long-term sustainability of public finances'.[27]

In light of these economic indicators and guidelines, the Cyprus government responded with its two main instruments of Europeanization of its macroeconomic policy: the National Convergence Plan (2005–2009 and 2006–2010)[28] (Table 6.1) and its National Lisbon Programme (2005).[29] These two programmes laid out objectives in the areas of fiscal, monetary and exchange rate policies as well as structural reforms. With regards to fiscal policy, there was emphasis on the sustainability of public finances via a redirection of public expenditure and the reduction of public deficit in order to comply with the EU criteria. Attention was given to the need to curtail current expenditure and restructure public spending in favour capital expenditure and research and education. Concerning monetary and exchange rate policy, there was emphasis in maintaining macroeconomic stability and low inflation – primarily with the use of the Exchange Rate Mechanism (ERM II). In regards to structural reforms, the aim was to enhance competition by strengthening the Commission for the Protection of Competition, rationalizing state aid, raising efficiency of the public sector, restructuring semi-governmental organizations with a view to enhancing their flexibility, encouraging foreign direct investment,[30] reducing the regulatory and administrative burden and improving the overall business climate; increase the diversification of the economy towards higher value added activities (via mainly an increased utilization of the comparative advantages of the island) by upgrading and diversifying the tourism product as well as diversifying towards other services such as banking and financial services, business services and education and health; promote R&D innovation and facilitation, mainly through the Research Promotion Foundation as well as the more effective coordination of government-funded academic and private sector research programmes; upgrading basic infrastructure; further developing human capital including the enhancement of the links of the

Table 6.1   The National Convergence Plan of Cyprus (2005–2009 and 2006–2010)

Expenditure	Revenue
Reduction of	*Increase of*
• government sector employment growth	• land and survey fees (for issuing title deeds, mortgaging, acquiring and inspecting immovable property).
• salary increases to civil servants (0%, 2004–2005; 2%, 2006; 1%, 2007).	• vat tax base
• pension expenditure (retirement age in the public sector shift from 60 to 63 years of age, and to 65 in the private sector).	• tax efficiency (better charge on land appreciation due to zoning changes; improving the of the Revenue Collecting Departments; revaluation of individual property at current market price; bating tax evasion)
• current expenditure (growth rate ceiling to 2%)	
• capital expenditure (growth rate ceiling to 6%)	• economic activities (regularisation of dividend income policy for semi-governmental organizations; improved utilization of government property)
• (in real terms) agricultural subsidies and transfers to semi-governmental organizations (fixed at the level of 2005 in nominal terms).	
• current transfers (ceiling on the rate of growth of 2%).	*Introduction of*
• compensation for overtime work in the public sector.	• taxation on non-developed land inside Town Planning areas
• net interest payments (brought by the reduction of stock of debt)	• mobile telecommunication tax
• government's contribution to the Social Security Funds (increase in contribution of private and public sector employees)	• mobile telecommunication licences
	One-off
	• tax amnesty
Abolition of	• concession for buildings erected with minor irregularities
• the unemployment benefit granted to retired public and private sector employees.	*Compensating expenditure transfers from the EU Budget*
Introduction of	
• *means testing* for certain social benefit schemes.	

Impact on the deficit							
2005	*2006*	*2007*	*2008*	*2005*	*2006*	*2007*	*2008*
0.2	−1.7	−0.3	−0.8	1.6	0.1	0.0	0.0

Source: adapted from data from Ministry of Finance, Cyprus.

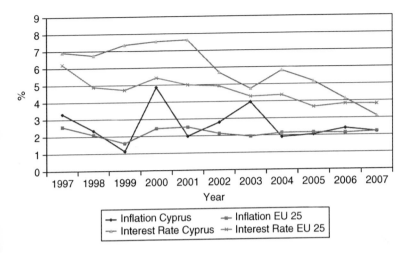

Source: data compiled from Eurostat (1997–2007).
Figure 6.5 Criteria for nominal convergence in Cyprus compared to the EU average: inflation and interest rates

educational system to labour market needs and wider use of information technology; developing a comprehensive national framework for life-long learning; upgrading and adapting skills to labour market needs; enhancing conditions for social cohesion and ensuring environmental sustainability; and reforming social security and health care systems in light of the prospective population ageing. Finally, there is also recognition of the need to further liberalize important sectors such as energy and the postal services as well as transforming cooperative societies into banks, since liberalization is expected to leave the cooperatives in a vulnerable position.

Cypriot inflation has most of the time been above the EU average (Figure 6.5). It reached its peak in 2000 (4.86 per cent) well above the EU average (2.44 per cent). Since membership of EMU makes it impossible to control inflation by manipulating interest rates, the only option (apart from enhancing liberalization and competitiveness) was to reduce the public deficit. The government's policy as outlined in the Convergence Plan was successful in reducing the deficit throughout the years (Figure 6.6). From a high 6.3 per cent in 2003 it has gradually converged on the EU average, being 1.8 in 2006 and 1.6 in 2007. As a result, inflation has also been reduced to 2.4 per cent in 2006 and 2.2 per cent in 2007, again converging with the EU average. Interest rates have also

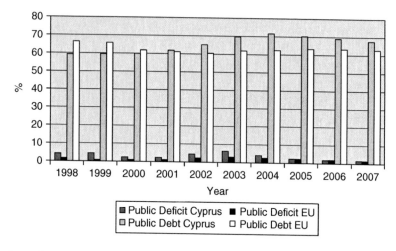

Source: data compiled from Eurostat (1998–2007).
Figure 6.6   Criteria for nominal convergence in Cyprus compared to EU average: public deficit and public debt

followed a similar pattern – while they have always been above the EU average, reaching a peak in 2001 (7.63 per cent), they are now gradually converging to the EU average with 4.12 in 2006 and 2.1 in 2007.

Identification of mechanisms, processes and dimensions of Europeanization

Many of the above reforms (e.g. liberalization of traditionally state-controlled sectors, interest rates and capital controls, reduction of public deficit, curbing inflation, independence of Central Bank) were generally favoured as long-term plans by successive Cypriot governments in order to deal with the effects of globalization, but there was little political will to implement them primarily because there were 'no serious problems to the economy' – they only actually came about in the early 00s as a result of the strong *rationalist* external incentive mechanisms outlined by the Maastricht criteria as a condition for participation in the eurozone, and which 'speeded up the process'.[31] The Association and Custom's Union agreements also worked as an external incentive for macro-economic reforms but their impact was comparatively smaller. Indeed, some policies such as the liberalization of the telecoms industry generated significant resistance from domestic actors such as semi-state organizations (e.g. Cyprus Telecommunication Authority) as well as left-wing political parties (e.g. AKEL and EDEK). Resistance was also generated in relation to the independence of the Central Bank particularly through the establishment of an 'external auditor' for the bank – in that case the government insisted that the Republic's independent General Auditor constituted such authority whereas the Commission insisted on the appointment of an external auditor from an international audit organization.[32] Moreover, *rationalist* external incentives also impacted on the openness of Cypriot economy and the quality and geographical orientation of Cypriot trade. In particular, the strengthening of institutional ties of Cyprus with the EU led to the opening of the Cypriot economy and an increase in both exports and imports. It also led to a qualitative shift of trade from agricultural to manufacturing products and a geographical shift of trade from the Middle East to European markets. Yet these mechanisms had little impact on increasing the competitiveness of the country's economy – Cyprus still ranks low in this area – with the *territorial* dimensions of the country such as its small, distant and peripheral status playing a key role in this. In particular, competitiveness in small Cyprus is undermined by its lack of natural resources – which means that local manufacturers depend heavily on imports of industrial supplies and raw material – as well as from its costly infrastructural development which discourages foreign direct investment. Its distant status further undermines competitiveness as local manufacturers endure higher costs of transport which raises costs of production and leads to time delays and additional costs such as warehousing.

Moreover, *constructivist* mechanisms were evident in the social learning process of Cypriot officials from the Ministry of Finance, Planning Bureau and the Central Bank with their counterparts at the EU level, as well as with Commission and European Central Bank officials played a significant role in instilling European beliefs, norms, ideas, and practices in national economic policy-making. National policy-makers have realized that their economic rhetoric and discourse at the domestic level is being closely monitored by officials at the highest level in Brussels and Frankfurt, and in many cases they were forced to 'tone down' disagreements concerning issues such as the Stability Pact and the euro.[33]

Furthermore, change was also induced through the *dual rationalist–constructivist* lesson-drawing mechanism where mimetism and learning from 'best' and 'worst' practices took place in the form of the establishment of EU Directorates within the Ministry of Finance and the Central Bank, macro-economic and fiscal policies on the adaptation of the euro and campaign strategies for the promotion of the euro. Lesson-drawing took place from other small states such as Ireland, perceived by economic domestic economic circles as a 'successful model' of a small and relatively poor country which adapted successfully the euro, absorbed effectively the EU's Structural and Cohesion Funds, and generally utilized its membership status to achieve a strong and competitive economy,[34] Slovenia as the state that preceded Cyprus in adopting the euro, and from Greece's 'successes and failures' in this regard.[35] Here again, the *territorial* and *temporal* dimensions of the country such as its small, southern and new status shaped the source of lesson-drawing (i.e. small Ireland, small and southern Greece; small and new Slovenia).

In regards to the *downloading* process of Europeanization, there has been an adaptation of institutions and policies with the aim of meeting the demands of the EMU and the Lisbon Process, whereas there was – as expected – little evidence of *uploading* any Cypriot economic policies at the EU level but there was evidence of *cross-loading* in the form of socialization of Cypriot economic officials as well as lesson-drawing both from perceived successful economic models such as that of Ireland, and less successful ones such as that of Greece.

The North–South development gap

At the time of the *de facto* ethnic division in 1974 per capita GDP in the north part of the island (that is, areas of the Republic of Cyprus in which the government does not exercise effective control) was about half that in the south. The discrepancy in labour productivity was even larger, with the level in the north estimated at slightly below 40 per cent that in the south. During the following two decades, the economy of the north moved from a largely agricultural base toward light manufacturing. Then, in the early 1990s, export-oriented services – tourism and higher education – took off. Nonetheless, the gap in living standards *vis-à-vis* the south appears to have continually widened further. Average annual GDP growth during 1977–2000 reached about 3.9 per cent against 4.9 per cent in the south while labour productivity in 2000 still stood at 40 per cent of the southern level (Demetriades *et al.*, 2003). By 2003, the north was generating a GDP of €1.1 billion, one-tenth of that in the south. Given a population of nearly 220,000 (under 30 per cent of that in the south), GDP per capita was some €5300, that is, one third of the southern level (Watson & Noe, 2005).[36]

Although studies (Watson, 2006) suggest that the income gap between the north and the south may in fact be narrowing due to an observed acceleration of growth in the north that supersedes that in the south (Table 6.2), this growth does not appear to be fully sustainable and

Table 6.2 Real GDP growth rates in the North and the South (%)

	2001	*2002*	*2003*	*2004*	*2005*
South	4.1	2.1	1.9	3.8	3.9
North	5.4	6.9	11.4	15.4	10.6

Source: Watson (2006: 3).

conventional wisdom remains that the north will continue to lag far behind the standards of the south for some time to come. Eichengreen *et al.* (2004), for example, indicate that even in a benign scenario, incomes in the north might still be only 62 per cent of levels in the south by 2020.

This persistent development gap with the south is even more striking if one considers the north's economic potential based on its fertile agricultural land, exceptional beaches, major historical sites, extensive tourist accommodation and key infrastructure (including a main port). This has been attributed to a range of factors, including international non-recognition, economic isolation and the limitations of direct trade with the EU since 1994 following a decision of the European Court of Justice on certification for products originating from Cyprus (Ayres, 2003). Yet these factors cannot explain this gap as the case of Taiwan – one of the most prosperous economies in South East Asia – indicates that non-recognition is not necessarily a barrier to economic growth (Ugur, 2003: 61). Non-recognition did not also stop tourism in this part of the island. In fact, net annual income tourism income in the north increased from US$30 million in 1977 to US$208 million in 2000.[37] Also, 'TRNC' exporters enjoyed the same level of preferences as their Greek-Cypriot counterparts in the EU, and especially the UK, market. The 1994 ruling of the European Court of Justice which requires certification of the 'TRNC' exports by the Cypriot government has been an important obstacle, but cannot explain the widening of the per-capita income gap, which had widened well before 1994. In addition, the EU continued to be the main destination for the Northern Cyprus exports despite the certification problem – absorbing 64 per cent in 1975 and 67 per cent in 1993. After the ruling, the traditional 'TRNC' exports to the EU have declined, but this decline was offset by improved market access secured in Turkey.

Thus, the widening gap between the north and the south can be better explained by other important factors. More specifically, it is related to the different economic policy responses of the two parts of the island after the trauma of 1974. For example, the south has deliberately encouraged entrepreneurship as a means of job creation and the labour force was incorporated into a corporatist structure to facilitate social conflict resolution and ensure that workers benefit from the economic growth to be achieved. Also, Greek-Cypriots were successful in combining an export-oriented development policy with capital controls, interest rate controls and tailor-made financial arrangements that kept interest rates low and maintained currency stability.

In contrast, the north chose a clientelistic strategy that involved employment by the state rather than the private sector and stifling of productive investment. Throughout the post-1974 period, total government expenditures in the 'TRNC' was higher than total tax revenue. As a result, the annual deficit financing ranged between 10 and 20 per cent of the GDP. As of 1997, the deficit/GDP ratio in the 'TRNC' (13.3 per cent) was two and a half times the deficit/GDP ratio in the south (5.1 per cent) and more than three times the deficit ratio in the EU (4.0 per cent). What is more striking, however, is the size of the public sector as employer and source of employment-related transfers. The share of wages, salaries and transfers in the GDP amounts to more than the share of government revenue, revealing that the TRNC's public employment bill and employment related transfers have been higher than its total revenue. This clearly indicates that the legitimacy of the 'TRNC' has been mainly based on the disbursement of quasi-private goods (employment and employment-related transfers) rather than public goods such as stable macroeconomic environment or social insurance (Ugur, 2003: 62).

The 'TRNC's heavy reliance on Turkish aid and economy is also of particular importance. Accordingly, foreign aid accounts for as much as 10 per cent of the GDP in the 'TRNC'. About 75–90 per cent of this foreign aid originates from Turkey. This makes the 'TRNC' vulnerable to any downward cycles that the Turkish economy experiences such as the financial crisis in the 1980, 1990 and 1994. But it also perpetuates Turkey's influence on economic and political choices of the 'TRNC' governments, something which undermines efforts for reunification and complicates the EU's and the Republic of Cyprus' task should a political solution be achieved. Thus, it is not surprising to observe that the widening of the income gap between the North and the South has been accompanied by continuous support for the political system of the North (Ugur, 2003: 63). In that sense, the widening gap between the North and the South has been mainly due to the inefficiency of the institutional/governance structures established in the North after the division;

and the synchronization with Turkey's financial markets as a result of the adoption of the Turkish currency as legal tender (Ugur, 2003: 62).

Economic convergence should be the aim for both communities as this would also lay the groundwork for a reunification of the island. As the Annan Plan referendum indicated, one of the factors that contributed to the 'No' vote of the Greek-Cypriot community was the perceived economic costs that reunification would entail – as a result of the transfer of funds and resources to the north – especially for the lower income classes of the south (Lordos, 2006: 18). A strategy for economic convergence before a settlement can ameliorate some of these Greek-Cypriot fears. Indeed, the economic gains from convergence can be substantial for both the south and the north. Although the two communities are specialized in similar sectors, there are significant synergies that can be realized, as well as complementary market niches they can exploit. In tourism, the north can draw in new and repeat visitors who will, in many cases, spend periods in both communities, including in markets such as eco-tourism. In exporting educational services, the two communities can potentially exploit complementary regional catchments. Convergence in the north will offer a valuable market for the south; and companies based in the south (including overseas investors) would be among those contributing to, and benefiting from, accelerated development in the north. In the labour and other production factor markets, there are significant potential synergies as well (Watson & Noe, 2005). Yet, successful integration in the north hinges on two conditions: a) substantial resource transfers that go beyond the north's entitlement to EU structural funds; and b) a conditionality clause that would be functional in breaking the path dependency by tying the resource transfer to modernization and institution building in the north (Ugur, 2003: 65).

The EU has an important role in contributing to the economic integration of the two *de facto* divided parts of the island. After the sudden but partial opening of the division line in April 2003, the Council on the basis of a Commission proposal approved the 'Green Line Regulation'[38] on 29 April 2004 which would facilitate the movement of persons and goods through the division line of the island.[39] On 7 July 2004, the Commission proposed a comprehensive package of aid and trade measures in order to promote economic integration of the island and improve contact between the two communities: the 'Aid Regulation'[40] aiming to boost economic development in the Turkish-Cypriot community and the 'Direct Trade Regulation'[41] aiming to establish special conditions of trade with the north such as opening Turkish-Cypriot sea and air ports to direct trade with the EU. After intensive debates, the Council approved the Aid Regulation on 27 February 2006 – due to the delayed adoption only €139 million (of the €259 million originally earmarked) were made available to the Turkish-Cypriots.[42] Finally, the Commission has implemented an Institution Building programme through the TAIEX instrument in order to help prepare the Turkish-Cypriot community for the future application of Community Law.[43]

This chapter examined the impact of Europeanization on the country's economy. It particularly focused on the country's economic policy institutions, macroeconomic and fiscal policy, competitiveness and trade patterns. It has also examined the impact of the EU on the economic development gap between the two communities. It has indicated that *rationalist, constructivist* and *dual rationalist–constructivist* mechanisms, as well as *downloading* and *cross-loading* processes were at work in effecting impact in these areas – in contrast, there was little evidence of *uploading* processes. It has also indicated that how the *territorial* and *temporal* dimensions of the country such as its small, southern, distant, peripheral and new status have mediated the impact of these mechanisms and processes.

7
Agricultural and Regional Policy

Introduction

There is an emerging literature on the regional and agricultural policies of states. In regards to the agricultural dimension, these studies have focused mostly on state–farmer relations, state structures, and on a European model of agricultural policy (Rynning-Roederer, 2007: 212). In regards to state–farmer relations, these studies have emphasized the strong, quasi-institutionalized, and exclusive partnerships between state and farmers; powerful national peak farm organizations, often generously subsidized by the state; and the exclusion of non-farm interests from agricultural policy-making. By virtue of these partnerships, farmers benefited from an extended discretionary power over decision-making, and overtook key areas of implementation. The state, in return, could count on the support of farmers to undertake the necessary restructuring of this sector while delegating to farm leaders the responsibility of administering painful reforms. In regards to state structures, there was a focus on how different state structures, defined with reference to the strong/weak states or centralized/decentralized state dichotomies, affect policy efficiency and the possibility for agency capture at the national level. Finally, there was also focus on how CAP has impacted domestic agricultural policy, that is, with mixed findings pointing towards radical reforms at the domestic level, but also, in some cases, resilience of distinctive national policy and a renationalization of the CAP. In regards to regional policy, studies have focused on how it has empowered regional and sub-national governments in Member States, albeit with the watchful eye and 'gate-keeping' role of national governments (Houghe, 1996; Marks *et al.*, 1996; Bache, 1998; Leonardi, 2005) and how EU conditionality has effected change in the regional policies and structures of candidate states (Hughes *et al.*, 2004; Jacoby, 2005).

Both agricultural and regional policies are areas that small states are known to prioritize (Goetschel, 1998: 69) because they gain considerable benefits from them. The former amounts to nearly half of the EU budget and the latter amounts to one-third (2006 figures). Also, small states are committed to the CAP because of their dependence on agricultural exports (Thorhallsson, 2006: 47) and to regional policy because structural and cohesion funds may have significant effects on the economic growth of small economies (as, for example, in the cases of Greece, Portugal and Ireland).

Agricultural policy

At the time of independence (1960–61), agriculture employed 40 per cent of the Cypriot labour force and produced 17.8 per cent of GDP. Agricultural and mineral products constituted the most important export product, accounting for 30 per cent of total exports. The contribution of agriculture to GDP increased during the early years of independence reaching a share of 20.9 per cent in 1965 while 40.6 per cent of the labour force was employed in agriculture in 1963. Agricultural exports reached a peak in 1972 when they accounted for 53.9 per cent of total exports, with potatoes (28.2 per cent), citrus fruit (56.1 per cent), grapes (4.6 per cent) and vegetables (6 per cent) being the main products. The events of 1974 severely disrupted the agricultural sector of the Republic of Cyprus as nearly 40 per cent of arable land was *de facto* lost. As a consequence, the proportion of the population employed in this sector decreased from 35 per cent in 1971 to 18 per cent in 1976. Agriculture's share in GDP also decreased considerably from 17.1 per cent in 1972 to 15.9 per cent in 1976. In the following years, Cyprus experienced rapid growth in other sectors of the economy resulting in a decrease in agriculture's share in the GDP and employment to 5.7 and 11.8 per cent respectively in 1993 (Michael & Zanias, 1999: 126). Nevertheless, agricultural exports remained a significant source of income for the island's economy which was partly the reason why Cyprus signed the AA with the EC which would ensure favourable access of Cypriot products to the important UK market.

Agricultural policy in Cyprus has been traditionally highly interventionist. There has been considerable protection from foreign competition, especially in the case of products where domestic production could satisfy domestic demand. Furthermore, wholesale and retail prices and margins for various products has been controlled by the state authorities such as the Vines Products Commission and the Cyprus Grain Commission, and the external and internal marketing of many products has been controlled by statutory marketing boards. As the accession process took its course, there was an understanding that many of these policies were unsustainable under the EU's CAP. Subsidies for cereals, feed grains and hay, vine growers, water supply, as well as fixed margins for retail and wholesale prices had to be abolished or restructured. Also, the various state-controlled commissions and marketing boards were in disharmony with the *acquis* which prohibited all forms of exclusive market arrangements.

The accession process effected significant changes in the country's agricultural regime. There were amendments of laws regarding horizontal issues, specifically, the creation of a Paying Authority in 2003, an Integrated Administration and Control System (IACS), a Farm Accountancy Data Network (FADN), quality policy, organic farming and state aid; the alignment of the Cypriot agricultural market organizations to that of the EU with regards to arable crops, fruit and vegetables, wine, olive oil, bananas, milk, beef, sheep and pigmeat and eggs and poultry; and as regards rural development. In the veterinary and phytosanitary field, there were also law amendments in regards to animal disease control, trade in live animals and animal products, animal welfare and zootechnics. Measures have also been implemented to align the agricultural sector with the European Agricultural Guidance and Guarantee Fund (EAGGF). There was also the establishment of an EU Directorate within the Ministry of Agriculture as well as other administrative mechanisms and procedures for the horizontal coordination of agricultural matters relating to Europe. Many of these mechanisms were borrowed from countries such as the UK and Netherlands – the former in particular being 'a model of organizational efficiency'.[1] Also, given the common agricultural challenges that southern Mediterranean Greece faces (e.g. lack of natural resources, limited agricultural land, uncompetitive agricultural products), it served as a model for alignment with the agricultural *acquis*. In this regard, Cyprus along with other southern Mediterranean countries (i.e. Greece, Italy, Spain, France, Portugal, Malta, Slovenia) has continuously sought to shape the EU's agricultural policy on the traditional products of this region (i.e. fruit, vegetables, wine and olive oil sectors) insisting on a 'slower pace of liberalization of the market'.[2] Finally, important measures have been implemented concerning some or all of the monopolistic elements of the Cyprus Grain Commission, the Cyprus Olive Products Marketing Board, the Cyprus Milk Industry

Organization and the Cyprus Vine Products Commission, the Cyprus Potato Marketing Board and the Cyprus Carrot and Beetroot Marketing Board.[3]

Accession also meant the convergence of prices and support payments, temporary derogations from the implementation of EU rules and exemptions to free circulation for very sensitive products. It also had a macroeconomic effect in that it affected agricultural prices (for both producers and consumers) and inflation. Moreover, membership affected the whole of the Cypriot agricultural trade, since all products which had been previously state controlled had to open up to a liberalized market, both with other EU countries and with third countries enjoying special trade relationships with the EU.

Membership also changed the pattern of external trade in agricultural products as Cyprus adopted the EU's policies. Community preference meant that many non-EU imports had to be replaced by those of the EU, with the Middle East, North African and Eastern Mediterranean trade patterns affected. In 1999, EC imports of agricultural products originating from Cyprus increased by 5 per cent to €108 million. EC exports to Cyprus increased by 16 per cent to €259 million. The trade balance in favour of the Community amounted in 1999 to €151 million compared to €120 million in 1998. In 2001, overall agricultural trade between Cyprus and the EC showed mixed tendencies. EC imports of agricultural products originating in Cyprus increased by 6 per cent to €107 million. EC exports to Cyprus decreased by 19 per cent to €266 million in 2001. The trade balance in favour of the Community amounted to €159 million compared to €229 million in 2000. EC imports were dominated by fruit and nuts and vegetables. Tobacco, beverages, spirits and vinegar, miscellaneous edible preparations, preparations of cereals, flour, starch or milk and diary products were the main export goods from the EC.

The structural effects on the Cypriot agricultural sector have been mixed. On the one hand, it can be argued that modernization was stimulated by EU accession. Investment increased substantially, but it was directed at increasing production rather than modernization per se. Although accession did force the abolition of some obsolete agricultural processes and their replacement by more advanced technology, the real benefits of the CAP came from greater production rather than structural adaptation. The first years of membership created expectations that Cypriot agriculture would benefit from the CAP's support and guarantee mechanisms, since 2003 the industry has been characterized by overproduction. One of the main existing problems is that Cypriot products are uncompetitive: Cyprus' agricultural productivity is 53 per cent of EU average, and this is most evident in the processed food market and high value added products where the trade balance has deteriorated since accession. Factors that have undermined the competitiveness of Cypriot agricultural products are related to production (i.e. low input use; under utilization of prevailing farm resources), support-services (i.e. under utilization of marketing and distribution systems; weak research and extension capacity) and macro-economic issues (i.e. market liberalization and structural adjustment; low investment in agriculture).[4] Other related factors are an ageing population, technological deficiencies, serious problems of soil erosion, water shortage, small farm units and rural depopulation.[5] As a consequence, while EU goods have penetrated Cyprus, the opposite occurred in a lesser degree.

Moreover, the economic importance of agriculture – both in terms of its percentage of GDP and workforce employed in the sector – has declined over the years (Figure 7.1), yet both of these indicators are still higher than the EU-25. For example, in 2005, the contribution of agriculture in the country's GDP and the percentage employed in the sector was 2.5 per cent and 22.2 per cent respectively, whereas that of the EU-25 was 2.3 per cent and 4.3 per cent respectively. Also, owing to the prevalence of Mediterranean products, the profile of Cyprus' agricultural product range still does not exactly match that of the EU as a whole (Figure 7.2) – potatoes, citrus, vegetables, grapes and olives are still the main export products of the country.

Overall, the process of EU accession and adaptation with the objectives of the CAP, has contributed to the modernization and restructuring of the Cypriot agricultural sector. That did not stop, however, the declining importance of this sector to the island's economy, both in terms of the workforce employed in this sector, as well as its overall share of the GDP. Also, Cypriot agricultural products have remained relatively uncompetitive in the European markets. At the same time, the nature of this sector has changed with greater emphasis on environmental functions, agrotourism and rural development schemes accompanied with changing norms in these areas (e.g. an 'environmental agricultural conscience') adopted from the European agricultural arena.[6]

Fisheries

Fisheries is a very small sector of economic activity contributing to only around 4 per cent of the total value added generated in the broader sector of agriculture and provided direct employment to around 1000 fishermen (2007 figures). Cyprus receives approximately 18 million euro from the European Fisheries fund for the period 2007–2013. In regards

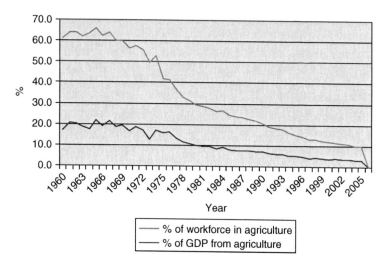

Source: data compiled from Statistical Service (1960–2005), Cyprus.
Figure 7.1 The declining importance of the agricultural sector in the Cypriot economy

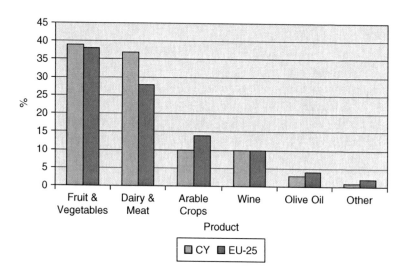

Source: data compiled from Statistical Service (2005), Cyprus & Eurostat (2005).
Figure 7.2 Composition of Cypriot agricultural products compare to EU total (2005)

to reforms in the fisheries sector regime, there were amendment of laws in the field of resource management, inspection and control, state aid laws, and the strengthening of the administrative capacity of the state in this sector. Moreover, there was a creation of a fishing boat register, the decrease of the number of deep sea fishing boats and the establishment for a satellite monitoring system.[7] Overall, there was emphasis in modernizing the professional fishing fleet as well as enhancing fishermen's methods with training programmes.[8]

Identification of mechanisms, processes and dimensions of Europeanization

Rationalist and *constructivist* mechanisms contributed towards reforms in the structure of the country's agricultural regime as well as in its agricultural production and trade patterns. In particular, a *rationalist* external incentives mechanism contributed towards the creation of new institutions and amendment of laws, the abolition of monopolistic elements of state-controlled authorities and the restructuring or abolition of state agricultural subsidies, with a view towards meeting the requirements of the CAP. Also, such mechanisms contributed towards a significant – though not complete – shift in the external trade patterns of agricultural products where preference was given to EU imports at the expense of those from the Middle East, North Africa and Eastern Mediterranean countries. Moreover, such mechanisms also contributed towards a change in the mode of agricultural production as well as a greater emphasis on environmental functions, agro-tourism and rural development schemes. It also contributed to the modernization of the fishing sector, including its safety and fishing methods. *Constructivist* social learning mechanisms induced changes among the agricultural community, at both state and private level, in developing more environmentally conscious methods in the sector. A *dual rationalist–constructivist* lesson-drawing mechanism was evident in the adoption of organizational mechanisms (e.g. EU Directorates) and agricultural practices from the UK, Netherlands and Greece. Here, the *territorial* and *temporal* dimensions of the country such as its small (i.e. Greece, Netherlands), southern (i.e. Greece) and post-colonial (i.e. UK) status shaped the source of lesson-drawing. At the same time, the limitations of these mechanisms were also evident in the continuing importance of the Middle East markets in the external agricultural trade patterns of the country as well as low competitiveness of agricultural products. Here again, the *territorial* dimension of the country such as its small, south (eastern) and peripheral status mediated for these limitations. In particular, the unique, in European terms, geographical proximity of Cyprus and the Middle East, as well as the traditional historical ties between them, were still important factors in their continuing trade relations despite the EU's preferential agricultural trade agreements with Cyprus. And most of the production, support/services and related macro-economic factors that are responsible for the low competitiveness of Cypriot agricultural products are also related to the small and southern status of the country.

Overall, there was significant evidence of the *downloading* process of Europeanization whereby the state reformed its institutions and policies in order to align with the requirements of the Common Agricultural Policy. There was also evidence of *cross-loading* Europeanization whereby an 'environmental conscience' was cultivated among state agricultural policy officials as well as the broader agricultural community and other social partners, and policy transfer and lesson drawing from countries such as the UK, the Netherlands and Greece. There was also evidence of *uploading* Europeanization in the efforts by the Cypriot Government to shape the CAP on the liberalization process of traditional Mediterranean agricultural products.

Regional policy

For the period between 2004 and 2006, the Republic of Cyprus was a recipient of 113.44 million euro in total from the EU's Structural and Cohesion Funds. From the Structural Funds, Cyprus received aid under Objective 2 (28.02 million euro) financing measures in underdeveloped rural and mountainous areas in the west and east of the island, as well as selected urban areas along the cease-fire line in Nicosia; and under Objective 3 (21.95 million euro) financing measures in education, training and employment, as well as measures supporting the fisheries sector. Under the Structural Funds, Cyprus also received aid from the Community Initiatives such as the INTERREG programme (4.3 million euros) supporting cross-boarder, transnational and interregional cooperation initiatives (e.g. Greece/Cyprus; Cyprus/Med countries; Zone South) as well as from the EQUAL programme (1.81 million euro) supporting the development of partnerships for equality in the labour market. Finally, Cyprus received economic aid from the Cohesion Fund (53.94 million euro) directed towards infrastructure projects involving the environment and transportation. During accession negotiations, the Cypriot Government went to great lengths to persuade the Commission to be categorized as an Objective 1 region – and thus be eligible for a greater amount of funding – highlighting the country's small, peripheral and distant status and the various structural weaknesses and problems in the economy.[9] More particularly, emphasis was given to the small size of its market which hinders the realization of economies of scale for mass product goods; to its lack of natural resources and a high dependence on imported raw material and export markets; to its weakness in the structure of production reflected in its considerable dependence on tourism (direct and indirect contribution to GDP estimated to 19 per cent in 2007) which is vulnerable to exogenous factors; to the decline of the competitiveness of the agricultural and manufacturing sectors due to comparatively low level of technology and productivity; to water scarcity which hinders development of tourism and agriculture; to the lack of indigenous conventional energy sources (with the notable exception of solar energy which covers 4 per cent of needs); to its weak infrastructural development of the protection of the environment (e.g. waste management policy); to its large distance (3700 km) from the GDP gravity centre of the EU, something which increases transaction and transportation costs for goods and people;[10] and to the relatively high costs for upgrading the existing transport infrastructure, in order to link Cyprus to the Trans-European Networks. These factors were emphasized by the Chief Negotiator at the time but the Commission's Directorate-General Regional Policy – and to the dissatisfaction of domestic officials – decided against granting an Objective 1 status citing the country's high per capita income (which is higher than all new and some old Member States) and high GDP growth, as well as territorial impracticality – due to the small size of the country – to divide it into two different Objective regions.[11] Efforts were renewed after membership and there was partial success when Cyprus received 'retrospective funds' under Paragraph 47 of the 2007–2013 financial framework increasing the total aid to 580 million euro.[12] Figures 7.3, 7.4 and 7.5 indicate the distribution of Structural and Cohesion Funds in Cyprus for each of these two financial periods, as well as comparatively. Given the evident importance and impact of these funds for the Cypriot economy (Figures 7.6 and 7.7), there is a great domestic incentive to absorb and manage them effectively.[13] Figure 7.6 indicates the increasing share of structural and cohesion funds as a percentage of the country's GDP and Figure 7.7 indicates the steady and positive impact of these funds on the country's productivity, that is, in terms of GDP/Labour.

In order to prepare for the absorption and management of these funds, the government – and in accordance with the Commission's Regular Reports – was required to implement significant reforms in the areas of territorial organization and the institutional and legislative framework of the country's regional policy. These reforms needed to be implemented

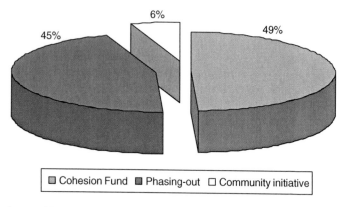

Cohesion Fund ■ Phasing-out □ Community initiative

Note: Structural Funds – Phasing out
Community Initiative – INTEREG
Source: data compiled from Eurostat (2000–2006).
Figure 7.3   Distribution of structural and cohesion funds in Cyprus (2000–2006)

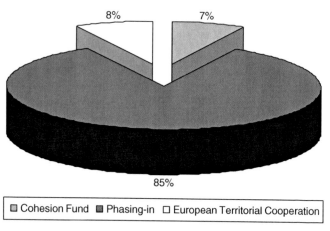

Cohesion Fund ■ Phasing-in □ European Territorial Cooperation

Note: Structural Funds – Phasing in
European Territorial Organization – INTEREG
Source: data compiled from Eurostat (2007–2013).
Figure 7.4   Distribution of structural and cohesion funds in Cyprus (2007–2013)

in accordance to the overarching principles of EU regional policy, that is, coordination, concentration, programming, additionality, partnership, and the 'federalist' EU principle of subsidiarity.[14]

In regards to territorial reforms, Cyprus complied with the requirements of the European Charter of Local and Self Government (1985) and the Communities Law (1999) dividing the island into six districts,

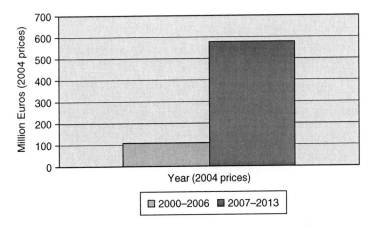

Source: data compiled from Eurostat (2004).

Figure 7.5   Comparative distribution of structural and cohesion funds

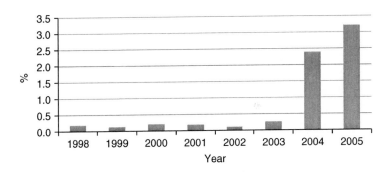

Source: data compiled from Eurostat (1998–2005).

Figure 7.6   Structural and cohesion funds as a % of Cyprus' GDP (1998–2005)

33 Municipalities and 576 Community Councils (village authorities), thus qualifying as a single Nomenclature of Units for Territorial Statistics (NUTS) 2 unit, its 6 districts qualifying for NUTS 3, while the municipal level qualified for NUTS 5. The Union of Municipalities of Cyprus participates regularly in sessions of the Committee of the Regions.

In regards to institutional and legislative reforms, significant measures were taken in 2001 with the division of government competencies regarding the management, programming, implementation, evaluation and monitoring, and financial management and control of structural and cohesion funds in Cyprus. More specifically, there was the creation

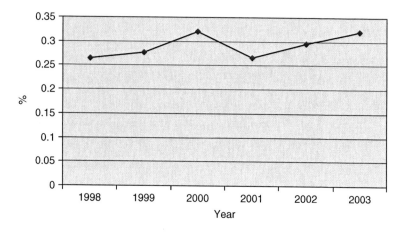

Source: data compiled from Eurostat (1998–2003).
Figure 7.7 Impact of structural and cohesion funds on Cyprus' productivity (GDP/Labour: 1998–2003)

and designation of Managing, Intermediate and Paying Authorities, Intermediate Bodies and an Internal Audit Board as well as a Monitoring Committee. Thus, the Planning Bureau and its Structural Funds Unit was designated as the Managing Authority; the Treasury and its Accounting and Financial Services Directory was designated as the Paying Authority; the Intermediate Authority for Objective 3 (the Social Fund) was designated to the Ministry of Labour & Social Security and its Social Fund unit; the Intermediate Authority for Objective 2 was designated to the Ministry of Interior; the Intermediate Body for the Fisheries Programme was designated to the Ministry of Agriculture, Natural Resources and Environment and its Fisheries Department; and the chair of the Monitoring Committee was designated to the Permanent Secretary of the Planning Bureau (Figure 7.8).[15] Moreover, since 1999 the Cypriot Government has been incorporating within its customary national Strategic Development Plans (SDP) for the economy, specific programmes aiming to satisfy the requirements for the Structural and Cohesion Funds.[16] Emphasis has been given to 'program oriented approaches', 'synergies', more effective 'project targeting' and involvement of social partners, as well as 'ex-ante and ex-post evaluation'. *Acquis* norms and principles such as 'equality', 'protection of environment', 'competition' and 'public procurement' were reinforced through the process of EU socialization and more effectively established in Cypriot policy-making. There was also an emulation of institutions from countries such as Ireland

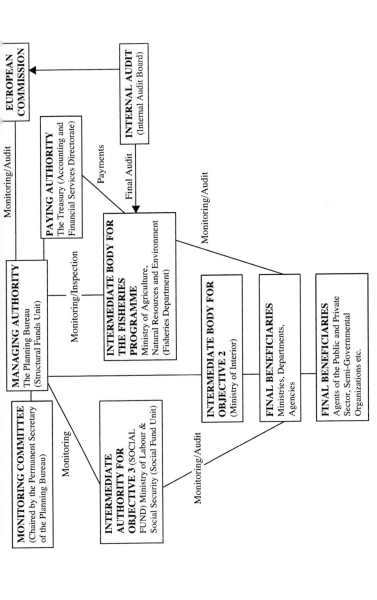

Source: author's compilation.

Figure 7.8 Organizational structure for the management of the EU's structural and cohesion funds in the Republic of Cyprus (e.g. organization of the Structural Funds unit) and Greece (e.g. adoption of a monitoring system).[17] There was particular emphasis on learning from Ireland's absorption mechanisms as, according to the Commission's annual reports, this country has consistently recorded the highest absorption capacity from the four original Cohesion countries (i.e. Greece, Spain, Portugal and Ireland).

In spite of these wide ranging reforms, questions are still raised in regards to the capacity of these institutional mechanisms to absorb fully and manage effectively these funds.[18] The absorption and effective management of these funds is a challenge that many new Member States are facing,[19] yet for a micro-state such as Cyprus, their loss can negatively impact economic growth. In particular, the lack of effective mechanisms to deal with these funds – and their subsequent loss – can prompt the EU to freeze or reduce the funding in the subsequent years. This may prove detrimental for the economy of the country given the fact that it competes for these funds with all the new Member States but also with old Member States such as Greece, Ireland, Portugal and Spain.

The literature on the capacity of Member and candidate states to absorb structural funds has been limited. From a public choice perspective, Herve and Holzmann (1998) investigated the capacity of economically less developed regions and countries to productively absorb large-scale transfers. In 2002, the Commission sponsored a set of studies (NEI, 2002a, b, c) which set key indicators and benchmarks for candidate states to manage effectively the EU's structural funds. These studies focused on the institutional set-ups and administrative resources required to manage these funds. And in 2003, the European Commission published studies where key indicators for the absorption capacity were tested in the ten Central and Eastern European countries, but not Malta and Cyprus.[20]

Absorption problems depend mostly on institutional factors at both the European and national level. At the EU level, there is a lack of transparency and coherence in the Commission's procedures regarding the allocation and management process of the Structural Funds, as well as inefficient coordination between the various units of the Commission (Bauer, 2001: 14). At the domestic level, factors such as the structure of the economy and the political system, wage setting institutions, administrative capacity and capability also determine the efficient management of these funds.

According to the Commission's study (NEI, 2002a), absorption capacity has three dimensions: (a) macroeconomic, defined and measured in terms of GDP levels to Structural Funds allocated; (b) administrative, defined as the ability and skills of central, regional and local authorities to prepare and decide on programmes and projects in due time, to ensure coordination among the principle authorities, to manage the administrative and reporting requirements of the Commission, to finance and supervise effective implementation and to avoid fraud and corruption in the process; and (c) financial, defined as the ability to co-finance EU programmes and projects, to guarantee these national contributions in multi-annual budgets and to collect these contributions from several partners (public and private) interested in a programme.

The study measures the administrative capacity with a distinction between structure, human resources, systems and tools (Table 7.1). *Structure* relates to the clear assignment of responsibilities and tasks to institutions, or better at the level of departments or units within these institutions. This assignment refers to a range of Structural Funds tasks, including management, programming, implementation, evaluation and monitoring, and financial management and control. Structure also relates to supervisory and ancillary bodies, such as Monitoring Committees, auditing tasks, partnership, etc. *Human resources* relate to the ability to detail tasks and responsibilities at the level of job descriptions, to estimate the number and qualifications of staff, and to fulfill the recruitment needs. Securing the timely availability of experienced, skilled and motivated staff is a key success factor in the management of the Structural Funds. Clearly, the conditions within the administrative system need to be favourable towards recruiting and retaining such professionals. *Systems and tools* relate to the availability of instruments, methods, guidelines, manuals, systems, procedures, forms, etc. In brief, these are all job-aids that can enhance the effectiveness of the functioning of the system. Systems and tools enable organizations to transform tacit and implicit knowledge (within the heads of individual people) into explicit knowledge that can be shared across organizations. Systems and tools therefore make organizations less vulnerable (e.g. when key staff is leaving), reduce the risk of malfunctioning and enhance overall effectiveness. Effective management of the Structural Funds requires that the above dimensions be taken into account: structure, human resources, systems and tools. Together these provide complementary elements of the management capability grid (NEI, 2002a: 4).

The study is essentially designed on the basis of the principles of *programming, concentration, partnership, additionality, co-financing, monitoring and evaluation*, introduced by the EU in 1988 being significantly shaped by the Jacque Delor Commission. These principles provide a framework within which these funds can be programmed and organized strategically, induce efficient coordination between the partners from the EU,

Table 7.1 The structural funds management grid

Indicators	Design			Functioning
	Structure	*Human resources*	*Systems & tools*	
Management	Designation of MAs	Staffing of MAs	Arrangement on delegating tasks	Existence of a modern civil service
Programming	Partnership already present	Capacity to carry out programming	Guidelines/manuals for programming exist	Existence and quality of NDP
Implementation	Assignment of Intermediate Bodies	Staffing of Intermediate Bodies	Existing operational project development and management process	Absorption of and project pipeline for pre-accession funds
Evaluation & Monitoring	Designation of monitoring and evaluation responsibilities	Availability of independent evaluation expertise	Existence of a computerized monitoring information system	Functioning and monitoring system for pre-accession funds
Financial Management & Control	Designation of Paying Authorities and functions	Accounting and auditing expertise secured	Existence of accounting system and financial procedures secured	Established practice in dealing with financial irregularities

Source: NEI (2002a: 7).

Table 7.2 Absorption capacity of Cyprus in comparison with CEE countries

	HU	CZ	SK	EST	SLO	CY	Total
1. Management (max. 24)	21 (87%)	18 (75%)	15 (63%)	21 (88%)	17 (71%)	17 (71%)	87%
2. Programming (max. 15)	12 (80%)	12 (80%)	6 (40%)	13 (90%)	12 (80%)	9 (60%)	71%
3. Implementation (max. 25)	18 (72%)	14 (56%)	13 (52%)	17 (68%)	13 (52%)	13 (52%)	59%
4. Evaluation and Monitoring (max. 16)	N/A	N/A	N/A	N/A	N/A	10 (63%)	N/A
5. Financial Management and Control (max. 22)	N/A	N/A	N/A	N/A	N/A	19 (86%)	N/A
Total Score (max. 102)	N/A	N/A	N/A	N/A	N/A	68 (67%)	N/A

Source: adapted from Horvat & Maier (2004: 14) to include Cyprus.

national and subnational levels of governance, and more generally lay a monitoring and evaluation system so as to ensure that these funds will meet their prescribed objectives.

On the basis of the Commission's Structural Funds Management Grid, studies were conducted to measure the absorption capacity of Central and Eastern European states such as Hungary, the Czech Republic, Slovakia and Slovenia (Horvat & Maier, 2004). A separate equivalent study for Cyprus was also conducted and the comparative results are indicated in Table 7.2.[21] The study indicates that the Cypriot Government needs to improve in the areas of programming and implementation – part of the problem is that the principles of subsidiarity and partnership have not yet been absorbed and assimilated by Cypriot policymakers.[22] In regards to programming and partnership, for example, a Programming and Economic Consultative Committee has been established aiming to bring together 'government ministries and departments, semi-governmental organizations and local authorities; economic and social partners as well as non-governmental organizations; and relevant Directorate-Generals of the European Commission'[23] – yet in practice these procedures have not been fully assimilated.[24] In other words, more needs to be done as far as delegating responsibility to local actors, involving them in the preparation, assessment and monitoring of programmes and holding them accountable for any shortcomings in the implementation process.[25] This state of affairs represents an example of a 'paper' partnership or 'thin' Europeanization (Bache, 2007) whereby the Cypriot state has rationally established these mechanisms but its officials have yet to normatively or sociologically adapt them. In other words, this 'regional deficit' is an indication of the limits of the 'external incentives' mechanism which gives credit to the argument of the 'myth of conditionality' (Hughes *et al.*, 2004).

Identification of mechanisms, processes and dimensions of Europeanization

Rationalist and *constructivist* mechanisms induced change in the country's regional policy in regards to territorial organization as well as in institutional and administrative mechanisms aimed to absorb regional and cohesion aid. In particular, a *rationalist* external incentives mechanism induced the reorganization of the regional and local level into units, as well as institutional and legislative reforms aimed for the management, programming, implementation, evaluation and monitoring, and financial management and control of structural and cohesion funds in Cyprus. *Constructivist* social learning mechanisms also induced the establishment of EU norms in regional policy such as 'equality', 'environmental protection', 'competition' and 'public procurement'. And a *dual rationalist–constructivist* lesson-drawing mechanism was evident in the adoption of institutions and policies from countries such as Ireland (i.e. organization of the Structural Funds unit) and Greece (e.g. adoption of a monitoring system). Here, the *territorial* dimension of the country such as its small and southern status shaped the source of lesson-drawing (i.e. small and southern Greece; small Ireland). At the same time, the limitations of these mechanisms were evident in the existing inadequacies in the domestic mechanisms for the absorption of the structural and cohesion funds, particularly in effectively adopting the principles of programming, partnership and implementation. Here, the *territorial* and *temporal* dimension of the country such as its small, southern and new status mediated this impact as many of these inadequacies are related to weak administrative capacities which are characteristics of small, southern and the new Member States.

Overall, there was significant evidence of the *downloading* process of Europeanization whereby the state reformed its institutions and policies in order to align with the requirements of the CAP as well as adopt regional and cohesion funds. There was also evidence of *cross-loading* Europeanization whereby an 'environmental conscience' was cultivated among state regional policy officials as well as local authorities and other social partners, and policy transfer and lesson drawing from countries such as Greece and Ireland. There was also evidence of *uploading* Europeanization in the efforts by the Cypriot government to shape the criteria and framework of Structural and Cohesion Fund aid.

This chapter has examined the impact of Europeanization on the country's agricultural and regional policies. In regards to agricultural policy, it has focused in the areas of the agricultural regime and institutions, production and trade patterns. In regards to agricultural policy, it has indicated that *rationalist, constructivist* and *dual rationalist–constructivist* mechanisms, as well as *downloading, uploading* and *cross-loading* processes were at work in effecting change in these areas. It has also indicated how the *territorial* and *temporal* dimensions of the country such as its small, southern, peripheral and post-colonial status has mediated the impact of these mechanisms and processes. In regards to regional policy, it has focused on the areas of territorial and institutional structures. It has indicated that *rationalist, constructivist* and *dual rationalist–constructivist* mechanisms, as well as *downloading, uploading* and *cross-loading* processes were at work in effecting change in these areas. It has also indicated how the *territorial* and *temporal* dimensions of the country such as its small, southern and new status mediate the impact of these mechanisms and processes.

8
Foreign Policy

Introduction

The existing literature on the Europeanization of national foreign policies has been limited (Wong, 2007). This is probably because the European Political Cooperation EPC/CFSP/ESDP has been, and still is, the least centralized decision-making executive in the EU, with the least impact on the domestic policy choices of Member States (Goetz & Hix, 2000: 6). It is also because it is difficult to isolate the 'EU effect' from other domestic or global influences impacting upon the nation-state (Major, 2005: 183).[1] Thus, it is not always clear whether Europeanization has 'overtaken domestic processes or just added to them' (Radaelli, 2004: 9). Nevertheless, a number of scholars have attempted to define and explain this notion as it relates to foreign policy. Tonra (2001: 229) defines Europeanization in foreign policy as 'a transformation in the way in which national foreign policies are constructed, in the ways in which professional roles are defined and pursued and in the consequent internalization of norms and expectations arising from a complex system of collective European policy-making'. Ladrech (1994: 69) also defines Europeanization in terms of national adaptation to EU membership where 'EC political and economic dynamics become part of the organizational logic of national politics and (foreign) policy-making'.[2] Fanes (2002) defined the Europeanization of foreign policy as 'the process of foreign policy change at the national level stemming from the adaptation pressures and the new opportunities generated by the process of European integration'.[3] Moreover, Europeanization of a national foreign policy also occurs through elite socialization whereby, elites involved in the inter-governmental bargaining process of EPC/CFSP internalize supranational norms and interests, feeding these back to their national capitals (Ohrgaard, 1997; Smith, 2000; Major, 2005).[4] Thus, a prolonged participation in the CFSP feeds back into EU Member States and reorients their foreign policy cultures along similar lines. Smith (2000) also added three more dimensions of change: bureaucratic restructuring, constitutional changes and changes in public perceptions about the desirability and legitimacy of CFSP/ESDP cooperation.

Furthermore, Europeanization of a national foreign policy can also occur through a bottom-up process where Member States influence European foreign policy, through 'national projection', that is, by exporting their national priorities and strategies onto EU institutions (Milward, 2000; Bulmer & Burch, 2001b; Laffan & Stubb, 2003; Major, 2005, Wong, 2007). Scholars, for example, indicate how Germany 'Europeanized' its low deficit, fiscally disciplined macro-economic policies into the EMU convergence criteria, how the UK Europeanized its sanctions against Argentina during the Falklands conflict in 1982, and how France projected its institutions into the early EC and its predecessor the European Coal & Steel Communits (ECSC) (Regelsberger *et al.*, 1997; White, 2001). Finally, there is also a 'cross-loading' dimension in the Europeanization of foreign policies (Major, 2005; Wong, 2007) which encompasses the socialization processes outlined earlier, but also involves mimicry, lesson-drawing or policy transfer between Member States. Table 8.1 outlines these three dimensions of foreign policy Europeanization.

In regards to the small state dimension of Europeanization of foreign policies, there is a consensus among scholars that small states generally favour the adaptation of a strictly rule-based European foreign policy. They view the CFSP/ESDP as a way to overcome their dependency on large states by constructing a system based on law, not power (Smith, 1998: 318). They view the European foreign and security policy as an opportunity rather than a constraint and as a way to increase their access to information and resources as well as to other international actors (Manners & Whitman, 2001: 10). As Tonra (1997: 183) points out, 'minor states usually lack significant intelligence or espionage capabilities and have smaller diplomatic staff from which to gather and analyze data' and thus access to CFSP/ESDP resources significantly 'boosts their foreign policy formulation'. Small states benefit from the 'politics of scale' (Haas, 1958) which increases their influence in the foreign policy process. This, in turn makes them more susceptible to the process of Europeanization, confirmed by studies that indicate that 'the substantial policy impact of CFSP has been stronger in small Member States' (Ohrgaard, 1997: 33).

Table 8.1   Three dimensions of foreign policy Europeanization

Aspects of Europeanization	National foreign policy (FP) indicators
I. Adaptation and Policy Convergence ('downloading')	(a) Increasing salience of European political agenda (b) Adherence to common objectives (c) Common Policy outputs taking priority over national *domains reserves* (d) Internationalization of EU membership and its integration process ('EU-ization')
II. National Projection ('uploading')	(a) State attempts to increase national influence in the world (b) State attempts to influence foreign policies of other Member States (c) State uses the EU as a cover/umbrella (d) Externalization of national FP positions onto the EU level
III. Identity Reconstruction and Policy Transfer ('cross-loading')	(a) Emergence of norms among policy-making elites (b) Shared definitions of European and national interests (c) Coordination reflex and 'pendulum effect' where 'extreme' national and EU positions are reconciled over time (d) Exchange of 'best practices' with other Member States

Source: Adapted from Wong (2007: 326).

The impact of Europeanization on Cyprus' foreign policy

The impact of Europeanization on Cyprus' foreign policy has been significant. One can observe an adaptation and policy convergence with the institutions and policies of the EU's CFSP and the ESDP. In particular, there was the establishment of the post of a European Correspondent within the Foreign Ministry in 1998 as well as an alignment of the state with the Union's CFSP/ESDP statements, declarations and demarches, with the country often taking national positions that were previously considered inconceivable. One such example was the implementation in September 1998 and 2000 of an oil and arms embargo, bans on flights and officials as well as financial sanctions on the Former Republic of Yugoslavia – a fellow Christian Orthodox country with historically close ties with the island. Despite the fact that this issue divided political parties and public opinion, the Cyprus government eventually aligned its foreign policy with that of the EU. Another such example regarded the Iraq War, Cyprus easily aligned itself with the February 2003 Common Position of the EU-15 which called for Iraq to 'disarm or face the consequences', a position that was taken under the Greek Presidency. Cyprus, however, along with other small and candidate states has consistently expressed its reservations concerning the extension of enhanced cooperation in defence issues (i.e. lowering minimal threshold, 'passarelle' clauses) in both the Treaty of Nice and the Constitutional Treaty (Sepos, 2005c). Finally, the May 2004 withdrawal of Cyprus from the Non-Aligned Movement (which it helped found in 1961) is also a direct result of membership.

Cyprus has also actively supported the various EU initiatives in conflict prevention, conflict transformation, peacekeeping and crisis management within the framework of the Petersberg Tasks. It has participated with military personnel in ESDP operations in Congo (Operation Artemis[5] & Operation EUFOR RD[6]), Sudan's Darfur (Operation Amis)[7] and in Police Missions in Bosnia-Herzegovina and the FYROM (Operation Proxima).[8] It is also jointly participating in a 1200 strong-combat EU Battlegroup (named HELBROC) with Greece, Romania and Bulgaria which became operational in May 2007, and which aims to enhance the capacity of these countries to conduct humanitarian and crisis-management missions. Finally, it has become a member of various ESDP agencies, such as the European and Defence Agency (EDA), the European Union Institute for Strategic Studies (ISS), the European Union Satellite Centre (EUSC) and the European Security and Defence College (ESDC).[9] Cyprus is not participating, however, in EU–NATO strategic cooperation in crisis management – based on the 'Berlin Plus' Agreement[10] – due to internal disagreements between right and left wing parties over applying to NATO and its related organizations (i.e. Partnership for Peace)[11] – as well as fears that any such application will be rejected by Turkey which has a history of vetoing Cyprus' participation in such and other international organizations (e.g. Organization for Economic Cooperation and Development [OECD], Missile Technology Control Regime [MTCR] and the Wassenaar Agreement).

Moreover, Cyprus' good relations with its Middle East neighbors have allowed it to play a constructive role in promoting security in the region within the framework of the EU's Euro-Mediterranean partnership (EMP) and, subsequently, its European Neighborhood Policy (ENP). It has contributed to the Middle East Peace Process by facilitating meetings between Israelis and Palestinians, helped diffuse the crisis surrounding the Bethlehem Church of the Nativity crisis in May 2002, while it also played a key role in the July 2006 Hezbollah–Israel conflict by facilitating – in coordination with the EU's Civil Protection Mechanism – the relocation of 60,000–70,000 Lebanese refugees and utilizing its military base 'Andreas Papandreou' for the purposes of the Franco-German aerial surveillance of post-war Lebanon.

Cyprus has historically and strategically tried to 'project' or externalize its national priorities, that is, the Cyprus problem, at the European level, as an associate, candidate and now full member of the EU. Its consistent efforts to 'Europeanize' its 'national problem' (εθνικό πρόβλημα) as a means to achieve a 'just and viable solution' to the conflict are well documented. This policy came about as a result of the realization that the other existing strategies of Greek-Cypriot foreign policy (i.e. inter-communal talks, internationalization of the problem, special relationship with Greece, American mediation,[12] a deterrent strategy) (Tsardanidis & Nicolau, 1999) were not sufficient, on their own, to produce 'a just and viable solution' to the Cyprus problem. The Cyprus government's effort to complement (or substitute entirely) these strategies by involving the EU factor rested on two pillars: (a) to show to the European and international community that the Greek-Cypriots are determined and committed to a solution of the problem and to bi-communal negotiations leading to this goal; and (b) to initiate closer ties with the EU through the signing of the Association Agreement, the conclusion of the Custom's Union and the launch of accession negotiations leading to membership (Vassiliou, 2004).

Since then, Cyprus has consistently used its candidate and Member State status as a means to pressure Turkey, the Turkish-Cypriot community, and to a lesser extent the UK, to change their position on the problem. In this process, it has been encouraged and had a strong ally in Greece, which as a Member State used every opportunity to set the Cyprus problem high on the EU agenda and to provide support for the positions of the Greek-Cypriot community. The two governments closely coordinated their positions on the island's accession process, as well as respective positions towards Turkey, though, particularly after accession there have also been signs of divergences and disassociation in their positions. Hence in 1986, Greece made it clear that it would not consent to the signing of the fourth financial protocol between the EC and Turkey, one of the key components of the EU's Mediterranean Policy, unless Turkey withdrew its military forces from the north of Cyprus (Ioakimidis, 1999: 159). And in the Corfu European Council in June

1994, Greece threatened to veto both the Central and Eastern European enlargement process, as well as Turkey's Custom's Union, unless Cyprus was included in the next wave of enlargement (Nugent, 2000: 134). Moreover, in the Helsinki European Council in December 1999, Greece consented to the EU's decision to grant Turkey a candidate status only when the Council made it clear that 'a political settlement to the Cyprus problem would not be a precondition to the island's accession to the EU'.[13] Greece and newly acceded Cyprus also influenced the content of Turkey's Customs Union (December 1995), 'Accession Partnerships' or 'Road Maps' (March 2001, December 2005), 'Negotiating Frameworks' (October 2004, October 2005), European Council Conclusions (June 1986, June 1994, December 1997, December 1999, December 2002, December 2004, December 2006, December 2007) and the Commission's Regular or Progress Reports (1998–2007) on Turkey as they relate to the country's accession process and its stance towards Cyprus. Within these documents, Cyprus insisted on the inclusion of general references urging Turkey to contribute positively to the solution of the Cyprus problem, but also more specific ones that would contribute towards the normalization of the relationship between the two countries.

Thus, in the period prior to the European Council in Brussels in December 2004, when the Council was contemplating whether to grant Turkey a date for the beginning of its membership negotiations, Cyprus reportedly threatened to veto the granting of any such date unless Turkey changed its position on the Cyprus issue.[14] When Turkey signed the Ankara Protocol extending its Custom's Union to the ten new Member States, but issued (on 29 July 2005) a unilateral declaration stating that its signature did not amount to formal recognition of the Republic of Cyprus[15], the Cypriot government urged for a strong EU condemnation of this stance, which resulted to an EU counter-declaration (on 21 September 2005) indicating that Turkey's declaration does not legally affect Turkey's obligations under the Additional Protocol.[16] Moreover, in the period prior to the 14–15 December 2006 European Council of the Finnish Presidency, Cyprus insisted that the EU set a specific 'time frame' for Turkey to fulfill its standing obligations under the 2005 Ankara Protocol – including the formal recognition of Cyprus, opening its air and sea ports to Cypriot vessels, and stop blocking the island's cooperation with and application to international organizations (e.g. NATO, OECD)[17] – or else it would not agree to the opening of the first chapters of Turkey's accession negotiations.[18] When Turkey insisted on its political declaration on the non-recognition of Cyprus and declared that it would open trade with Cyprus only when the latter lifts its embargo against the

'TRNC', Cyprus insisted on the total suspension of Turkey's accession negotiations. In that process, it lobbied its position and found allies in other Member States such as Germany and the Netherlands which called for a fall-back position of 'privileged partnership' with Turkey, Austria which called for a 'breathing pause' from negotiations, and France which called for the 'suspension of 17 chapters'. Eventually, the EU compromise led to the suspension of Turkey's membership negotiations on eight chapters of the *acquis*.[19] A key part of that deal, was the insertion at the bi-communal negotiating table of a process – suggested by the Finnish Presidency – that would potentially and gradually lead to the lifting of the trade embargo in return of the Varoshia (a prominent coastal area which includes the city of Famagusta) to Greek-Cypriot administration.[20]

Since its newfound membership in 2004, it became evident that Cyprus sought to influence the parameters of the Cyprus problem not only through its Greek connection but also through its increasing political weight as a new Member State. The government sought to prevent states such as Azerbaijan and Kyrgyzstan from recognizing the 'TRNC' by influencing the content of their Association Agreements – in regards to international law – with the EU.[21] And it is one of only four states in the EU-27 (the other being Spain, Greece, Romania) that has declined to recognize the independence of Kosovo fearing that it would set a precedent for other break-away states such as the 'TRNC'.[22] Furthermore, the Cypriot government sought to establish coalitions with powerful Member and non Member States – permanent members of the UN Security Council and nuclear powers – but also strengthen its ties with smaller Member and non-Member States. Thus, on 28 February 2007, Cyprus signed a bilateral defence agreement with France which foresaw, among other things, the creation of permanent or temporary bases to French air and sea forces. The two countries had closely and successfully cooperated to relocate refugees from Lebanon during the Hezbollah–Israel conflict the previous year and since then had conducted joint military exercises in the Eastern Mediterranean.[23] Moreover, apart from signing important bilateral economic agreements, Cyprus has also succeeded in intensifying the involvement of China in the resolution of the Cyprus problem, more recently, with the joint Greek–Chinese declaration on the parameters of a 'fair, sustained and pragmatic settlement'.[24] Russia has always been a traditional ally to Cyprus given its common Christian Orthodox heritage. The two countries have signed numerous bi-lateral economic and defence agreements (for example, the purchase of the controversial Russian S-300 missile system) and the close relations of the two countries are well documented throughout the Cold War Era.[25] Yet, while

Russia has always been one of the strongest supporters of the island's efforts on the Cyprus problem, particularly within the Security Council, it has not always succeeded in playing the decisive counter-balance role to the Anglo-American influence that the Greek-Cypriots have hoped for. This was not only due to the dominance of the Anglo-American axis within the Council, the diminishing role of USSR/Russia in world affairs, but also due to the fact that Russia never really saw Cyprus as a crucial geo-strategic partner in the Eastern Mediterranean and Europe in general. With the island's newfound membership, however, the growing importance of the Union as a world power, and the rising EU–Russia tensions (e.g. the Ukraine issue), Russia is now more eager to look to Cyprus for additional support within the EU bloc and at the same time be a more forceful ally to the island's positions on the Cyprus problem. In that regard, President Papadopoulos hailed Russia's 'steady and unwavering position in achieving a just and viable solution to the Cyprus problem'.[26] And he also strongly encouraged the interest of Russia and China in joining the government's efforts to explore and exploit oil and gas reserves off the shores of the island, hoping to cash in the form of side-payments and support on the Cyprus issue.[27] Cyprus' close relations and supportive positions towards Russia and China within EU circles is often seen as a counter-balancing act to the 'Atlanticist' position of most of the new Member States (i.e. Visegrad and Baltic States).[28] These initiatives essentially signify the intention of the Cypriot government to distinguish itself from the Anglo-American influence on the affairs of the island and more actively involve other powerful players of the international arena. EU membership has provided the island with an added international value and clout to increase the likelihood of success of such initiatives.

At the same time, these examples are not meant to argue that the Cypriot government has ceased to value the importance of the Anglo-American variable in the Cyprus problem and the need to 'win over' these two countries on the issue. Indeed, the historically tense relationship of Cyprus with the US over the latter's close political, economic and military ties with Turkey as well as the ambiguous American role in the events of 1974 and thereafter is well documented.[29] This is perhaps one of the reasons why Cyprus has more of a 'Europeanist' than 'Atlanticist' identity with respect to EU and trans-Atlantic relations. At the same time, Cypriot foreign-policy makers have been careful not to overstate this identity and there have even been reports that suggest that Cyprus has secretly accommodated the Americans on a number of occasions on the Iraq War and the 'War on Terror',[30] that extend beyond the role of the sovereign British military bases on the island. Certainly, however, EU membership has provided the political clout to the Cypriot government to be more assertive on its positions *vis-à-vis* the Americans. This stance has been further reinforced by the presidency of Papadopoulos – re-knowned for his historically critical positions on American foreign policy – and his centre-left coalition government. When, in February 2005, a US business/embassy delegation visited the 'TRNC', Papadopoulos stressed that such actions 'would have a negative effect on US–Cyprus Relations'.[31] And in the period prior to the UN-sponsored Annan Plan referendum, Papadopoulos fiercely resisted Anglo-American pressure to endorse what he – and much of the Greek-Cypriot population – perceived as an 'unworkable' and 'unfair' Plan, remaining unapologetic for its dismissal and in fact criticizing these two countries for their role in drafting many of its provisions and promoting it within Cypriot society. He also reprimanded Kofi Annan (in a letter, 7 June 2004)[32] for allowing those he had entrusted as 'honest brokers' (i.e. the Anglo-Americans) to become 'active participants' in the negotiation process.[33]

Though Papadopoulos' assertive stance towards the Americans has been criticized on the domestic front for not being very constructive for the 'national cause',[34] it would not have been possible without the added clout that EU membership provides to his government. Indeed, one cannot discount the important influence of left-wing and traditionally anti-US AKEL – the largest party in the government coalition – on the positions and rhetoric of Papadopoulos, yet AKEL was also in the ruling government between 1988–93 and Cypriot foreign policy was clearly less assertive during that pre-accession era. At the same time, however, it is also important to indicate that, as with his predecessors, President Papadopoulos still perceives (and values) the quality of relations of the Cyprus government with these two countries as one of the most important factors for the solution of the Cyprus problem.

The relationship with ex-colonial power Britain – which has long-standing strategic interests in the island – has been equally tense and Cyprus membership has brought these tensions and antagonisms to the front. On 19 April 2007, the House of Representatives unanimously called for the government to take the necessary international legal measures against the British government for its non-payment of rent for the use of British Bases,[35] as provided by the Treaty of Establishment in 1960, and prepare the ground for the ultimate dismantling of the bases in the island. This motion came about following mounting tensions between the two countries since accession, from mass public demonstrations on the potentially harmful environmental and health effects of the British military bases in the island – and the subsequent detention of a Cypriot MEP by the British authorities on Cyprus – to accusations from the Cypriot government on the shady role of the British government (Lord David Hannay) in drafting controversial provisions in the 2004 Annan Plan; the 'incredible and unjustified pressure' on the Greek-Cypriot side to endorse the Plan, and its subsequent 'concerted efforts to discredit' the Cypriot government after the 'No' vote in the Plan;[36] the legal row from the purchase of Greek-Cypriot property in the 'TRNC' by British citizens (where in one case the British Prime Minister's wife acted as a barrister); the refusal of President Papadopoulos to meet with British Foreign Secretary Jack Straw – delegating instead the meeting to Cypriot Foreign Minister George Jacovou – after the latter's decision to meet with Turkish Cypriot leader Mehmet Ali Talat at his 'so called presidential palace';[37] culminating with the leader of largest party in the coalition government (i.e. AKEL) to call Britain, 'Cyprus' long-time nemesis' which 'historically exploited rival nationalisms for its own purposes of divide and rule'.[38] Such public rhetoric, discourse and actions from the government and the House of Representatives would have been unthinkable in the pre-accession era, where candidate Cyprus depended on the approval of the British government for its EU application process. The issue of the British Bases came to the fore in the period just before accession when Britain – eager to secure its guarantee role and influence the island's affairs – insisted on and secured the inclusion of Protocol 3 in Cyprus' EU Accession Treaty (16 April 2003) ensuring that the sovereignty of the British Bases be maintained with the island's accession and that a substantial portion of EU law would apply to the territory.[39] During that time, the Cypriot government perceived that it could not afford to jeopardize its accession process by adopting a confrontational stance towards the UK and hence did not raise any objections[40] yet after membership, and with the newfound political weight that this entails, Cypriot elites are increasingly pushing for the 'opening of this long-standing issue' and generally challenging the conventional 'soft' foreign policy stance towards former colonial power Britain. When Britain signed a Strategic Partnership with Turkey in October 2007 which agreed to 'help end the isolation of the Turkish-Cypriots'[41] – ultimately aiming to elevate the status of the 'TRNC' in the EU and international community[42] – the Cypriot government angrily declared that it would begin a process of 're-evaluation of the long-standing political relationship with Britain', including a 're-examination of the status of the British Bases' and the 'possibility of withdrawing from the British Commonwealth'.[43] Cyprus' more assertive foreign policy and rhetoric towards Britain is significantly attributed to Europeanization and the political weight and capital that EU membership bestows on small states.

Furthermore, a direct consequence of the Europeanization of Cyprus' foreign policy has been the disassociation of the country's foreign policy from Greece. As indicated earlier, the latter has always been at the forefront of Cyprus' accession process and has been its most staunch supporter. However, since the late 1990s there seems to be a desire from both countries to disassociate their national policies and become more independent from each other. A series of reasons and events have contributed to this shift of policies. On the part of Greece, there were specific reasons to begin a rapprochement with Turkey which necessitated the 'toning down' of the national rhetoric and discourse in regards to the Cyprus issue *vis-à-vis* Turkey and EU circles. Firstly, the Greek aim of participating in the euro zone necessitated budgetary cuts in Greece, in particular in defence spending. Since Turkey was the main focus of Greek defence expenditures, a rapprochement with Turkey would allow a reduction in such expenditures, thereby paving the way for Greek entry into the euro zone. Secondly, there was a realization in Greece that the Cyprus problem was something of a 'liability' for Greek interests in the EU – asking for concession on Cyprus among its EU partners meant weakening Greece's bargaining power on other important issues (e.g. structural and cohesion funds; the euro; justice and home affairs). Thirdly, there was a realization among Greek policy-makers that the improvement of bilateral relations between the two countries and the resolution of major issues between them (i.e. territorial and sea-bed issue in the Aegean; protection of respective ethnic minorities) passed through the Europeanization of Turkey. The 'democratic peace' thesis that a more Europeanized and democratized Turkey will also be more cooperative, moderate and peaceful in its foreign policy underpinned this shift in Greek foreign policy.[44] The rapprochement between the two countries was also facilitated by non-political events such as the near simultaneous earth-quakes that devastated the two countries in the summer of 1999 and when mutual sentiments of solidarity and sympathy, as well as common efforts in rescue operations, lead to the so-called 'earthquake diplomacy' for the search of further common solutions to common problems. In that regard, the change of Greece's foreign policy towards Turkey – and Cyprus – has to be understood as taking place within a process of Europeanization of its own policies (Economides, 2005).

Similarly, as Cypriot foreign policy became more Europeanized through the years – with the country forging stronger institutional links with the EU – the more disassociated its policy became from Greece. These differences in policies have been evident in many cases. For example, in 1997 Cyprus purchased the Russian-made S-300 missile defence system – a move which was opposed by Greece, which feared an escalation of tensions with Turkey, and was only resolved when Greece offered to install them on the island of Crete.[45] In 2005, the Cypriot government went ahead and staged a major military exercise that had been cancelled over the previous years despite strong opposition from the Greek government.[46] Perhaps, the most prominent example of this disassociation was in the two year period leading up to the April 2004 referendum of the Annan Plan, that is, 2002–2004. The newly formed Cypriot government (February 2003) headed by Tassos Papadopoulos strongly lobbied against the Plan whereas the leader of the strongest parties in Greece, George Papandreou of the Panhellenic Socialist Movement (PASOK) and incoming new Prime Minister Costas Karamanlis of right-wing New Democracy openly supported the Plan which was also endorsed by Turkey. Eager to continue the process of the Greek-Turkish rapprochement Greek policy-makers pushed for an early settlement despite being aware of the deep opposition to the Plan among the Cypriot government and much of the Greek-Cypriot population.[47] When the Plan was eventually rejected by the Greek-Cypriots, the mutual disassociation of Greek and Cypriot foreign policy was cemented. Thus, while PM Costas Karamanlis and President Tassos Papadopoulos agree on the main parameters and principles of the solution of the problem, they have a different approach in regards to the process of doing so. While Greece is eager and pushes for a fast-track comprehensive solution of the problem which would help improve its relationship with Turkey and relieve itself from a 'taboo-like' issue in the negotiating table of the EU–Greek policy process, Cyprus prefers a slow and incremental approach towards a solution which would ensure its national interests to the greatest degree. This policy divergence which signifies the beginning of a more mature and independent relationship of Cyprus from 'mother-country' Greece was also evident in the issue of the exploration and exploitation of hydrocarbon reserves (oil and gas) in the southern and eastern economic zone of the island. In this issue, the Cyprus government made it clear that this was an exclusive national interest of the Republic and went ahead and signed a bi-lateral agreement with Lebanon without prior consultation with the Greek government,[48] even though the issue clearly has wider implications on Greek–Turkish relations.[49]

At the same time, one has to indicate that the two governments still work very closely on national issues. Their relationship, however, has been certainly transformed whereby both countries can also openly disagree on major national issues. This has been a direct result of the impact of Europeanization on both countries, that is, Greece revising its position on Turkey in order to cater to its own particular interests in Europe, and Cyprus using its new political weight as a new Member State to promote its national policies, even if those policies often disrupt and create tensions in Greece's rapprochement process with Turkey.

Another dimension of the Europeanization of Cypriot foreign policy relates to the position of the Cypriot government towards the Turkish-Cypriot community. Since 2004 the Cypriot government has been keen to reach out to the Turkish-Cypriot community. Thus, in the months that followed the rejection of the Annan Plan, and under the negative European response towards the Greek-Cypriot community, President Tassos Papadopoulos initiated a number of confidence building measures directed towards the Turkish-Cypriots, as for example, measures for facilitating the movement of Turkish-Cypriot vehicles and goods as well as measures for the creation of new crossing points, de-mining landmines, and unmanning of areas along the ceasefire.[50] These measures were adopted in response to the Council's 'Green Line' Regulation[51] aiming to facilitate the movement of persons and goods across the so-called 'Green Line', that is, the boundary which divides the two parts of the island, ultimately aiming towards the gradual integration of the Turkish-Cypriot community in the Republic's European vocation. And Papadopoulos has been eager to indicate to the EU his keenness to participate in the UN-sponsored July 8 process aiming to re-ignite bi-communal negotiations extending an invitation to the Turkish-Cypriot leader Mehmet Ali Talat. Also, Papadopoulos' main opponents in the February 2008 Presidential elections, Ioannis Kasoulides and Demetris Christofias, both stated that their main priority after the elections is to engage constructively with the Turkish-Cypriot leadership. Newly elected President Demetris Christofias (February 2008),[52] whose party has a political history of a rapprochement with the Turkish-Cypriot community, reaffirmed that committment.[53] This indicates the overall consistent and sustained impact of the EU on moderating the positions of conflicting parties.

Furthermore, Cypriot foreign policy has been Europeanized in the sense that EU norms and identities are beginning to penetrate and shape domestic dynamics, identities and preferences. The socialization process of Cypriot elites and officials was evident during the controversy between the Cypriot government and EU Health Commissioner Markos Kyprianou, the son of the late and founding leader of the centre party that President Papadopoulos headed. More specifically, Kyprianou criticized President Papadopoulos for not being persuasive enough and even alienating some EU Member States, following an 'unconstructive', 'blackmailing' and 'confrontational' approach on the Cyprus problem, specifically in regards to the accession process of Turkey.[54] He was referring to the position of the Cypriot government before the December 2006 European Council that it would veto the continuation of Turkey's accession negotiations unless the latter formally recognizes the Republic under the Ankara Protocol. In return, Papadopoulos' closed circle criticized Commissioner Kyprianou for not being 'assertive' enough in his promotion of the country's national interest at the EU level.[55] This example indicates how Cypriot officials embraced and adapted – through their socialization in Brussels – the EU agenda of constructively engaging Turkey and the Turkish-Cypriots rather than the more confrontational approach of the past, and even engaged in a persuasion process of their domestic counterparts about the legitimacy and value of this approach. One can observe a transformation in Kyprianou's rhetoric before and after his appointment in Brussels. Finally, there was borrowing of 'best practices', particularly from the UK and Greece, such as the creation of an EU and CFSP unit within the Ministry of Foreign Affairs as well as the post of the European Correspondent in 1998. There was also an acquiring of technical expertise from the Nordic and Baltic states which have experience in setting and organizing humanitarian and crisis-management missions.[56]

Moreover, another clear consequence of Europeanization has been the country's changing relationship with and perception of NATO. Traditionally, the relationship of Cyprus with NATO has been tense due to Turkey's membership since 1952 and also of the alliance's quiet support of Turkey's military intervention in the island in 1974. Archbishop Makarios repeatedly denied the installation of NATO bases in Cyprus and political parties, with left-wing AKEL being the most vocal, have consistently denied this prospect. Yet, with EU membership and the realization that any real influence within the CFSP/ESDP presupposes membership or at least a close relationship with NATO – given the close coordination, resource overlap and capability dependence between the two strategic organizations[57] – Cypriot policy-makers are gradually warming up to the idea that sooner or later the island will need to follow the route that other neutral (e.g. Sweden, Finland, Ireland) or former foes (Central and Eastern European countries) have done in recent years, that is, forging a closer relationship with the Organization and its projects (i.e. the Partnership for Peace) as a way to exert more influence within Europe's foreign and security policy arm. This, however, again presupposes that Turkey will not veto such willingness to participate.

Finally, Cyprus' assumption of the EU presidency – jointly with Poland and Denmark – in 2012 is expected to further Europeanize the island's foreign policy as state executives will be forced to think beyond the 'national problem' and will be expected to help provide solutions to 'European problems'. Indeed, the intensity and pace of convergence and Europeanization is particularly high when Member States hold presidencies. In that regard, it would be of value to observe how a Cypriot Presidency will deal with Turkey's accession process in 2012 – in case the latter is still not a member – that is, to what extent would it disassociate itself with its 'national problem' in favour of a more 'European approach' towards Turkey.

Identification of mechanisms, processes and dimensions of Europeanization

Overall, *rationalist* and *constructivist* mechanisms have resulted in institutional and administrative reforms but also qualitative changes of the country's foreign policy towards the principle actors of the Cyprus problem but also towards other major players in the European and international arena. The *rationalist* external incentive mechanism was significantly evident in the adaptation of the institutions and policies of Cyprus with the CFSP/ESDP objectives. Thus there was an establishment of the post of the European correspondent in the Foreign Ministry as well as alignment with EU common policies and decisions on issues such as the Iraq War and the oil and arms embargo on the Former Republic of Yugoslavia. The country has also participated in various peace-keeping, conflict-resolution, humanitarian and crisis-management initiatives within the framework of the Petersberg Tasks and the ENP (i.e. in Congo, Bosnia-Hezegovina, Former Yugoslavian Republic of Macedonia [FYROM], Lebanon, Israel–Palestine) and became a member of various ESDP agencies (i.e. (EDA), ISS, ESDC) and EU battle groups (i.e. HELBROC). Yet there was reluctance in endorsing further integration initiatives with other vanguard fast Member States – in the form of enhanced cooperation – within the area of defence. In this case, the *temporal* dimensions of the country such as its slow status mediated for this position. More importantly, the limitation of this mechanism was evident in the lack of significant change in the core of Cyprus' foreign policy on its national problem. In this case, while Greek-Cypriot elites engaged more constructively with the Turkish-Cypriot community, promoting and implementing confidence-building measures, and while also generally supporting, under strict conditions, the European orientation of Turkey – all these being policies and objectives of the EU – they remained steadfast in their core national position on the Cyprus problem, strategically influencing the EU's foreign and enlargement policy towards Turkey and its Negotiating Framework, first as a candidate state through its Greek connection, and secondly as a Member State with the use of the veto threat. Here, the *territorial* and *temporal* characteristics of the country such as its small, southern and post-colonial status – which are all linked to its national problem – mediated the deficiency of this mechanism. Also, evidence point to the argument that EU membership status has also made Cyprus' foreign policy more assertive towards Britain and the US and more independent from Greece. This status has also been used to recruit support on its national problem from countries which have tense and competitive relationships with the EU, such as Russia and China, as well as shape the policies of other nations vying for closer ties with the EU, such as Azerbaijan and Kyrgyzstan. Finally, Cyprus has not hesitated to break EU unity on international issues which may have implications on its national problem such as the independence of Kosovo.

Constructivist social learning mechanisms were also at work with the change in the rhetoric and position of Cypriot elites and the government towards the Turkish-Cypriot community and Turkey. In this case, the rhetoric became less confrontational and closer to the position and concerns of the EU in regards to the Turkish-Cypriots, particularly on the issue of their economic isolation. Also, there was adherence with the (broader) EU belief that Turkey's accession process is beneficial for the democratization of the country and stability in the region, including the prospects for the solution of the Cyprus problem.

The *dual rationalist–constructivist* lesson-drawing mechanism was evident in the borrowing of 'best practices', particularly from the UK and Greece, such as the post of an EU and CFSP Unit within the Foreign Ministry and technical expertise from the Nordic and Baltic states which have experience in organizing and conducting humanitarian and crisis-management missions. Here, the *territorial* and *temporal* dimensions of the country such as its small, southern and post-colonial status determined the source of lesson-drawing (i.e. small Baltic and Nordic States; small and southern Greece; colonial UK).

At the same time, the change towards a more assertive and independent Cypriot foreign policy towards Britain and Greece respectively, and a more moderate position towards the Turkish-Cypriots cannot be solely explained by these mechanisms of Europeanization. One can argue that these transformations are also partly a result of internal processes of democratization, ethnic reconciliation and other internal dynamics such as the strengthening and maturity of the sovereignty and the political, economic and social institutions of the state, its civil society, political culture and democratic discourse as well as Cypriot identity. These processes are also a result of the general developmental trajectory of a relatively young democracy, which is in a process of nation and state-building in its post-colonial era, which in the process of breaking away from the influence of its colonial ruler, disassociating itself from the Greek mother-land and re-establishing positive relations with the opposite community, while also establishing itself as a truly sovereign and independent state with particular interests and ambitions in the international arena. Indeed, the Europeanization and democratization processes in Cyprus – and many other countries with similar backgrounds – existed separately but they also fueled each other, strengthening even more their effect in the country. The fact that Cyprus sought and achieved its European vocation can be a result of its internal democratization process where elites realized that this process could be better achieved through the European integration process. And it is also a result of the state and its elites seeking to address its geo-political and economic challenges stemming from globalization through the umbrella and protection of a regional organization.

As far as the *downloading* process of Europeanization, it was evident in the reforms of the institutions, procedures and substance of Cyprus' foreign policy. The *uploading* process of Europeanization was evident in the state's projection of its national preferences onto the EU (and global) level by influencing the EU's foreign and enlargement policy towards Turkey – as it related to the Cyprus problem – first as a candidate state through its Greek connection, and secondly as a Member State with the use of its veto threat. The *cross-loading* process was evident in the socialization of Cypriot officials to the norms and ideas of the EU on Turkey and the Turkish-Cypriots, as well as a policy and institutional transfer from the ministerial structures of Member States such as Greece and the UK, particularly as it relates to the organizational structure of the ministry of foreign affairs, but also from other small Member States such as the Baltic and Nordic States in regards to technical expertise in organizing humanitarian and crisis-management missions. In that sense, the policy transfer dimension of the *cross-loading* process of Europeanization was shaped by the country's *territorial* and *temporal* dimensions such as its small, southern and post-colonial status.

This chapter has examined the impact of Europeanization on the country's foreign policy. It has focused on the institutions and nature of the Cypriot foreign policy, with emphasis on its relations with the principle actors of the Cyprus conflict, that is, the Turkish-Cypriot community, Turkey, Greece and the UK, as well as its relations with other EU Member States, world powers such as the US, Russia and China and states in the EU Neighbourhood. It has indicated that *rationalist, constructivist* and *dual rationalist–constructivist* mechanisms, as well as *downloading, cross-loading* and *uploading* processes were at work in effecting change in these areas. It has also indicated how the *territorial* and *temporal* dimensions of the country such as its small, southern, slow and post-colonial status has mediated the impact of these mechanisms and processes.

9
Justice and Home Affairs

Introduction

Europeanization also has a significant impact on the justice and home affairs policies of states (Monar, 2003; Lavenex, 2007). Bigo (2001) stresses the role of transgovernmental networks of law and order officials in strengthening the security practice and discourse linking migration and security, while Huysmans (2000) and Waever *et al.* (1993) and Waever (1995) highlight a broader, more structural impact of European integration. According to Huysmans (2000: 753), 'the explicit privileging of nationals of Member States in contrast to third-country nationals and the generally restrictive regulation of migration sustains a wider process of de-legitimating the presence of immigrants, asylum-seekers and refugees. EU policies support, often indirectly, expressions of welfare chauvinism and the idea of a cultural homogeneity as a stabilizing factor'. Waever (1995: 404) also detects a tension between European integration, national identities and migration: 'a nation will only allow integration when it is secure that its national identity will not be threatened, that it may even be strengthened by its exposure to different identities'. From a more institutionalist perspective, Geddes (2000) and Guiraudon (2000) review contending explanations (e.g. intergovernmentalist vs neo-functionalist logic) for the shift of asylum and immigration policies from the national to the European level. Combining a social-constructivist focus on the role of policy frames with institutionalist approaches, Lavenex (2001b) argued that in order to achieve a de-securitization of European asylum cooperation, institutional reforms should be accompanied with traditionally normative foundations of the asylum right in the EU framework as evident, for example, in the Charter for Fundamental Rights. Finally, the impact of EU requirements and policies on the asylum policies of individual Member States (Baldwin-Edwards, 1997; Nascimbene, 2000; Schuster, 2000; Vink, 2002) but also non-EU countries and international organizations (Lavenex & Ucarer, 2002; Boswell, 2003) were examined in a number of studies.

The impact of Europeanization on Cyprus' justice and home affairs policy

The impact of Europeanization on Cyprus' justice and home affairs policy has been significant. There were reforms in the institutions and policies of the country in order to align with the requirements of the third pillar of the Union, i.e. Police Judicial Cooperation in Criminal Matters (PJCCM).[1] In particular, the state adopted the various Schengen provisions and aligned its legislation with the adoption of numerous European and international conventions as well as the amendment and creation of new laws in the following areas: data protection, visa policy, external borders, migration, police cooperation and combating organized crime, fight against terrorism, fight against fraud and corruption, drugs and money laundering, customs cooperation, judicial cooperation in civil and criminal matters and human rights legal instruments. In that regard, Cyprus has been part of the Schengen Information System (SIS II) established in order to help new Member States align with the Schengen *acquis* and a Supplementary Information Request at the National Entries (SIRENE) Bureau[2] was established (in April 2005) within the Police Department in order to help with this transition (will be fully operational in 2008). With regards to data protection, there has been the establishment of the Office of the Commissioner for Data Protection; in regards to border control there was the establishment of the Cyprus National FRONTEX Point of Contact (NFPOC) within the Police Department,[3] an upgrade of border control equipment (e.g. radars, helicopters and patrol boats), improved training of personnel (e.g. Odysseus, Oisin, Falcone programmes), the installation of the Automated Fingerprint Identification System (AFIS), and the conclusion of cooperation agreements with Poland, France and Russia. Yet on this issue, and despite fulfilling the requirements, Cyprus – along with Britain and Ireland – is the only new Member State that has chosen to opt-out from the implementation of the Schengen Agreement on overland borders, seaports and airports.[4] This is due to administrative, infrastructural and political considerations linked to the ability of the state to ensure the effective policing of its borders with the 'TRNC'.[5] In regards to visa policy, there was the introduction of the Airport Transit Visa and the introduction of visa obligations for countries such as Russia, the Gulf states, Ukraine, Belarus and Syria. With respect to migration, there have been various amendments to the Aliens and Immigration Regulations and the establishment of the Centre for Information, Discussion and Exchange on the crossing of frontiers and immigration. In this area, the issue of the resident status of Third Country Nationals (TNC) *vis-à-vis* EU citizens and that of illegal immigration has been of notable importance. The upward trend in the number of migrant workers has been discernible for a number of years in Cyprus, particularly prior to accession in 2004. Workers from India, Pakistan, Bangladesh, Sri Lanka, the Philippines, Russia and the former Soviet Republics, are favoured as a cheap labour market, occupying positions in the labour force that Cypriots will not take. On this issue, Cypriot immigration policy has always being protectionist in nature and formulated to ensure that migrants' stays remain short-term (i.e. six years), temporary and restricted to specific sectors (Trimikliniotis & Demetriou, 2005). While their contribution to the economy is undeniable, their presence has exposed a number of social problems in the country such as racism, xenophobia, exploitation and human trafficking. Thus, when the EU issued a new directive (2003/109/EC) on long-term residence status of TCNs, which would have allowed these nationals to reside permanently in the given EU country after five years, the Cypriot government swiftly responded with a new legislation that lowered the short-term stay to four years, so as to minimize the number of immigrant workers residing permanently in the country (Thomson, 2006). The issue of illegal immigration is important[6] because it is linked with the division of the island since nearly 90 per cent of illegal or undocumented migrants originate from the 'TRNC'.[7] This has created another area of dispute between the Greek and Turkish communities in Cyprus with the former eager to curb this flow of immigrants, many of whom are originating from mainland Turkey (as the only country which recognizes the 'TRNC'). In light of the fact that the Green Line is not a *de jure* but nonetheless a *de facto* external border of the EU – given the lack of control of the Republic of Cyprus to the area occupied by the 'TRNC' – the country faces particular challenges from implementing the Schengen *acquis* as border control to curb illegal immigration may also affect bi-communal contacts along the border.[8] Moreover, in regards to asylum, various institutions have been created such as the Asylum Unit, the Refugee Authority and the Review Authority, a national visa registration unit, while there has also been Cypriot participation in European institutions of such matters such as European Monitoring Centre for Drugs and Drug Addiction (EMCDDA) and Dublinet.[9] In these two areas, that is, illegal immigration and asylum, the Cypriot government has taken pains to emphasize the particular challenges that stem from its unique situation with the division of the island as well as its peripheral status as the most distant (from the core) and one of the most sensitive frontiers of the Union and has demanded 'more commitment from the part of the Union to safeguarding its south-eastern borders'.[10] In regards to combating organized crime, there has been an improved cooperation and coordination between the police and the prosecuting and judicial bodies, as well as with Europol – a special department has been established within the Police Department in this regards.[11] In regards to the fight against drugs, there has been an upgrade of the Drug Law Enforcement Unit within the Police Department, the establishment of the post of the Drugs Liaison Officer, as well as a Anti-Drug Council and Fund which is responsible for leading the National Drug Strategy of the state and for coordinating public and private initiatives in the field of drug demand reduction and drug supply reduction, while there has also been Cypriot participation in European information networks on drugs and addiction (e.g. Reitox).[12] In regards to the fight against money laundering, there has been the establishment of various special units within the Police Department (i.e. the Crime Intelligence Unit, the Crime Prevention Squads, the Drug Law Enforcement Unit, and the Mobile Immediate Action Unit), a Unit for Combating Money Laundering (MOKAS) within the Law Office of the Republic and a Special Investigation Unit within the Department of Customs and Excise. In regards to the fight against terrorism, various bodies such as MOKAS and special anti-terrorist units within the police are jointly-coordinating on this matter, while measures are taken for the establishment of a National Central Office on Terrorism which will coordinate their activities. And in regards to judicial cooperation in civil and criminal matters and human rights legal instruments, there has been the establishment of a Unit of International and Legal Cooperation in the Ministry of Justice and Public Order and an Equality Committee for the equal treatment of men and women.[13] It is also worth noting that Cyprus has chosen not to sign the Prűm Treaty (27 May 2005), that is, a variable geometry initiative (i.e. outside the EU framework) between seven Member States on furthering cross-border cooperation, focusing in the combat of terrorism, cross-border crime and illegal immigration.[14] Finally, these institutional changes were accompanied with socialization processes of Cypriot ministry officials, judges, prosecutors, lawyers, police officers and border guards with their counterparts at the EU level, though 'more time is needed to change established norms and mentalities' in this area.[15]

At the same time, Europeanization has had a limited impact on eradicating corruption and clientelism in the country which still runs deep through the socio-economic and political system and culture of the country.[16] The roots of clientelism in Cyprus can be traced as early as the Ottoman Empire where the local *muchtar* or elected village headman served as the leader and patron of the local Christian population as well as an actor of Ottoman repression in case of disobedience, thus defining a patron-client structure which persisted and spread horizontally and vertically in society and politics in the post-Ottoman era. Due to Ottoman rule the island never fully experienced the process of liberalization and modernization that accompanied the Enlightenment period in the 18th century, and which essentially contributed to the dissolution of such structures. Though some argue that these structures were eventually dissolved by British rule (Faustmann, 1998; Richter, 2003), overwhelming contemporary evidence indicate otherwise.[17] Other southern European states which also belatedly experienced these democratization and modernization processes have also maintained such structures.[18] On the one hand, reform and modernization – the eradication of corruption, clientelism and nepotism – are seen as favourable developments from the Cypriot public and is in fact a popular topic in political discussions. On the other, there is an underlying concern, among the public and the government, that were clientelism to be completely eradicated, the Cypriot people would be deprived of one of the main avenues they have to benefit from the state.[19] In fact, there is evidence to suggest that in countries where government institutions are weak (e.g. young democracies) and patron-client relationships are strong (e.g. small, southern countries) citizens are more likely to support corrupt governments and leaders from which they receive tangible benefits (Manzetti & Wilson, 2007). Yet the short and long-term effects of these forms of bureaucratic pollution are evident: lack of interpersonal and government trust, profound cynicism and feelings of hopelessness towards the state, a weak collective civic behaviour and inefficiency of the state machine.[20] Also, there is a strong positive correlation between corruption and negative economic growth (Drury *et al.*, 2006). Measures resulting from pressures of Europeanization such as the establishment of a Corruption Coordination Body (April 2003), closer links with the European Fraud Prevention Office (OLAF) and Cypriot participation in the Group of States Against Corruption (GRECO) have done little to alleviate the problem. At this point, the creation of a Permanent Commission Against Corruption and the launch of a long-term strategy from the state which would involve strong coordination among the government, the private sector and civil society in anti-corruption efforts and good governance, the creation of educational programmes that would help change the roots of these elements in the country's political culture, lesson-drawing from corruption-free countries[21] and the signing of the United Nations Convention Against Corruption are some of the necessary steps that need to be taken if the state is to function efficiently, effectively and democratically alongside its fellow partners in the EU.

Moreover, Europeanization had a mixed impact in the strengthening of civil society and social capital in the country. While there have been some positive developments with the creation of Cypriot Civil Society Organizations (CSOs) and Non-Governmental Organizations (NGOs) (e.g. Action for Equality, Support and Anti-Racism) dealing with issues such as worker's rights, detention and treatment of asylum seekers, women's rights and racism, as well as others dealing with the promotion of bi-communal peace and the protection of the environment, there have been little activity in regards to promotion of good governance, transparency, poverty and socioeconomic inequality. Studies confirm this, revealing a 'weak' Cypriot civil society and low and uneven (urban vs rural) levels of public participation in organized forms of volunteering. These organizations have been closely linked to political parties which hinders their autonomy and impact, and low levels of corporate philanthropy and social responsibility.[22]

Identification of mechanisms, processes and dimensions of Europeanization

Rationalist and *constructivist* mechanisms have induced changes in the country's Justice and Home Affairs regime. In particular, *rationalist* mechanisms have encouraged the adaptation of the various Schengen provisions on data protection, external borders, migration, police cooperation and combating organized crime, fighting against terrorism and against fraud and corruption, drugs and money laundering, customs cooperation, judicial cooperation in civil and criminal matters and human rights legal instruments. At the same time, the limitations of these mechanisms were evident in the opt-out of Cyprus from the implementation of the Schengen Agreement on overland borders, seaports and airports, as well as its reluctance to sign the Prüm Treaty on furthering cross-border cooperation. Here, the *territorial* and *temporal* dimensions of the country, such as its small, southern, post-colonial and slow status, mediated for these positions. In particular, Cyprus opted out from Schengen partly as a result of its institutional and administrative affinity with colonial UK and partly due to political considerations stemming from the Cyprus problem which is linked to the country's small, southern and post-colonial status. Also, its reluctance to join further integration initiatives in this area, such as the Prüm Treaty is linked to its slow status. Similarly, the *constructivist* social learning mechanism was evident in the socialization processes of Cypriot ministry officials, judges, prosecutors, lawyers, police officers and border guards with their counterparts at the EU level in establishing justice and home affairs norms but had limited impact in reducing corruption and dissolving patron-client structures and mixed impact in reinforcing core values of civil society. The *territorial* and *temporal* dimensions of the country such as its small, southern and post-colonial status mediated this limited and mixed impact. In particular, corruption and clientelism are characteristics evident in other small and southern states in Europe, particularly those which were under colonial Ottoman rule. Similarly, a weak civil society is associated with young post-colonial states which are still in the process of democratization. The *dual rationalist–constructivist* lesson-drawing mechanism was evident in the borrowing of 'best practices', particularly from the UK, in regards to the reorganization of the Ministries of Interior and Justice (i.e. establishment of EU units) as well as the adoption of common institutions with the UK, Malta and Ireland (i.e. the 'Common Law Club') in dealing with the Schengen *acquis*. Here, the *temporal* dimensions of the country such as its post-colonial status defined the source of lesson-drawing (i.e. the UK, Ireland, Malta).

Downloading processes of Europeanization took place whereby there were reforms in the institutions and policies of the country in order to align with the requirements of the third pillar of the Union, i.e. Police Judicial Cooperation in Criminal Matters (PJCCM). In regards to *uploading* processes, Cyprus has actively sought to shape the policy environment of the ENP in order to address its particular interests in this area, more specifically, on the sensitive issue of immigration and asylum. For example, during accession negotiations, Cyprus began discussions with Italy to sign an agreement within the framework of the ENP to curb illegal immigration stemming from Syria, Egypt and Lebanon (Kasoulides, 2007). Cyprus also signed an agreement with new Member State Poland to enhance their cooperation in regards to asylum seekers.[23] And it has consistently reminded the EU of Turkey's responsibilities as a candidate state to curb illegal immigration from 'TRNC' in the areas controlled by the Republic of Cyprus, an issue which touches upon the country's political problem.[24] Finally, Cyprus[25] – along with Greece and Malta – have played a critical role in shaping the legal framework on ship source pollution arguing that this would endanger their maritime and shipping interests (Monar, 2006: 111–12).[26] In that sense, Cyprus' *territorial* (i.e. small, south-eastern) and *temporal* (i.e. new, post-colonial) dimensions have defined its national preferences and state coalitions and mediated the *uploading* processes of Europeanization in this area.

In regards to *cross-loading* processes, EU socialization had limited impact in dissolving patron-client structures and mixed impact in reinforcing core values of civil society. Policy transfer and lesson drawing also occurred within the context of the so-called 'Common Law Club' (established in January 2006) consisting of Cyprus, the UK and other post-colonial states such as Malta and Ireland – countries that have retained the British legal system and traditions established during colonial years – and which deal with common challenges stemming from the adaptation of the Schengen *acquis* in these systems.

This chapter has examined the impact of Europeanization on the country's justice and home affairs policy. It has focused on reforms conducted for the adoption of the Schengen *acquis* in areas such as external borders, immigration, organized crime and drug trafficking, terrorism, corruption, judicial cooperation in civil and criminal matters and human rights. It has indicated that *rationalist, constructivist* and *dual rationalist–constructivist* mechanisms, as well as *downloading, uploading* and *cross-loading* processes were at work in effecting change in these areas. It has also indicated how the *territorial* and *temporal* dimensions of the country such as its small, southern, new, post-colonial and slow status has mediated the impact of these mechanisms and processes.

Conclusion

The beginning of the book highlighted how *rationalist* and *constructivist* mechanisms and *downloading*, *uploading* and *cross-loading* processes are effecting change in Member States, candidate states and even third countries. It also indicated how their *territorial* dimensions such as their size and geographical location and *temporal* dimensions such as their time of accession and their historical trajectory of development, that is, whether a communist, authoritarian or colonial past has mediated change in these countries. In examining the case of Cyprus, it became evident that these mechanisms, processes and dimensions were critical in shaping the response of the country towards the Europeanization process.

Thus, in regards to the area of government, these mechanisms and processes led to reforms in the executive, legislative and judicial branch of the government. *Rationalist* mechanisms were evident in the various government reforms in the executive, legislative and judicial authorities which were outlined in the Association Agreement, Accession Partnership and the Commission's Regular Reports and in light of the strong incentives of pre-accession aid (the four Financial Protocols) and institutional ties (Association, Custom's Union, candidacy and membership). They were evident for example, in the creation of joint Cyprus-EU institutions (e.g. Association and Custom's Union Committees, Joint Parliamentary Committees), the Office of the Ombudsman and the International Office of the Planning Bureau. The *constructivist* social learning mechanism was evident in the context of Cyprus' Structured Dialogue whereby 'soft money' and a process of deliberation and persuasion contributed to capacity-building (e.g. TAIEX), policy-networking of Cypriot officials (e.g. working committees) exchange of information and institutional building. It is also evident in the participation of Cypriot officials at various stages of EU policy-making (i.e. working groups, COREPER, Council of the EU). The *dual rationalist–constructivist* lesson-drawing mechanism was evident in the adoption of best practices from the UK, Ireland and Slovenia such as the creation of EU directorates within government ministries and mechanisms for meeting the responsibilities of the EU's Presidency, even though these were not requested by the Commission. Overall, in this area there was much evidence of *downloading* and *cross-loading* processes of Europeanization but little evidence of an *uploading* process.

Concerning the area of political parties and public opinion, these mechanisms and processes led to reforms in the Cypriot parties' policy/ programmatic content, organizational structures, patterns of party competition, party-government relations and relations beyond the national party system; and shaped specific and diffuse support of the Cypriot public towards the EU. In particular, the *constructivist* social learning mechanism and the *dual rationalist–constructivist* lesson-drawing mechanism were at work in inducing change in the parties policy/programmatic content (i.e. more pro-European programmes; emphasis on European issues and agendas such as environment and gender equality), organizational structures (i.e. creation of EU units and think tanks), patterns of party competition (i.e. adoption of European campaign methods) and party–government relations (i.e. EU party affiliations, participation in European party federations). The *constructivist* social learning mechanism was also at work in inducing diffuse support from Cypriots towards the EU, while *rationalist* external incentives had less of an impact, particularly in the post-accession period, in inducing specific support from Cypriots. Overall, in this area there was evidence of the *cross-loading* and *uploading* process of Europeanization though little evidence of *downloading*.

With respect to public opinion, these mechanisms and processes shaped specific and diffuse support of the Cypriot public towards the EU. In particular, the *constructivist* social learning mechanisms were at work in shaping diffuse support of the Cypriot public opinion towards the EU as evident from the consistent high recordings of trust towards the EU. In contrast, the *rationalist* external incentives mechanism was mostly at work in shaping specific support of the Cypriot public opinion towards the EU in the pre-accession period, as evident from the lower recordings on the value and benefits of EU membership after accession. Overall, in this area there was evidence of *cross-loading* process of Europeanization though little evidence of *downloading* or *uploading*.

In regards to the area of economy, these mechanisms and processes led to reforms in macro-economic fiscal and monetary policy, market liberalization and change in trade patterns. In particular, the *rationalist* external incentive mechanism led to the liberalization of traditionally state-controlled sectors, interest rates and capital controls, reduction of public deficit, curbing inflation and independence of Central Bank. Moreover, *rationalist* external incentives also contributed to the openness of Cypriot economy (i.e. increase in exports and imports) and to a shift on the quality (i.e. from agriculture to manufacturing) and geographical orientation (i.e. from the Middle East to Europe) of Cypriot trade. *Constructivist* mechanisms were also at work inducing change in domestic economic rhetoric regarding the country's accession to the eurozone and meeting the demands of the Stability Pact. And a *dual rationalist–constructivist* lesson-drawing mechanism was at work in emulating economic institutions and policies (i.e. EU Directorates, macro-economic and fiscal policies on euro convergence; campaign strategies on promotion of euro) from Ireland, Slovenia and Greece. Overall, in this area there was much evidence of *downloading* and *cross-loading* processes of Europeanization but little evidence of *uploading* processes.

In regards to the area of agricultural policy, these mechanisms and processes led to reforms in the structure of the country's agricultural regime as well as in its agricultural production and trade patterns. In particular, a *rationalist* external incentives mechanism contributed towards the creation of new institutions and amendment of laws, the abolition of monopolistic elements of state-controlled authorities and the restructuring or abolition of state agricultural subsidies, with a view towards meeting the requirements of the CAP. Also, such mechanisms contributed to a change in the external trade patterns of agricultural products where preference was given to EU imports at the expense of those from the Middle East, North Africa and Eastern Mediterranean countries. Moreover, such mechanisms also contributed to a change in the mode of agricultural production as well as a greater emphasis on environmental functions, agro-tourism and rural development schemes. They also contributed to the modernization of the fishing sector, including its safety and fishing methods. *Constructivist* mechanisms induced changes within the agricultural community, at both the state and private level, in developing more environmentally conscious methods in the sector. A *dual rationalist–constructivist* mechanism was evident in the establishment of organizational structures and policies from countries such as the UK, Netherlands and Greece. Overall, in this area there was much evidence of *downloading, cross-loading* and *uploading* processes of Europeanization.

In regards to the area of regional policy, these mechanisms and processes led to reforms in territorial organization as well as the institutional and administrative regime. In particular, a *rationalist* external incentives mechanism induced the reorganization of the regional and local level into units, as well as institutional and legislative reforms aimed for the management, programming, implementation, evaluation and monitoring, and financial management and control of structural and cohesion funds in Cyprus. *Constructivist* mechanisms also induced the establishment of EU norms in regional policy such as 'equality', 'environmental protection', 'competition' and 'public procurement'.

And a *dual rationalist–constructivist* lesson-drawing mechanism was evident in the adoption of institutions and policies from countries such as Ireland (i.e. organization of the Structural Funds unit) and Greece (e.g. adoption of a monitoring system). Overall, in this area there was much evidence of *downloading, cross-loading* and *uploading* processes of Europeanization.

In regards to the area of foreign policy, these mechanisms and processes led to institutional and administrative reforms but also qualitative changes to the country's foreign policy towards the principle actors of the Cyprus problem and towards other major players in the European and international arena. In particular, a *rationalist* external incentive mechanism was significantly evident in the establishment of new institutions in the Foreign Ministry and the alignment with EU common policies and decisions on issues such as the Iraq War and the oil and arms embargo on the Former Republic of Yugoslavia. The country has also participated in various peace-keeping, conflict-resolution, humanitarian and crisis-management initiatives within the framework of the Petersberg Tasks and the ENP (i.e. in Congo, Bosnia-Hezegovina, FYROM, Lebanon, Israel-Palestine) and became a member of various ESDP agencies (i.e. EDA, ISS, ESDC) and EU battle groups (i.e. HELBROC). Yet there was less evidence of a significant change in the core of Cyprus' foreign policy on its national problem. In this case, while Greek-Cypriot elites engaged more constructively with the Turkish-Cypriot community, promoting and implementing confidence-building measures, and while also generally supporting, under strict conditions, the European orientation of Turkey – all these being policies and objectives of the EU – they remained steadfast in their core national position on the Cyprus problem, strategically influencing the EU's foreign and enlargement policy towards Turkey and its Negotiating Framework, first as a candidate state through its Greek connection, and secondly as a Member State with the use of the veto threat. Also, evidence points to the argument that EU membership status has also made Cyprus' foreign policy more assertive towards Britain and the US, more independent from Greece, while this status has also been used to recruit support on its national problem from countries which have tense and competitive relationships with the EU, such as Russia and China, as well as to shape the policies of other nations vying for closer ties with the EU, such as Azerbaijan and Kyrgyzstan. Finally, Cyprus has not hesitated to break EU unity on international issues which may have implications on its national problem such the independence of Kosovo. *Constructivist* mechanisms were also at work with the change in the rhetoric and position of Cypriot elites and the government towards the Turkish-Cypriot community and Turkey. In this case, the rhetoric became less confrontational and closer to the position and concerns of the EU with regards to the Turkish-Cypriots, particularly on the issue of their economic isolation. Also, there was adherence with the (broader) EU belief that Turkey's accession process is beneficial for the democratization of the country and stability in the region, including the prospects for the solution of the Cyprus problem. The *dual rationalist–constructivist* lesson-drawing mechanism was evident in the adoption of best practices and institutions from Greece and the UK in regards to the organizational structure of the foreign ministry as well as from the Nordic and Baltic states in regards to humanitarian and crisis management expertise. Overall, in this area there was much evidence of *downloading*, *cross-loading* and *uploading* processes of Europeanization.

Finally, in regards to the area of justice and home affairs, these mechanisms and processes led to institutional and administrative reforms as well as changes in the country's policies towards key areas of PJCCM. *Rationalist* and *constructivist* mechanisms have induced changes in the country's Justice and Home Affairs regime. In particular, *rationalist* mechanisms have induced the alignment with the various Schengen provisions on data protection, external borders, migration, police cooperation and combating organized crime, fight against terrorism, fight against fraud and corruption, drugs and money laundering, customs cooperation, judicial cooperation in civil and criminal matters and human rights legal instruments. Similarly, the *constructivist* social learning mechanism was evident in the socialization processes of Cypriot ministry officials, judges, prosecutors, lawyers, police officers and border guards with their counterparts at the EU level in establishing Justice and Home Affairs norms. The *dual rationalist–constructivist* lesson-drawing mechanism was evident in the borrowing of 'best practices', particularly from the UK, in regards to the reorganization of Ministries of Interior and Justice (i.e. EU units) as well as the adoption of common institutions with the UK, Malta and Ireland (i.e. the 'Common Law Club') in dealing with the Schengen *acquis*. Overall in this area, there was much evidence of *downloading*, *cross-loading* and *uploading* processes of Europeanization.

Both *rationalist* and *constructivist* mechanisms were evident in all stages of the accession process, yet those associated with the *constructivist* social learning mechanism and the *dual rationalist–constructivist* lesson-drawing mechanism were more evident in the later stages where the strengthening of institutional ties also fostered an increase in interaction between national and EU policy-makers as well as processes of policy transfer Also, the *rationalist* mechanism was met with greater domestic resistance than the other two mechanisms. Examples where there was notable domestic resistance to reforms included the liberalization of the telecoms industry, the independence of the central bank, the reform of the pension system and the termination of state aid to arable crops and fisheries. There was also restriction of hunting rules as well as in the establishment of environmental standards in the maritime and shipping industry. Similarly, *downloading, cross-loading* and *uploading* processes of Europeanization were evident in all stages of the accession process, though *cross-loading* and *uploading* were more evident in the later stages where the strengthening of institutional ties fostered socialization and policy transfer and provided the country an opportunity to shape EU policies and institutions from within, by participating as an equal member in the decision-making institutions of the EU.

Moreover, the *territorial* and *temporal* dimensions of Cyprus have all mediated and shaped the way in which these mechanisms and processes impacted the country. Its *territorial* dimensions such as its 'small', 'southern Mediterranean', 'peripheral', 'distant', 'dependent', 'outsider' status, as well as its *temporal* dimensions such as its 'new', 'slow' and 'post-colonial' status have all shaped the way in which the country responded to but also influenced the EU. Thus, for example, in regards to government, the *territorial* and *temporal* dimensions of the country such as its small, southern and post-colonial status mediated deficiencies of these mechanisms and processes in establishing an efficient and effective national coordination system, implementation and institution-building, and shaped any lesson-drawing of mechanisms and institutions within the executive, legislative and judicial authorities from countries such as the UK, Ireland, and Slovenia. In regards to political parties, the *territorial* and *temporal* dimensions of the country such as its small, southern, post-colonial and new status mediated the deficiencies of these mechanisms and processes in the lack of the effective dismantling of patron–client patterns in party behaviour, including their practices in exercising power, and in the persistent gender gap in regards to the participation in Cypriot politics, while they also shaped diffuse and specific support towards the EU. In regards to public opinion, the *territorial* and *temporal* dimensions of the country such as its small, southern, post-colonial and new status shaped mediated the deficiencies of these mechanisms and processes in sustaining specific support for the EU in the post-accession period. In regards to the economy, the *territorial* and *temporal* dimensions of the country such as its small, southern, distant and new status mediated the deficiencies of these mechanisms and processes in increasing the competitiveness of the economy and shaped any lesson-drawing of economic institutions and policies from countries such as Greece, Ireland and Slovenia. In regards to agricultural policy, the *territorial* and *temporal* dimensions of the country such as its small, southern and post-colonial status mediated lesson-drawing of agricultural institutions and policies from countries such as Greece, Netherlands and the UK. Also, the small, southern and peripheral status of the country mediated for the limitations of these mechanisms and processes to shift the agricultural trade patterns of the country from the Middle East to the EU markets, as well as increase competitiveness of the Cypriot agricultural products. In regards to regional policy, the *territorial* and *temporal* dimensions of the country such as its small, southern and new status mediated the lesson-drawing of regional and cohesion policy institutions from countries such as Greece and Ireland as well as deficiencies in the management and absorption of structural and cohesion funds. In regards to foreign policy, the *territorial* and *temporal* dimensions of the country such as its small, southern, post-colonial status mediated the lesson-drawing of foreign policy institutions from countries such as the UK, Greece and the Nordic and Baltic States, as well as the limitations of these mechanisms in effecting significant change in the country's foreign policy towards its national problem. Its slow status also mediated the (op)position of the state in further integration initiatives in the area of defence. Finally, in regards to justice and home affairs the *territorial* and *temporal* dimensions of the country such as its small, southern and post-colonial status mediated the deficiencies of these mechanisms and processes in eradicating corruption and clientelism in governance and society, strengthening civil society, as well as the its opt-out from parts of Schengen. Also, the *temporal* dimension of the country such as its post-colonial status mediated the lesson-drawing of justice and home affairs institutions from countries such as the UK and Ireland, and its slow status mediated its reluctance to participate in further integration initiatives on cross-border cooperation such as the Prüm Treaty.

Finally, it is important to indicate that many of these effects on the country are not entirely associated with Europeanization but with other forces as well, such as globalization and democratization. For example, the declining importance of the agricultural sector – in terms of GDP share and workforce – is a world trend in developing nations that is partly due to globalization and technological development. And in regards to foreign policy, the change towards a more assertive and independent Cypriot foreign policy towards Britain and Greece respectively, as well as a more moderate position towards the Turkish-Cypriots is also partly due to internal processes of democratization and ethnic reconciliation.

This book has indicated the importance of a country's *territorial* and *temporal* dimensions in responding to *rationalist, constructivist, dual-rationalist–constructivist* mechanisms as well as *downloading, cross-loading* and *uploading* processes of Europeanization. Countries, whether inside or outside the EU, which have similar dimensions are likely to respond in similar ways to these processes and mechanisms of Europeanization and share some of the same Europeanization experiences. Hence, one can distinguish various regional constellations in Europe such as the Franco-German, Anglo-American, Alpine, Central, Baltic, Nordic, Mediterranean, Balkan and Wider Europe. At the same time, one has to bare in mind that the cross-cutting influence of these mechanisms, processes and dimensions of Europeanization are unique in each country and that even within these regional constellations, there is a significant differentiation in terms of membership and belonging in the new Europe.

Notes

1. Introduction: Conceptualizing and Theorizing Europeanization

1. The book follows the standard international usage of 'Cyprus' to mean the Republic of Cyprus, recognized under international law and the United Nations, to have authority over the entire island of Cyprus and the 'Cypriot government' to refer to the government of the Republic of Cyprus, which has been controlled by the Greek-Cypriots since 1963. The 'Turkish Republic of Northern Cyprus' ('TRNC') refers to the regime run by the Turkish-Cypriots in the north of the island, and which is recognized only by Turkey (hence the use of quotations). The main argument for 'non-recognition' of the 'TRNC', which has been proposed by the UN and subsequently by the EC/EU, is that under the principle of *jus cogens* in international law, an entity is not recognized if it is a result of an 'illegal act' or 'aggression' as the military intervention in the island was characterized by United Nations Resolutions. For more on this issue see Dugard, J. (1987) *Recognition and the United Nations* (Cambridge: Cambridge University Press).

2. With the same logic one can also distinguish 'thin' processes of Europeanization whereby actors, following the logic of optimality, rationally and strategically act and respond to Europe in order to realize their preferences; and 'thick' processes of Europeanization whereby actors, following the logic of appropriateness, act on the basis of patterns of behaviour and ideas that they deem suitable to their purposes (Vink, 2003; Bache, 2007).

3. *Coercion* has rationalist roots and is the response to such pressures as a government mandate or dependence on key organizations, that is, an organization will tend to become similar to those organizations on which it depends. *Mimetism* has both rationalist and constructivist roots and stems from the need to cope with uncertainty by imitating organizations perceived to be more legitimate or more successful. *Normative pressures* has constructivist roots and is induced by professionalization, that is, professionals, their associations and the mechanisms of formal education, socialization and recruitment produce a common cognitive base and a shared legitimation of occupational autonomy which make organizational structures similar to one another (Radaelli, 2000b: 28).

4. *Institutional compliance* or *positive integration* has rationalist roots and it is the mechanism where the EU prescribes concrete institutional arrangements with which Member States must comply. *Changing opportunity structures or negative integration* has rationalist roots and it is the mechanism where the EU affects the domestic arrangements by altering the rules of the game, whereby changes in domestic opportunity structures may successfully challenge existing institutional equilibria. *Policy framing* or *framing integration* has constructivist roots and is the mechanism which affects the domestic arrangements even more indirectly by altering the beliefs and expectations

of domestic actors which in turn may affect the strategies and preferences of these domestic actors, potentially leading to corresponding institutional adaptations (Knill & Lehmkuhl, 1999: 2).

5. *Judicial review* acts as a mechanism of change by providing the right of any affected party to challenge deficient implementation of Community Law before national courts (Weiler, 1991) whereas *regulatory competition* acts as a mechanism of change by triggering the dismantling of trade barriers which provides firms with exit options from national jurisdictions (Majone, 1996).

6. 'The goodness of fit' between the European and the domestic level determines the degree of pressure for adaptation generated by Europeanization on Member States. The lower the compatibility between European and domestic processes, policies and institutions, the higher the adaptational pressure (Caporaso *et al.*, 2001).

7. In its broad definition, *conditionality* refers to 'the use of fulfilment of stipulated political obligations as a prerequisite for obtaining economic aid, debt relief, most-favoured national treatment, access to subsidized credit or membership in coveted regional or global organizations (Schmitter, 2001: 42).

8. *Gate-keeping* has a rationalist root and refers to the EU's strongest conditionality tool, that is, providing a state access to different stages of the accession process, particularly achieving candidate status and starting negotiations. *Benchmarking and Monitoring* has a rationalist root and refers to the EU's instruments in influencing policy and institutional development through ranking the applicant's overall progress, benchmarking in particular policy areas, and providing examples of best practice that the applicants seek to emulate. *Provision of Legislative and Institutional Templates* has a rationalist root and refers to the EU's detailed identification of institutional weaknesses of the candidate state and detailed guide for the required reforms for the full adoption of the *acquis*. *Aid and Technical Assistance* has both rationalist and constructivist roots and refers to the EU's efforts in providing conditional financial aid for the strengthening of the candidate state's existing institutions and the creation of new ones as well as for the training and socialization of national officials with EU institutions and procedures. *Advice and Twinning* has both rationalist and constructivist roots and refers to the EU's efforts to help candidate states to learn from Member States experiences in building institutions and implementing the *acquis* encouraging both the adaptation of 'best practices' and the socialization of candidate state officials with their counterparts in those Member States (Grabbe, 2001:1020–4).

9. Some of the conditions that can facilitate normative diffusion and policy transfer and the activation of these 'social learning' and 'lesson-drawing' mechanisms are: perceived policy failures that opened windows of opportunity for learning, active transnational entrepreneurship on the part of policy-makers and epistemic communities, pressure to incorporate the norms of groups and institutions to which states belong or aspire to join, close correspondence between domestic priorities and the imported policy lesson, and relatively weak or diffuse conditionality or linkage with material interests (Andonova, 2005: 155).

10. 'Families of Nations' are distinguished in terms of shared geographical, linguistic, cultural and/or historical attributes leading to distinctive patterns in public policy outcomes.

11. 'Centre and Periphery' structures are respectively distinguished by a 'privileged' territorial location within Europe characterized by a military–administrative and economic advantage as opposed to an 'unprivileged' location characterized by distance, difference and dependence.

12. 'Constellation' structures are distinguished between 'insiders' and 'outsiders', 'poles' and 'non-poles' distinguished in terms of 'size of population and territory, resource endowment, economic capability, military strength, political stability and competence'.

13. Clusters of Europeanization' refers to multi-country groupings that are characterized by high levels of intra-regional commonality and inter-regional differences in both substance and modes of Europeanization.

14. There have been many definitions of 'smallness' because it is not an absolute but a comparative idea (Amstrup, 1976: 165) but factors such as size of population, geographical area, economic and military capacity, 'vulnerability' and 'perceptual size' have been presented as key variables (Damijan, 1997; Castello *et al.*, 1997; Holl, 2000; Antola & Lehtimäki, 2001; Archer & Nugent, 2002; Crowards, 2002; Thorhallsson, 2006). Note that EU-27 consists of 21 small Member States.

15. These views are not unchallenged as there are those that argue that small-state peripherality should not be exaggerated. Numerous coalitional analyses in the EU-27 reveal coalitions between 'pro-integrationist versus less-integrationist' and 'left-wing versus right-wing' governments (Mattila, 2004), 'north versus south' (Kaeding & Torsten, 2005; Naurin, 2007), 'net contributors versus net receivers' (Kaeding & Torsten, 2005), between regional constellations such as the Baltic, Visegrad and Nordic States (Hosli, 1996; Kaeding & Torsten, 2005; Naurin, 2007), and a Franco-German axis (Naurin, 2007), but not a distinct small (or large) state coalition. Instead, there is a situation where both small and large Member States co-exist in different constellation groups, a conclusion also supported by constellation theory (Mouritzen & Wivel, 2005). Empirical case studies (Hanf & Soetendorp, 1998; Ingebritsen, 1998; Antola & Lehtimaki, 2001; Gstöhl, *et al.*, 2007) also indicate the divergence between the views and policies of small Member States.

16. Again, these views are not unchallenged, however, as there are those who theoretically call into question the analytical utility of notions such as 'Mediterranean Europe', or the idea that Southern Europe should be seen as distinctive (apart from the obvious fact of geographical location) (Closa & Heywood, 2004: 240) and those who indicate that there is no empirical evidence of differentiation as, for example, in the structure and function of parties in Southern Europe (Ignazi & Ysmal, 1998).

17. A number of studies have focused on the common Europeanization experiences of these new Member States in the areas of central government administration (Lippert *et al.*, 2001; Agh, 2003; Laffan, 2003; Goetz, 2001b; Fink-Hafner, 2005; Lippert & Umbach, 2005), civil service (Dimitrova, 2002; Verheijen, 2002; Bossaert & Demmke, 2003; Scherpereel, 2003), political parties (Agh, 2002; Taggart & Szczerbiak, 2004; Henderson, 2005; Lewis, 2005), territorial organization (Brusis, 2002; Hughes *et al.*, Hughes, 2003, 2004 & Keating), monetary and budgetary policy (Dyson, 2006; Dimitrov *et al.*, 2006), social policy (Guillen & Bruno, 2004; Lendvai, 2004; Leiber, 2005), environmental policy (Carmin & VanDeveer, 2004) and justice and

home affairs (Grabbe, 2000; Lavenex, 2001a; Lavenex & Ucarer, 2004). Other comparative studies have also revealed common patterns across countries and sectors (Andonova, 2004; Dimitrova, 2004; Hughes *et al.*, 2004; Agh, 2005; Vachudová, 2005; Schimmelfenning & Sedelmeier, 2005).

18. It is important to indicate that while Soviet communist domination in CEE shares similarities with former colonial and imperial powers (e.g. Roman and British Empire), in order to avoid conceptual stretching (Sartori, 1970) it is not categorized as such. One can point out, for example, that much like US domination in Cold War Western Europe, it did not involve the acquisition of foreign territory and population settlements but rather the exercise of political, economic and military control and influence over these countries.

19. In terms of ethnic conflicts, Malta is a lone and notable exception. For more on the common experiences of post-colonial states see Van de Goor, L. *et al.* (1996) (eds) *Between Development and Destruction: An Inquiry Into the Causes of Conflict in Post-Colonial States* (London: Mcmillan Press Ltd); Wimmer, A. (1997) 'Who Owns the State?: Understanding Ethnic Conflict in Post-Colonial Societies', *Nations and Nationalism*, vol. 3(4), pp. 631–666.

20. Another related factor to the mode of EU policy-making regards the degree and extent of the *acquis* that needs to be adopted by states. At different stages of the integration process, there was much greater emphasis on the part of the Union on the adoption and full implementation of the *acquis* prior to accession. Thus, adopting the *acquis* in the last enlargement process was a greater challenge than in the case of other enlargements in the 1980s.

21. One can add, however, that this distinction is difficult to observe given the interaction between domestic, European and international processes. In particular, globalization and democratization are processes that exist in parallel, complementary, overlapping, cross-cutting, mutually reinforcing but also competing manner with Europeanization. Their definition, however, is useful for the purposes of this distinction. Globalization is variously defined (Harvey, 1989; Giddens, 1990; Hirst & Thompson, 1996; Scholte, 2000; Gilpin, 2001) but it can be simply understood 'as the widening, deepening and speeding up of worldwide interconnectedness' (McGrew, 2005: 20). Democratization has also been variously defined (Sorensen, 1993; Potter, 1997; Grugel, 2001; Schmitter, 2003) but it is best understood as 'a complex, long-term, dynamic and open-ended process, consisting of progress towards a more rule-based, more consensual and more participatory type of politics' (Whitehead, 2002: 27).

2. The Making of Modern Cyprus: An Overview

1. With the end of the Ottoman rule in 1878, the Muslim community consisted of 46,000 people (20 per cent of population) compared to 180,000 Christians. With the end of the British rule in 1960 and the independence of the island, Greek-Cypriots comprised 78 per cent of the population, Turkish-Cypriots 18 per cent and Maronites/Latins and Armenians 4 per cent out of a total population of 573,000. In 2007, more than three decades after the division

of the island, the respective percentages for each community remain out of a total population of 788,457 (July 2007 estimates).

2. During this period, there was an impressive rise of ecclesiastic/monastic holdings through the accumulation of land, with the Kykko monastery epitomizing the Church's economic dominance among the local population (Rizopoulou-Egoumenidou, 1996: 194).

3. 'Εκκλησία, Κοινωνία, Πολιτεία', *Πολίτης*, 1 September 2007; 'Παραμέτρους μη εμπλοκής εθεσε ο Αναστασιάδης', *Φιλελεύθερος*, 31 August 2007; 'Η Εκκλησία έιμαι εγώ', *Πολίτης*, 14 August 2007;

4. For more on clientelism in contemporary Cypriot society see 'Chapter IX: 'Justice and Home Affairs'.

5. The British initially acquired the island in 1878 as a loan from the Ottoman Empire in exchange for protecting the latter against possible Russian aggression. With the fall of the Ottoman Empire in 1925, however, and the 1923 Treaty of Lausanne where the Turkish Republic renounced its claims to formerly Ottoman possessions beyond its borders, Cyprus officially became a Crown colony.

6. For example, the British were unwilling to recognize the Archbishop as the political representative of the Greek-Cypriots, due to their devotion to the doctrine of separation of religion and politics.

7. Note that in spite of this antagonistic state of affairs, 37,000 Cypriots (from both communities) volunteered for the British Armed Forces against the Germans in the Second World War, including Glafkos Clerides – the later President of the Republic – who became a prisoner of war while serving in the British Royal Air Force as a fighter pilot (Mallinson, 2005: 11).

8. According to the Plan, each community would run its own communal affairs through its own House of Representatives. The administration, however, of the island as a whole would be directed by a Council composed of the British governor, representatives of the Greek and Turkish governments, and six Cypriot ministers, four elected from the Greek House of Representatives and two from the Turkish. The British governor, in consultation with the representatives of the Greek and Turkish governments, would have reserved power to deal with external affairs, defence and internal security. More importantly (for the Greek-Cypriots), the plan postponed the notion of self-determination for seven years and gave Turkey a veto for *Enosis* at the end of that period, while providing no central legislative power to the Greek-Cypriot majority (Stephens, 1966: 150–66).

9. Britain, which had already lost its colonial possessions of Jordan and Palestine in the late 1940s and was in dispute with the Egypt over the Suez canal, saw its role dramatically decline in the Middle East and was eager to hold on to Cyprus to avert further loss of influence in the region. Prime Minister Anthony Eden's speech at Norwich in 1956 on the lines of 'no Cyprus no oil' in the Middle East provided the British public with a simple explanation of the strategic importance of the island for the economic and political interests of Britain in the Middle East; Whitehall deemed that Cyprus had a 'stabilizing role' to play as a bastion of British power in the region and its retainment was necessary if Britain was to remain a 'first class power'. Thus, despite the fact that the island did not have a deep water port, it was still important

for Britain for 'strategic, political and psychological reasons' (Hatzivassiliou, 2006: 202–203).

10. Its military campaign began on 1 April 1955 and while its main target was the British military, EOKA also targeted pro-British Cypriots, informants, Communists, *Taksim* (partition) supporters, and members of Turkish Resistance Organization (TMT). Over 30,000 British troops were assigned to combat the organisation, which officially claimed the lives of 104 British military personnel. In addition, the conflict also claimed the lives of 90 EOKA fighters, 50 policemen and 238 civilians.

11. TMT was also supported with arms and money from Turkey.

12. For example, in the police mobile reserve units there were no Greek-Cypriots and in the auxiliary police there were 56 Greek-Cypriots compared to 1281 Turkish-Cypriots. Another notable point is that the Greek-Cypriot comprador bourgeoisie who controlled the trade sector saw their interests threatened by the anti-colonial movement and also sided with the British. And the Church which acted as the focal point of the anti-colonial struggle filled a political vacuum and further strengthened its power (Panayiotopoulos, 1999: 40).

13. More specifically, the constitution provided for a Greek-Cypriot President and Turkish-Cypriot Vice President elected by the two communities respectively; the Council of Ministers functioned with a 7:3 ratio, consisting of ten members, seven chosen by the President and three by the Vice-President with the Turkish-Cypriots acquiring at least one major ministry (in practice defence); decisions in the Council of Ministers were to be taken by absolute majority, with the President and the Vice-President having the power of veto over decisions relating to foreign affairs, defence or internal security; the legislative system was unicameral, with the House of Representatives consisting of 50 members, 35 Greek-Cypriots and 15 Turkish-Cypriots, and two communal chambers with separate competencies on education, religion and culture and tax issues; the judicial system was headed both by the Supreme Constitutional Court and by the High Court of Justice, each consisting of Greek and Turkish Cypriot judges, as well as a neutral president from the international community (who should not be Cypriot, Greek, Turkish or British). Finally, the constitution recognized the bi-communal nature of Cyprus in its arrangement of a public administration with a 7:3 participation ratio for the Greek and Turkish-Cypriot communities respectively; and a mixed Cypriot army and police.

14. The two bases are Akrotiri and Dhekelia in total of 99 square miles. Approximately 14,000 people live in sovereign area of the bases, including 7,000 Cypriots from both communities.

15. For more on the common experiences of post-colonial states see Van de Goor, L. *et al.* (1996) (eds) *Between Development and Destruction: An Inquiry Into the Causes of Conflict in Post-Colonial States* (London: Macmillan Press); Wimmer, A. (1997) 'Who Owns the State?: Understanding Ethnic Conflict in Post-Colonial Societies', *Nations and Nationalism*, vol. 3(4), pp. 631–66.

16. For more on the construction of Cypriot identity see Papadakis, Y. (1993) 'The Politics of Memory and Forgetting in Cyprus', *Journal of Mediterranean Studies*, vol.3(1), pp. 139–54; Kizilyurek, N. (1993) *Cyprus Beyond the Nation* (in Turkish & Greek) (Ploutis Servas); Mavratsas, C. (1997) 'The Ideological Contest Between Greek-Cypriot Nationalism and Cypriotism, 1974–1995:

Politics, Social Memory and Identity', *Ethnic and Racial Studies*, vol. 20(4), pp. 717–37; Calotychos, V. (1998) 'Interdisciplinary Perspectives: Difference at the Heart of Cypriot Identity and its Study' in Calotychos, V. (ed.) *Cyprus and its People: Nation, Identity and Experience in an Unimaginable Community, 1955–1997* (Colorado Press); Peristianis, N. (2006) 'Cypriot Nationalism, Dual Identity and Politics', in Papadakis *et al.* (eds) *Divided Cyprus: Modernity, History and an Island in Conflict* (Bloomington: Indiana University Press).

17. For more on this issue see 'Chapter 5: Political Parties and Public Opinion'.

18. An estimated 400 Turkish-Cypriots and 180 Greek-Cypriots were killed or went missing in 1963–64 alone.

19. Approximately, 60,000 Turkish-Cypriots fled their homes to live in enclaves.

20. The force was introduced following the UN Security Council Resolution 186 (1964). The UNFICYP mandate was originally defined in the following terms: 'in the interest of preserving international peace and security, to use its best efforts to prevent a recurrence of fighting, and if necessary, to contribute to the maintenance and restoration of law and order and a return to normal conditions'. That mandate was subsequently and periodically extended by the UN Security Council. For more on the role of UNFICYP during the 1964-1974 inter-communal conflict see Lindley, D. (2001) 'Assessing the Role of UN Peace-keeping Force in Cyprus' in Richmond, O. & Ker-Lindsay, J. (eds) *The Work of the UN in Cyprus* (Basingstoke: Palgrave Macmillan).

21. For more on UN mediation during 1964–1965 see Richmond, O. (2001) 'UN Mediation in Cyprus, 1964–1965: Setting a Precedent for Peacemaking?' in Richmond, O. & Ker-Lindsay, J. (eds) *The Work of the UN in Cyprus* (Basingstoke: Palgrave Macmillan).

22. Chossudovsky, M. (2006) 'Triple Alliance: The US, Turkey, Israel and the War on Lebanon', *Global Research*, 6 August.

23. Including the purchase of Soviet made arms.

24. Nikos Sampson was a key member of the EOKA guerrilla struggle against Britain in 1955–59 and of Grivas' National Guard forces which were involved in the inter-communal clashes of 1963–7. Since 1970 he was also a member of the House of Parliament and leader of the Progressive Party. When Grivas died in January 1974, he took a lead role in EOKA B activities.

25. The code name given by the Turkish forces to this military intervention was 'Operation Attila'. Turkish and Turkish-Cypriot discourse perceives this military intervention as a 'Peace Operation' whereas Greek and Greek-Cypriot discourse perceives this military intervention as an 'Attila Invasion'. This book will use the UN term 'military intervention' to describe these events.

26. During the events in 1974, UNFICYP resorted to *ad hoc* operations to ensure the ceasefire between the opposing forces and inspect opposing forces, cease fire lines and buffer zones.

27. Since then, the *de facto* boundary dividing the two communities is known as the 'Green Line'.

28. On February 1975 Turkey and the Turkish Cypriots declared that territory as the 'Federated Turkish State' and in November 1983 the 'Turkish Republic of Northern Cyprus'. Neither of these entities have been recognized by the UN.

29. For more on the role of the US and Britain in the events of 1974 see Mallinson, W. (2007) 'US Interests, British Acquiescence and the Invasion of Cyprus', *British Journal of Politics and International Relations*, vol. 9, pp. 494–508.

30. For the particulars of the Association Agreement see 'Chapter 3: The Evolution of Cyprus' Relations with the EU'.
31. The number now reduced following DNA tests and cooperation between the two communities.
32. For more on the effects of the war on Cyprus' economy see Chapter 6: Economy.
33. For more on this see 'Chapter 3: The Evolution of Cyprus' Relations with the EU.
34. For more on the north–south development gap see Chapter 6: Economy.
35. Makarios died of natural causes in August 1977.
36. For more on the role of UN mediation during this period see Ker-Lindsay, J. (2005) *EU Accession and UN Peacemaking in Cyprus* (Basingstoke: Palgrave Macmillan).
37. The plan was revised on 10 December 2002, 26 February 2003 and 29 March 2004. Revisions dealt with minor issues – the core principles of the plan remained in its final version.
38. Cyprus would speak in the European Union with a single voice produced by the coordination and cooperation of the two component states and the federal government on the basis of the Belgian Cooperation Agreements. Thus, on issues falling under the competencies of the common state, Cyprus will be represented by a federal official appointed by the Presidential Council. On issues falling under the competencies of the component states, Cyprus will be represented by a representative of the component state, by rotation. In cases of disagreement on the common position that Cyprus would adopt in the EU, Concertation Committees – comprised of ministerial representatives of the two component states, at first instance, at then of the President and Vice-President at second instance – would be formed in order to try to settle the dispute. If there is still no agreement, Cyprus would abstain in the Council of the EU.
39. For the full text of the plan see http://www.unficyp.org/
40. It is important to indicate that prior to the referendum in 2004, the Turkish-Cypriot community demonstrated widely in December 2002 and January 2003 against their leader Rauf Denktash who was strongly opposed to the Annan Plan (refusing to put it on a referendum) and demanded a resolution of the conflict through the acceptance of the plan and simultaneous membership to the Union. Under intense domestic pressure, Denktash surprised many by partially opening the borders along the Green Line (in April 2003) allowing nearly 300,000 Greek-Cypriots to visit the northern part of the island. He continued, however, to oppose the Annan Plan up until its referendum. Following the referendum, Denktash announced that he will not seek a further term as 'President' of the 'TRNC'.
41. Markides, A. (2002) 'UN Secretary General Plan for the Settlement of the Cyprus Problem: Comments for the Preliminary Information of the National Council' (in Greek), Office of the Attorney General of the Republic of Cyprus, 12 November 2002.
42. Lordos, A. (2006) 'Rational Agent or Unthinking Follower', paper presented in the *ECPR Joint Sessions Workshop: Cyprus: A Conflict at the Crossroads*, Nicosia, 25–30 April.
43. In regards to the crucial issue of security, the Greek-Cypriot perception was that the Plan's retainement of the 1960 'three guarantee power' provision

was in direct contradiction to any contemporary notion of sovereignty and independence. This clause would provide these powers the right to unilaterally (and militarily) intervene – in case of a breach of the agreement – and would constitutionally allow foreign involvement in the domestic affairs of the country, a unique constitutional provision in international affairs. On the same note, there was concern over the provision in the plan that Cyprus's territory cannot be used militarily by any international organization (including the EU) without the consent of Turkey. This effectively meant that Cyprus would need Turkey's consent for participating in any operations of the EU's Security and Defence Policy, again raising question of the sovereignty and independence of the new state.

44. In regards to the withdrawal of Turkish forces, the Greek-Cypriot side perceived the time frame for the withdrawal of 35,000 Turkish troops to be too long (i.e. 2018) and its conditional link with the accession of Turkey to the EU to be unsatisfactory, given that it would keep the country militarized (along with other Greek forces) for some indefinite time and dependent on the progress of Turkey's accession process.

45. In regards to the issue of reinstatement of property, there were concerns from the Greek-Cypriot side that the proposed provisions would effectively deny the right of many Greek-Cypriot refugees to reinstate ownership of their properties which would be under the Turkish-Cypriot jurisdiction after the solution. The plan provided for compensation but the perception was that it did not do justice to those Greek-Cypriot refugees who lost their homes and which now happen to be included in the Turkish Cypriot zone.

46. In regards to the issue of settlers, there was great concern from the Greek-Cypriot side that the provisions of citizenship – as outlined in the plan – would allow all the settlers in Cyprus to gain citizenship of the new state, some immediately with the effect of the agreement, and others after a short period of time (7 years). This would occur as the Turkish Cypriot canton, will have the right under those provisions to provide the existing settlers with work permits which would allow them after 7 years to achieve the status of 'legal residents' and effectively become citizens of Cyprus. This was perceived to effectively legalize the status of these people in Cyprus.

47. In regards to the issue of power-sharing, there was concern from the Greek-Cypriot side that the 4:2 ratio in the executive will make decision-making problematic as it will increase the likelihood of deadlocks and even lead to a paralysis of the state. It was felt that it would be much more difficult for both communities, but especially for the Greek-Cypriot side to sway in its favour a vote from the opposite side within the 4-2 ratio rather than the 6-3 ratio. In other words, it would be easier to persuade one out of three Turkish-Ministers rather than one out of two to vote in your favour. Whether it was a 4:2 or another proposed ration (i.e. 6:3), the fact that it effectively provided the 20 per cent Turkish-Cypriot minority the power to veto the proposals and decision of the government, raised doubts among Greek-Cypriots that such kind of arrangement would promote effective governance of the state, when it came to decision-making. Problems in decision-making would have important repercussions when Cyprus is called upon to decide about the common position that it would adopt at the EU level. When the two communities

could not decide on a common position, then Cyprus would need to abstain, effectively loosing its voice at the EU level.

48. In regards to the arbitration mechanism, there was concern from the Greek-Cypriot side that the three foreign judges composing the Court (even if they were not nationals of the three guarantee powers) would constitute a political anomaly as it would effectively allow foreign involvement in the internal affairs of the country. This is an element in the proposal that is unique in constitutional terms, as there is no other example of a state (federal or unitary) which gives authority to foreign nationals to settle domestic disputes.

49. In regards to the issue of residency, there was concern from the Greek-Cypriot side that the plan's general restrictions on this issue – whereby each community has the right to restrict the number of residents from the opposite side to 1/3 of the total population of its own cities and villages – would effectively allow the Turkish-Cypriot canton to forbid a great number of Greek-Cypriot refugees from returning to their homes, which would be against the EU principle of the free movement of people. Also, there were concerns over the residency restrictions within the transitional period of 20 years, whereby, only a small percentage of refugees would be allowed to return to their homes (the first year 1 per cent and an increase of 3 per cent every three years). This would significantly reduce the rate of returning refugees in the next 20 years.

50. In regards to the territorial issue, there was concern from the Greek–Cypriot side that the percentages outlined in the two maps (28.5 and 28.6 per cent) did not reflect the actual population percentages of the two communities (i.e. 80 and 20 per cent respectively).

51. For more on this see Eichengreen, B. *et al.* (2004) 'Economic Aspects of the Annan Plan for the Solution of the Cyprus Problem' Report to the Government of the Republic of Cyprus, 17 February 2004.

52. It is worth noting, however, that the party initially supported the Plan when it was first presented, only to change its policy in the later process reluctantly recommending a 'no' vote arguably to maintain the coherency with the rest of the parties of the ruling coalition (i.e. DIKO and EDEK) who rejected the Plan.

53. 'Greek premier pledges support as leadership discusses Annan Plan', Cyprus News Agency, 15 April 2004. Greek opposition leader George Papandreou actively supported the plan.

54. Following the referendum, UN Secretary General Kofi Annan recommended on September 2004 a reduction of the 1224 UNFICYP forces to that of 860 and a more mobile and efficient concept of operations while also extending its mandate until December 2007. His recommendations, which were approved by the Council, came after questions were raised by the international community regarding the value added of UNFICYP's 43-year old presence, particularly in light of absence of significant progress in the political process for the resolution of the conflict.

3. The Evolution of Cyprus' Relations with the EU

1. The Agreement came into force in 1 June 1973.
2. For more on this see Chapter 2: The Making of Modern Cyprus.

3. The Protocol came into force on 1 January 1988.
4. Cypriot Parliamentary Debates, Second Parliamentary Period, Third Meeting, no. 16, 11 January 1973 (as cited in Tsardanidis, 1991: 42).
5. Interview of Mr Orak in *Halkin Sesi* (Turkish-Cypriot daily), Public Information Office, Turkish-Cypriot Administration, Press Release, 20 January 1972.
6. *Agence Europe*, No. 586, 16 February 1972.
7. Article 5 of the AA provided that trade rules between the signatories should not discriminate in any way against other Member States, citizens and private companies of those states, and citizens or private companies of Cyprus.
8. At that time, there were no demands from the 'TRNC' for direct trade between the north and the EEC.
9. The Republic of Cyprus, established in October 1960, with a population of 749,200 (1 December 2005 est. Eurostat.), effectively controls 63 per cent of the island's total territory (9,250 sq. kil), although, according to international law it has jurisdiction over the whole of the island, being the only recognized government by the United Nations. The 'Turkish-Republic of Northern Cyprus', established in November 1983, with a population of approximately 300,000 (more than half being Turkish-born settlers) is only recognized by Turkey.
10. See Guney, A. (2004) 'The USA's Role in Mediating the Cyprus Conflict: A Story of Success or Failure?', *Security Dialogue*, vol. 35 (1), pp. 27–42.
11. See Chapter 2: The Making of Modern Cyprus and Chapter 6: Economy.
12. The criteria, set in the Copenhagen European Council in June 1993, are the rules that define whether a state is eligible to join the European Union. The criteria are: a) stable institutions guaranteeing democracy, the rule of law, human rights, and respect for and protection of minorities; b) functioning market economy as well as the capacity to cope with competitive pressure and market forces within the Union; c) the ability to meet the aims of the political, economic and monetary Union (European Council, 1993).
13. Commission of the European Communities, *Regular Report from the Commission on Cyprus' Progress Towards Accession*, Office for the Official Publications of the European Communities, Luxembourg, 1998.
14. Commission of the European Communities, *Regular Report from the Commission on Cyprus' Progress Towards Accession*, Luxembourg: Office for the Official Publications of the European Communities, 1998.
15. European Parliament (1995) 'Resolution on Cyprus's Membership Application to the European Union', 12 June 1995.
16. Commission of the European Communities (1997) 'Europe's Agenda 2000: Strengthening and Widening the EU', 16 July 1997.
17. European Council Conclusions, Luxembourg, 12–13 December 1997.
18. The French term *acquis communautaire* refers to the complete body of EU legislation, that is, the rights and obligations deriving from EU treaties, laws, and regulations. It consists of over 100,000 pages of legislation published in the Official Journal of the European Communities. For the purpose of the negotiations, it is divided into 31 chapters, each dealing with different policy areas (e.g. agriculture, environment, competition policy etc.). Applicant countries must be prepared to accept the *acquis communautaire* as it exists at the time of accession, although transitional periods and derogations are provided in

certain policy areas, and in exceptional cases, to countries which are unable or unwilling to accept the whole of the *acquis*. In the case of Cyprus, short transitional arrangement were agreed for nine chapters, due to the inability of the state to harmonize its legislation by the time of accession.

19. The last regular report was published on 9 October 2002.
20. European Council Conclusions, Helsinki, 10–11 December 1999.
21. European Council Conclusions, Helsinki, 10–11 December 1999.
22. Accession Partnerships were established with the other candidate states as well, that is, the Central and Eastern European Countries and Malta.
23. European Council Conclusions, Copenhagen, 12–13 December 2002.
24. European Council Conclusions, Athens, 16–17 April 2003.
25. This means inter alia that these areas are outside the customs and fiscal territory of the EU. The suspension has territorial effect, but does not concern the personal rights of Turkish Cypriots as EU citizens, as they are considered as citizens of the Member State Republic of Cyprus. Also, the dividing Green Line is not considered as an external border of the EU due to the non-recognition of the 'TRNC'.

4. Government: Executive, Legislative and Judicial Authorities

1. The exercise of power by the legislative branch to control, influence, or monitor government decision-making (Holzhacker, 2007: 143).
2. Commission of the European Communities, *Regular Report from the Commission on Cyprus' Progress Towards Accession*, Office for Official Publications of the European Communities, Luxembourg, COM (2002) 700 final.
3. The Ministerial Committee for EU Affairs presided over by the President of the Republic and composed of the Chief Negotiator, the Attorney General, the Ministers of Foreign Affairs and Finance, all Ministers who have a vertical competence on any one of the subjects involved in the accession process as well as the Governor of the Central Bank of Cyprus. Senior officials from the departments headed by the members of the Committee also participate in the meetings. The Committee allows the ministers to be informed on all aspects of Cyprus-EU relations and exchange views on various subjects. Since its creation in 1991, the EU Ministerial Committee has been activated four times, once in each Presidency (Interview with Permanent Secretary of the Planning Bureau, 7 January 2004).
4. The Cyprus Academy of Public Administration (CAPA) was created with the aim to improve the efficiency and effectiveness of the civil service through training and technical assistance programmes. Since July 1996, in view of Cyprus' efforts to join the EU, CAPA focused exclusively its activities on EU issues.
5. The Office of the Ombudsman was established with the task to investigate, report and recommend on acts or omissions of the administration, including local authorities, as well as on alleged ill-treatment by members of the police.
6. The European Institute of Cyprus was established as an independent non-profit institution with the aim of promoting the study, training and information on issues relating to the EU.

7. The Office of the Chief Negotiator played a key role during membership negotiations. The Office was headed by the ex-President of the Republic, George
Vassiliou, who was responsible for: a) the guidance and management of the
accession negotiations; b) the supervision and coordination of the harmonization process; and c) keeping the House of Representatives, the private
sector, the various organizations and the public at large informed on the
progress of the negotiation procedure and the tasks that the accession creates.
The Chief Negotiator was in charge of a small negotiating team composed of
less than ten officials drawn from the Ministry of Foreign Affairs, the Planning Bureau, and the Law Office of the Republic, together with the Permanent
Secretary of the Planning Bureau, the Permanent Secretary of the Ministry of
Agriculture and some of his own advisors. He was also assisted in his task by
thirty working groups that had previously served the implementation of the
Association Agreement and the structured dialogue which were upgraded or
redesigned. The Chief Negotiator had no executive power but mainly coordinated the execution of the various tasks relating to EU accession as well as
supervised and conducted the actual negotiations with the European Commission and other Member States. All major political decisions, including
the approval of Cyprus' negotiating positions were taken by the Council of
Ministers.

8. With the end of the accession negotiations in December 2002, and following presidential elections in March 2003, the newly elected President of the
Republic appointed Takis Hadjidimitriou, a former MP, as the new head of the
renamed (as of June 2003) Office of the Coordinator for Harmonization of
Cyprus to the EU. In May 2004, Hadjidimitriou resigned, citing his disagreement with the government's position on the UN sanctioned re-unification
plan (*The Annan Plan*). Since then the post has been vacant and the Office is
maintained by a few low-ranking administrative staff whose role is excluded
in the monitoring of the domestic transposition process of EU legislation.

9. The Diplomatic Office was established in 2003 to assist the President in
his/her wider duties regarding: a) monitoring of international developments
and the international relations of Cyprus; b) the exercise of his/her powers
in accordance with the Constitution regarding the enactment and application of the laws by the House of Representatives regarding foreign affairs and
the decisions of the Council of Ministers; c) to monitor and coordinate the
actions and the activities of the state in relations to the Cyprus Problem. It is
staffed by the Director of the Office and other political advisors selected by
the President.

10. These two bodies are largely independent, though with close ties with the
Ministry of Finance and the Ministry of Justice respectively. The Planning
Bureau is headed by a Permanent Secretary and the Law Office is headed by
the Attorney General of the Republic.

11. In accordance with the 1960 Constitution there are 11 ministries in the
Republic: Ministry of Foreign Affairs; Ministry of Finance; Ministry of Interior; Ministry of Labour and Social Insurance; Ministry of Defence; Ministry
of Justice and Public Order; Ministry of Education and Culture; Ministry
of Commerce, Industry and Tourism; Ministry of Health; Ministry of Communications and Works; and Ministry of Agriculture, Natural Resources
and the Environment. There are also 11 independent institutions of central

administration: Attorney-General of the Republic; Commission for the Protection of Competition; Office of the Coordinator for Harmonization of Cyprus to the EU; Office of the Commissioner for Public Aid; Office of the Data Protection Commissioner; Office of the Ombudsman; The Audit Office; The Central Bank of Cyprus; The Educational Service Commission; The Planning Bureau; and The Public Service Commission.

12. Interview with Head of EU Directorate, Ministry of Foreign Affairs, Republic of Cyprus, 9 February 2004 & 22 February 2007.

13. Titos Phanos acted as the first Permanent Representative of Cyprus to the EU.

14. During Cyprus' shared Presidency of the Council, membership is likely to expand even further.

15. The Committee consists of 31 members, 19 of whom are members of the EP and 23 are members of the Cypriot House of Representatives.

16. During accession negotiations, a total of 1,197 legislative proposals were examined by the Committee and were forwarded for plenary vote in the House of Representatives.

17. The Committee meets to examine these issues 4–5 times in each Presidency. It obtains the proposed EU legislation through 'Extranet', an internet governmental network (Interview with officials of the European Affairs Committee, 27 February 2008).

18. For more on this see Emiliou, N. (2004) 'Impact of EU Accession on the National Legal Orders of New Member States: The Case of Cyprus' in De Zwaan, J. *et al.* (eds) *The European Union: An Ongoing Process of Integration* (London: Asser Press).

19. The EU Directorate also works closely on cross-cutting issues with the Directorate for the Cyprus Problem and Euro-Turkish Affairs as well as the Directorate for Political Affairs, all within the structure of the Foreign Ministry.

20. During membership negotiations the Chief Negotiator was also part of this group (Interview with Michael Attalides, former Permanent Representative of Cyprus to the EU and Dean of School of Humanities, Social Sciences and Law of Intercollege, Nicosia, Cyprus, 28 December 2003; Interview with Officials of the Diplomatic Office of the President, 6 March 2008).

21. Interviews with Head of EU Directorate, Ministry of Foreign Affairs, Republic of Cyprus, 9 February 2004 & 22 February 2007; and Head of EU Directorate, The Planning Bureau, 21 February 2008.

22. Interview with H.E. Nicos Emiliou, Permanent Representative of Cyprus to the EU, 9 November 2007.

23. This evidence is based on insights gathered from interviews with Cypriot officials in the Foreign Ministry using Metcalfe's (1994) policy coordination scale. This Guttman scale measured EU coordination capacity on the basis of nine levels of coordination (the highest signifies the greatest capacity): 1. Independent decision-making by ministries; 2. Communication to other ministries (information exchange); 3. Consultation with other ministries (feedback); 4. Avoiding divergences among ministries; 5. Search for agreement among ministries; 6. Arbitration of policy differences; 7. Setting limits on ministerial action; 8. Establishing central priorities; 9. Government Strategy. Accordingly, Cyprus has a level 5 coordination capacity, in contrast with countries such as UK, France and Denmark who have a level 8.

24. That said, coordination efficiency at the domestic level is not a guarantee for effectiveness at the EU level (that is, the achievement of favourable policy outcomes in the various stages of EU decision-making) as other non-organizational factors also come into play (Sepos, 2005a). In addition, the designation of a clear central coordination mechanism may also lead to 'inter-bureaucratic fights' – between and within ministries – which may even spill over to the political realm (Interview with Head of EU Directorate, Ministry of Foreign Affairs, Republic of Cyprus, 9 February 2004 & 22 February 2007).

25. Interview with H.E. Theofilos V. Theofilou, Permanent Representative of Cyprus to the EU, 12 January 2004. This issue has been the focus of the abrupt resignation (28/5/2004) of Permanent Representative Theofilou from his post in Brussels. In his resignation letter, he cited that his appeal for 'the quantitative and qualitative reinforcement of the embassy was ignored in the past two years despite the continuously increasing workload and difficulties resulting from the demands and obligations of EU membership' (*Simerini*, 16 June 2004). This point has also been emphasized by H.E. Nicos Emiliou, Permanent Representative of Cyprus to the EU, 9 November 2007.

26. For example, the average travel time to Brussels, by air, from the EU capitals has been calculated at around one hour and forty-five minutes, while the travel time to Brussels from Cyprus, with one intermediate stop, is ten and a half hours. This distant status not only adds greater travel costs for the participation of Cypriot civil servants in the policy-making process in Brussels but it also affects day-to-day business given the different time zones between the two capitals (Interview with H.E. Nicos Emiliou, Permanent Representative of Cyprus to the EU, 9 November 2007).

27. For example, for the year 2003, 663 Cypriot ministerial civil servants participated in overseas training programmes conducted through Bilateral Cooperation Agreements, the TAIEX, the Third Pillar programmes and the Twinning programmes on institution buildings. Nearly half of these participants originated from the mentioned ministries (Internal Documents of the Planning Bureau). On the same year, 669 Cypriot ministerial civil servants participated in domestic training programmes conducted by the Cyprus Academy of Public Administration with the aim of acquainting them with the EU structures and policies. Again, the mentioned ministries occupied the majority of these positions (Internal Documents of the Cyprus Academy of Public Administration). It is indicative that for the year 2007, all of the 50 civil servants who participated in the TAIEX programme originated from these three ministries.

28. Interview with H.E. Nicos Emiliou, Permanent Representative of Cyprus to the EU, 9 November 2007.

29. The 1960 constitution prohibits the establishment of junior ministerial positions across all policy areas.

30. Their power and status, however, varies greatly. Some are senior civil servants, others are politicians with a rank of a Secretary-General of Ministry, others are Minister-Delegates attached to the Minister of Foreign Affairs, and still others are directly responsible to the Prime Minister. In most Member States, these officials have the greatest knowledge of European issues than anyone else in their governments but they do not always carry enough weight to have these issues highly placed on the agenda. Also, with few exceptions

European Ministers do not have the authority to represent their governments at the EU level. Proposals (as early as 2000) from former German Chancellor Gerhard Schröder to create a uniform system throughout Europe of Ministers for European Affairs have not yet materialized.

31. Interview with officials of the Diplomatic Office of the President of the Republic, 6 March 2008.

32. Currently, the Committee has 4–5 meetings per Presidency. It participates and is informed only on government deliberations that take place at the Council of Ministers level (Interview with officials of the European Affairs Committee, 27 February 2008).

33. Cyprus is one of the first countries to have reached the Commission's 1.5 per cent transposition deficit target (Internal Market Commission Scoreboard 16, July 2007).

34. Cyprus had 30 infringement proceedings in 2007 alone (Internal Market Commission Scoreboard 16, July 2007).

5. Political Parties and Public Opinion

1. Indeed, the absence of a genuine European level party system explains the insularity of national party systems from the impact of European integration.

2. A two-round majority system is currently in force for the election of the President of the Republic.

3. The Communist Party was formed in 1924, banned in 1931, and reappeared as AKEL in 1941.

4. Dunphy & Bale (2007) demonstrate how the party's origins and development, as well as leadership skill and the special circumstances of a small, divided island, have contributed to the organizational and ideological flexibility that help explain its relative success.

5. Founded in 1970 by Ahmet Mithat Berberoglu and now led by the current 'President' of the 'TRNC' Mehmet Ali Talat.

6. Founded in 2004 though it has its roots in the late-1980s under its former name and led by Alpay Durduran.

7. Other major existing Turkish-Cypriot parties are the centre-right National Unity Party founded in 1975 by Rauf Denktash and now led by Dervis Eroglu; the centre-right Democratic Party founded in 1992 by Serdar Denktash, the son of Rauf Denktash; the Freedom and Reform Party founded in 2006 by former members of the National Unity Party and the Democratic Party and now led by Turgay Avci; the United Cyprus party founded in 2002 and led by Izzet Izcan; and the Communal Democracy Party founded in 2007 with the merger of the Peace and Democracy Movement (of Mustafa Akinci) and the Communal Liberation Movement and now led by Mehmet Cakici.

8. Cypriot Parliamentary Debates, Second Parliamentary Period, Third Meeting, no. 16, 11 January 1973.

9. Proceedings of AKEL's 17th Congress, 3–7 October 1990. George Vassiliou was elected in 1988 with the backing of AKEL. An economist, Vassiliou's platform was based on economic reform, restructuring of the public service, and a more flexible approach towards the bi-communal talks, the latter being a primary target of AKEL. Eventually, Vassiliou proved to be one of the major

proponents and architects of Cyprus' membership bid, as he later served in 1998 as the Chief Negotiator for Cyprus Accession bid.

10. Proceedings of AKEL's 18th Congress, 16–19 November 1995. See also http://www.akel.org.cy/English/eu.html

11. Proceedings of AKEL's 19th (7–10 December 2000) and 20th (24–27 November, 2005) Congresses. In 2000, AKEL voiced its concerns regarding the benefits from 'catalytic role' of the EU on the Cyprus problem while at the same time it stressed for the rights of the 'working people' during the harmonization process. In 2005, AKEL rejected the Constitutional Treaty arguing that it represented 'a constitutional imposition of neo-conservatism on the working people', 'the dismantling of the social state' and the 'subjugation of Europe to American influence'.

12. It is worth noting, however, that the party initially supported the Plan when it was first presented, only to change its policy in the later process urging a 'no' arguably to maintain the coherency with the rest of the parties of the ruling coalition (i.e. DIKO and EDEK) who rejected the Plan.

13. This decision, however, was ignored by many party members (60 per cent of DISY supporters voted against the Plan) and it triggered severe internal party divisions which led, after the Annan Plan referendum, to the formation of two smaller break-away parties (i.e. European Party and European Democracy) from former DISY members, and others, who objected to the Annan Plan. For more on how the Greek-Cypriot political parties voted on the Annan Plan see Lordos, A. (2006) 'Rational Agent or Unthinking Follower? A Survey-Based Profile Analysis of Greek-Cypriot and Turkish-Cypriot Referendum Voters', paper presented at the ECRP Joint Sessions Workshop, Nicosia, 25–30 April.

14. http://www.diko.org.cy

15. The party consists of splinter group members of DISY, and dissolved right-wing nationalist parties ADISOK and New Horizons.

16. The party consists of splinter group members of DISY.

17. The party, headed by Michalis Papapetrou (since 2005), was the only staunch supporter of the Annan Plan.

18. For the specific positions of Cypriot political parties on the island's integration process since the early 1970s see 'Chapter 3: Evolution of Cyprus' Relations with the EU'.

19. The decisive role of the EU factor in shaping Cypriot politics was evident in the 2006 Parliamentary Elections where 18.5 per cent of registered voters changed their preferences compared to the previous elections. This was the greatest movement of voters registered since the first parliamentary elections in 1960. Evidence indicates that this change was a result of the cross-cutting dynamics of the landmark events of Cyprus' accession to the EU and the reunification efforts with the UN-sponsored Annan Plan. Of this change, the centre parties (DIKO, EDEK, EUROKO, Greens) gained at the expense of the two largest parties (left-wing AKEL and right-wing DISY).

20. The example of DIKO MEP Marios Matsakis who was arrested on two occasions by Turkish and British forces respectively for crossing the Green Line and protesting the presence of British forces in the island is indicative. On one of these occasions his Polish colleague reported the incident in the EP plenary. Also, a delegation of the European Parliament Transport Committee in

Cyprus, led by DISY MEP Ioannis Kasoulides, urged Turkey to open its sea and air ports and recognize the Republic. For more on this form of 'parliamentary diplomacy' at the EU level see Stavridis, S. (2006) 'Towards a European Solution of the Cyprus Problem? Assessing the views of some (Greek) Cypriot MEPs', Working Paper (Fundacion SIP Zaragoza).

21. For example, the participation of women in the Cypriot House of Representatives has increased from 5 per cent in 1996 (3 out of 56 positions) to 16 per cent in 2006 (9 out of 56 positions), while their participation in municipal councils has increased from 17 per cent in 1996 (65 out of 384 positions) to 20 per cent in 2006 (84 out of 414 positions).

22. For example, in the first 36 years of independence only eight women were elected as members of the Cypriot House of Representatives – and only two women were appointed government ministers (Agapiou-Josephides, 1998: 145).

23. More specifically, at the national level, in the 2008 ministerial cabinet of newly elected (February 2008) President Demetris Christofias there is one woman (out of 11 positions), there are three women (out of 11 positions) heading the independent central government authorities and there are nine women (out of 56 positions) as members of the House of Representatives. At the local level, there are 84 women (out of 414 positions) as municipal councillors and two (out of 33 positions) as mayors (2006 elections). Note also that there are no Cypriot women Members of the European Parliament (out of six positions). Christofias' new government, however, has nominated the first Cypriot woman EU Commissioner, Androula Vassiliou in the DG Health, as replacement of Commissioner Marcos Kyprianou who took the position of foreign minister of the Republic.

24. Cyprus is the only country in the EU where the employment rate gap between men and women has increased. In particular, in 2004–2005, employment rate among men increased from 82.9 per cent to 83.2 per cent whereas for women, there was decrease from 66.1 per cent to 62.7 per cent (European Commission, Eurostat, 2005).

25. European Commission, 'Eurobarometer: National Report for Cyprus' (areas under the control of the Cyprus Government), Spring 2007; European Commission, 'Eurobarometer: National Report for Cyprus' (areas under the control of the Cyprus Government), November 2006.

26. Easton (1965: 343) further observed that each form of supports spills over to the other and influences it and he hypothesized that specific support comes first and diffuse support later while others (Lindberg & Scheingold, 1970; Ingelhard, 1970) argued that diffuse support develops before or at least at the same time, with specific support.

27. Other indicators that may reveal diffuse support relate to unification and identity – though the latter is contested as being a weak indicator. Thus questions such as 'Are you in favour of European unification?' and 'Are you proud to be European?' are used to tap into such attitudes.

28. Data for Cyprus in Eurobarometer are only available since 2001.

29. High Cypriot support for membership, as well as the perceived benefits from it, was evident in a Cypriot poll conducted prior to accession which revealed a strong favourable view towards the EU as 85 per cent of Cypriot citizens believed that accession to the EU would contribute positively to the solution

of the Cyprus problem. Only eight per cent believed that accession would have a negative effect on the solution of the problem, with seven per cent undecided. Also, 68 per cent of Greek-Cypriot citizens stated that they would feel more secure once Cyprus accedes to the EU, 16 per cent less secure, 11 per cent would feel no difference in terms of security, and 5 per cent undecided. Moreover, at that time, 75 per cent agreed with the decision to pursue EU membership and 25 per cent disagreed. The percentage of those who agreed was higher among the high and middle socioeconomic layers of society and among men. Finally, 60 per cent believed that membership would bring more advantages to Cyprus while 30 per cent believed that it would bring more disadvantages (Public Opinion Survey, Office of the Chief Negotiator for Cyprus' Accession to the EU, July 2002).

30. This trend of a high level of diffuse support continued until 2007. Thus, in 2007 there was a positive net trust of 33 per cent compared to the EU-27 average of 25 per cent. This meant that 61 per cent of Cypriots stated that they tended to trust the EU as opposed to 28 per cent who did not.

31. Using the weaker indicator of diffuse support, that is, identity one further observe some useful facts in the area. In general, Cypriot citizens accept their identification with Europe and feel proud of their national origin. In particular, in 2007 the majority (58 per cent) see themselves as being both Cypriot and European citizens, 50 per cent feel pride when identifying themselves with Europe, while only 38 per cent of the population state that they have never felt being European. One can argue that the readiness of Cypriots to embrace the European identity partly has to do with the widely contested and ambiguous notion of what 'Cypriot' identity (See Chapter 2: The Making of Modern Cyprus) which renders the attachment with a strong collective identity such as the 'European' easier.

32. This decreasing trend in net benefit continued until 2007. Thus, in 2007 net benefits was a negative 15 per cent compared to 29 per cent of the EU average, the lowest recording in the EU-27. This meant that 52 per cent of Cypriots stated that the country has not benefited from membership as opposed to 37 per cent who stated that it had.

33. This decreasing trend in net evaluation continued up until 2007. Thus, in 2007 net evaluation was 27 per cent compared to the EU average of 42 per cent, the 19th lowest recording in the EU-27. This meant that 44 per cent of Cypriots stated that membership is a 'good thing' as opposed to 17 per cent who indicated that it is 'bad'.

34. The decline of support for EU membership also has to do with the fact that this lack of progress on the Cyprus problem comes in light of the fact that Turkey – the actor that Greek-Cypriots hold responsible for the current *status quo* – has began accession negotiations.

35. These figures and indices do not include the views of the Turkish-Cypriot community. Separate Eurobarometer surveys (2005–2007), however, reveal that 72 per cent of Turkish-Cypriots think the EU is a 'good thing' and 76 per cent believe that EU membership will be advantageous, in particular by increasing their standard of living (80 per cent), as well as the export (79 per cent) and services (74 per cent) sector, though 18 per cent believe that their security will be adversely affected. Yet, 59 per cent of the population stated that the EU leads to 'feelings of hope and trust', most of them trusting

the EU (51 per cent) more than the UN (41 per cent). Moreover, when asked what the EU means to them personally, Turkish Cypriots gave the following answers: economic welfare (53 per cent), peace (40 per cent), social protection (40 per cent) and democracy (29 per cent). Among them, there is also strong support for the idea of a political union (72 per cent), the EU Constitution (53 per cent) and further enlargement (61 per cent), with a high percentage supporting Turkey's membership (86 per cent). However, 47 per cent do not think the role of the EU in world peace is positive, compared to 60 per cent of EU-27. Finally, there is less identification with Europe than the Greek-Cypriot community, with three-quarters of Turkish-Cypriots stating that they are very proud of their Turkish-Cypriot identity, and only 32 per cent proud of their European affiliation.

6. Economy

1. In an effort to minimize time delays in deliveries, Cypriot enterprises stock their industrial supplies in large quantities in warehouses.
2. For more on this issue see Chapter 7: Agriculture and Regional Policy.
3. The Ottoman *muchtar* system allowed the elected village headman (or *muchtar*) to serve as the leader of and patron of the local Christian population. It spread horizontally and vertically on all dimensions of the society including economic structures.
4. The Ottoman *millet* system which allowed religious authorities to govern their non-Muslim populations.
5. See Chapter 9: Justice and Home Affairs.
6. In 1971, it was as high as 12.8 per cent.
7. In 1974, 20,000 Greek-Cypriots remained in the north – that number is now 350. Nearly all Turkish-Cypriots living in the south (51,000) were transferred to the north in an agreement between the two communities and the United Nations.
8. See also Andreou, E. (1996) 'The Cyprus Economy in the Last Three Decades (1960–1994): An Applied Econometric Approach', in V. Karageorghis & D. Michaelides (eds) *The Development of the Cypriot Economy: From the Prehistoric Period to the Present Day* (Nicosia: Lithiographica).
9. The Planning Bureau, 'Five Year Development Plan', 1990, p. 3.
10. See also Hudson, J.R. & Dymiotou-Jensen, M. (1989) *Modeling a Developing Country: A Case Study of Cyprus* (Aldershot, UK: Avebury).
11. GDP growth in 2006 was 3.8 per cent, 3.9 per cent in 2007 with an expected growth of 3.8 per cent in 2008. Eurostat, European Commission, Country Reports, Cyprus. http://epp.eurostat.cec.eu.int
12. Department of Merchant Shipping, Cyprus, 3 April 2006.
13. European Commission, *Regular Report from the Commission on Cyprus' Progress. Towards Accession*, Office for the Official Publications of the European Communities, Luxembourg, 1998–2003. See also, Featherstone, K. (2001) 'Cyprus and the Onset of Europeanization: Strategic Usage, Structural Transformation and Institutional Adaptation' in Featherstone, K. & Kazamias, G. (eds) *Europeanization and the Southern Periphery* (London: Frank Cass).

14. Interview with Head of EU Unit, Central Bank of Cyprus, Nicosia, 7 August 2007 & 28 January 2008.
15. Iraq was one most significant trade partners of Cyprus, amounting to nearly half of total trade with Middle Eastern countries in 1985. Since the Cypriot government aligned itself with the American foreign policy of sanctions towards Iraq, the island's trade with this country diminished to negligible levels in 2006.
16. 'China, Cyprus sign agreement on economic cooperation', People's Daily Online, 21 August 2006.
17. The OECD defined competitiveness as 'the degree to which a country can, under free and fair market conditions, produce goods and services which meet the test of international markets, while simultaneously maintaining and expanding the real incomes of its people over the long term'. See OECD (2002) *Technology and the Economy – The Key Relationships* (Paris: OECD).
18. Interview with Head of EU Unit, Central Bank of Cyprus, Nicosia, 7 August 2007 & 28 January 2008.
19. The four Maastricht criteria are: (a) *price stability*, measured according to the rate of inflation of the three best performing Member States; (b) *long-term interest rates* close to the rates in the countries with the best inflation results; (c) an annual *budget deficit* which does not exceed 3 per cent of Gross Domestic Product (GDP) and *total government debt* which does not exceed 60 per cent of GDP or which is falling steadily towards that figure; and (d) *stability in the exchange rate* of the national currency on exchange markets. The exchange-rate mechanism of the European Monetary System requires this stability to be demonstrated and sustained for two years.
20. Ministry of Finance, Republic of Cyprus, http://www.mof.gov.cy
21. The agreement on participation of the Cyprus pound in ERM II was based on a firm commitment by the Cypriot authorities to pursue sound fiscal policies, including lowering the high debt level, which are essential for preserving macroeconomic stability and ensuring the sustainability of the convergence process.
22. Ministry of Finance, Republic of Cyprus, http://www.mof.gov.cy. The Economist Intelligence Unit foresees that these indicators will remain within the Maastricht criteria (Economist Intelligence Unit: Country Report on Cyprus, 2006/7).
23. Murray, A. & Wanlin, A. (2006) *The Lisbon Scorecard: Can Europe Compete?* (London: Centre for European Reform).
24. For more on Cyprus' R&D capacity see Hadjimanolis, A & Musyck, B. (2005) 'Towards a Knowledge-Based Economy: Does the Cyprus R&D capability meet the challenge?', *Science & Public Policy*, vol. 32 (1), pp. 65–78.
25. It is indicative that Cyprus is the only country in the EU where the employment rate gap between men and women is increasing. In particular, in 2004-2005, employment rate among men increased from 82.9 per cent to 83.2 per cent whereas for women there was decrease from 66.1 per cent to 62.7 per cent (European Commission, Eurostat, 2005).
26. DG Economic & Financial Affairs – Country Reports: Cyprus, European Commission, 29 April 2006. http://ec.europa.eu/economy_finance/about/activities/countryeconomy/cyprus_en.htm

27. European Commission (2007) Recommendation for a Council Opinion on the updated convergence programme of Cyprus, 2006–2010), Brussels, 23 January 2007, SEC 2007, 70 final.

28. 'Convergence Programme of the Republic of Cyprus, 2005–2009 & 2006–2010', December 2006, Ministry of Finance, Republic of Cyprus; http://www.mof.gov.cy

29. 'National Lisbon Programme for the Republic of Cyprus: Part A', 10 November 2005. Ministry of Finance, Cyprus; http://www.mof.gov.cy

30. On this important issue, the establishment of a Cypriot Investment Support and Promotion Agency would be a useful measure. A similar agency has been established in regards to promoting tourism in Cyprus (Cyprus Tourism Organization) with successful results.

31. Interview with Head of EU Unit, Central Bank of Cyprus, Nicosia, 7 August 2007 & 28 January 2008.

32. Ibid.

33. Interview with Head of EU Unit, Central Bank of Cyprus, Nicosia, 7 August 2007 & 28 January 2008.

34. It is important to indicate that some of these perceptions may not accurately reflect the reality. While Ireland's convergence with the EU economy has been remarkable, beginning with a 60 per cent of EU's average in GDP per capita since becoming a member in 1973, and while it has demonstrated an ability to win and absorb effectively nearly 21 billion euro in Structural and Cohesion Aid, it has benefited tremendously from factors which are not EU-related. In particular, there are those that argue that the main driving force behind Ireland's economic success is not its EU membership but its territorial dimensions (i.e. geographical location and English language) which has allowed it to be part of the 'Atlantic Economy' driven by the US and UK, benefiting in particular from US direct investment in electronics, pharmaceuticals and financial services sectors and the export of these products (O'Hearn, 2001). Also, Ireland has consistently recorded one of the lowest scores in the EU in regards to Research & Development, a key factor for a strong, self-sufficient and sustainable knowledge-based economy. Indeed, there are those that argue that Ireland's economic success story (i.e. the 'Celtic Tiger') is unsustainable in the long-run given its over-dependency on a few products, heavy dependency on the US economy and US inward investment – the first showing strong evidence of a slowdown and the second a re-direction of multinational investment to an expanding EU periphery (O'Hearn, 2001). In addition, if one also takes the position that the recent outcomes in Irish society such as the break-up of social partnership, growing poverty, social injustice and dislocation and environmental pollution are not accidental side-effects of Ireland's economic boom, but intimately linked to the logic of the Irish economic model, then one should be wary in modeling Ireland as a showcase for successful development of other latecomers (Kirby, 2004: 219) such as Cyprus.

35. Ibid.

36. These data do not take into account a possibly sizeable unrecorded economy in the North, which in the mid-1990s was estimated at up to 70 per cent of GDP (Bicak, 1996).

37. 'TRNC', http://www.trncgov.com/

38. Council Regulation (EC), No 866/2004, L161, 30 April 2004.
39. Inter communal Green Line trade remains limited, however, approximately €2 million per year (COM(2006) 551 final, 25 Sept. 2006).
40. Council Regulation (EC), No 389/2006, L65/5, 27 February 2006.
41. Commission Proposal, COM 2004/0466/final.
42. At the time of writing, the 'Direct Trade Regulation' has not been adopted by the Council. The Greek-Cypriot community has objected to its adoption arguing that this will reinforce the international standing of the Turkish-Cypriot authorities. It has also pointed out that Turkey has failed to fulfill its Custom's Union obligations towards the Republic of Cyprus, among other things, opening its sea and air ports to the Cyprus flagged vessels and aircrafts.
43. This would pave the way for the withdrawal of the suspension of the *acquis* in case of a settlement as provided for in Protocol 10 of the Accession Treaty.

7. Agricultural and Regional Policy

1. Interview with Head of EU Unit, Ministry of Agriculture, Natural Resources and Environment, Republic of Cyprus, 29 January 2008.
2. Ibid.
3. Commission's Regular Reports on the Progress of Cyprus Towards Accession, 1998–2003.
4. Interview with Head of EU Unit, Ministry of Agriculture, Natural Resources and the Environment, Republic of Cyprus, 31 January 2008.
5. Interview with Director of Cyprus Agricultural Institute, Nicosia, 3 August 2007 & 28 January 2008.
6. Interview with Director of Cyprus Agricultural Institute, Nicosia, 3 August 2007 & 28 January 2008.
7. Commission Report SEC(2001) 1745.
8. Note, however, and this relates to the notion of 'street implementation' mentioned earlier, that Cyprus was one of seven Member States which has been subject to an infringement procedure for failing to send catch data on bluefin tuna fishing in the Mediterranean (IP 07/1399, Brussels, 26 September 2007).
9. Interview with Head of Structural Funds Unit, The Planning Bureau, 29 August 2007.
10. For example, the average time needed for the transportation of goods from the EU area to the EU GDP gravity centre is 20 hours, while from Cyprus it takes more than four times, i.e. 85 hours. This disadvantage is even more apparent regarding the cost of transportation in value terms. While the average cost for the transportation of goods within the EU is approximately EUR 1100, from Cyprus the cost rises to approximately EUR 5100, i.e. nearly five times higher. Also, the average travel time to Brussels, by air, from the EU capitals has been calculated at around one hour and forty-five minutes, while the travel time to Brussels from Cyprus, with one intermediate stop, is ten and a half hours.
11. Interview with Head of Structural Funds Unit, The Planning Bureau, 29 August 2007. Note that Cyprus is the only new Member State which is not under Objective 1 status, and among handful of Member States (i.e. France and the Netherlands) which do not receive any such aid.

12. Paragraph 47 of the 2007–2013 financial framework stipulates that Cyprus should have been eligible for Objective 1 funds in 2004–2006 based on the revised figures for the period 1997–1999. (European Commission, DG Regional Policy – Cyprus; See also 'EU leaders make deal on 2007–2013 budget', *Financial Mirror*, 19 December 2005).

13. In order to calculate these figures an Ordinary Least Square (OLS) regression method was employed.

14. For a definition of these principles see European Commission's DG Regional Policy web site.

15. European Commission, *Regular Report from the Commission on Cyprus' Progress Towards Accession*, Office for the Official Publications of the European Communities, Luxembourg, 2001. And 'National Strategic Reference Framework for Cohesion Policy, 2007–2013', The Planning Bureau, April 2007.

16. Those programmes are articulated in the 'Single Programming Documents', three for each objective. The Planning Bureau, Cyprus, http://www.planning.gov.cy

17. Interview with Head of Structural Funds Unit, The Planning Bureau, 29 August 2007.

18. 'Διαρθρωτικά Ταμεία Ε.Ε. και Κύπρος', *Σημερινή* (*Greek-Cypriot Daily*), 9 November 2003; 'Προτροπές του ΕΒΕ Λευκωσίας για τα Διαρθρωτικά Ταμεία της Ε.Ε.', *Σημερινή*, 13 March 2004; 'Χάνουν τις επιδοτήσεις της Ε.Ε.', *Πολίτης* (Greek-Cypriot Daily), 6 October 2005.

19. See for example, Horvat, A. & Maier, G. (2004) 'Regional Development, Absorption Problems and the EU Structural Funds: Absorption capacity in the Czech Republic, Estonia, Hungary, Slovakia and Slovenia' (Ljubljana: National Agency for Regional Development of Slovenia).

20. European Commission, 'Administrative Capacity Study Phare Region – Phase 2', Country Reports, March 2003.

21. The study was based on a structured Commission questionnaire which was distributed by the author to the Head of the Structural Funds Unit within the Planning Bureau of the Republic (9 February 2007).

22. Interview with Head of Structural Funds Unit, The Planning Bureau, 29 August 2007.

23. 'Single Programming Documents', three for each objective. The Planning Bureau, Cyprus, http://www.planning.gov.cy

24. Interview with Head of Structural Funds Unit, The Planning Bureau, 29 August 2007.

25. Ibid.

8. Foreign Policy

1. Endogenous factors that may cause change in a country's foreign policy can be national administrative reform project (e.g. reform of the military), influence of pressure groups (e.g. associations of the defence industry), public pressure or political events. Exogenous factors, other than the EU, causing change can be globalization and economic cooperation, global historic developments (e.g. end of Cold War) and other international institutions (e.g. NATO) (Major, 2005: 184).

2. White (2001: 6) also points out that foreign policies of Member States have been significantly changed, if not transformed, by participation over time in foreign policy-making at the European level.

3. Fanes warns, however, that one has to isolate the 'EU-effect' from other changes in the global, bilateral and national spheres (Bulmer & Lequesne, 2002: 18), i.e. the risk of conceptual stretching (Sartori, 1970: 1034–35) of attributing to Europeanization any change one detects in policy.

4. More specifically, Smith points out that a Europeanization of foreign policy takes place through: (a) elite socialization; (b) bureaucratic reorganization; (c) constitutional change; and (d) increase in public support for European political cooperation (Smith, 2000).

5. Posted one senior military officer in its Operational Headquarters (OHQ) in Paris.

6. Posted two military officers both in the Operations Headquarters (OHQ) in Potsdam, Germany and in the Force Headquarters (FHQ) in Kinshasa in the airfield of N'Dolo.

7. Posted one military officer in its Operation Headquarters (OHQ) in Khartoum.

8. Posted four police officers.

9. Cyprus is also a participant in the non-EU Organization for Security and Cooperation in Europe (OSCE).

10. An agreement, signed in 16 December 2002, outlining a comprehensive package of agreements between NATO and the EU, including, (a) NATO–EU Security Agreement; (b) Assured Access to NATO planning capabilities for EU-led Crisis Management; (c) Availability of NATO assets and capabilities for EU-led CMO; (d) Procedures for Release, Monitoring, Return and Recall of NATO Assets and Capabilities; (e) Terms of Reference for DSACEUR and European Command Options for NATO; (f) EU-NATO consultation arrangements in the context of an EU-led CMO making use of NATO assets and capabilities; and (g) Arrangements for coherent and mutually reinforcing Capabilities Requirements.

11. A project by NATO in 1994 aimed at building closer links and trust between NATO and other states in Europe and the former Soviet Union. It is considered the 'waiting room' for full NATO membership.

12. For more on this issue see, Guney, A. (2004) 'The USA's Role in Mediating the Cyprus Conflict: A Story of Success or Failure?', *Security Dialogue*, vol. 35 (1), pp. 27–42.

13. European Council Conclusions, Helsinki, 10–11 December 1999.

14. 'Cyprus' Papadopoulos threatens to veto EU talks with Turkey', *Middle East International*, no. 754, 2004, pp. 1–18. Note that this took place even after the 'No' vote on the Annan Plan from the Greek-Cypriots that reportedly created dissatisfaction among some EU circles.

15. European Commission, '2005 Enlargement Strategy Paper', COM 2005 (561) final, 9 November 2005.

16. Ibid. For more on the controversy surrounding these declarations see Talmon, S. (2006) 'The European Union – Turkey controversy over Cyprus or a Tale of Two Treaty Declarations', *Chinese Journal of International Law*, vol. 5(3), pp. 579–616.

17. Turkey insisted that Cyprus be excluded from the EU-NATO strategic cooperation in crisis management, conducted within the framework of the ESDP.

Also, Turkey continued to impose its veto on Cyprus' membership to international organisations and regimes such as the Organization for Economic Cooperation and Development (OECD), the Missile Technology Control Regime (MTCR) and the Agreement on the Code of Conduct on Arms Exports and on Dual Use Goods, thus hampering the functioning of the single market in the areas covered by the agreement (European Commission's 2006 Progress Report on Turkey, COM (2006) 649 final, Brussels, 8 November 2006).

18. *Guardian*, 'Cyprus vetoes Turkey's talks to gain EU entry, 10 June 2006; *EU Observer*, 'Cyprus threatens to block EU deal on Turkey talks', 1 December 2006.

19. European Council Conclusions, 14–15 December 2006, Brussels.

20. BBC, 'The Cyprus Peace Process', 6 December 2006.

21. Interview with Foreign Affairs officials, Nicosia, 2 August, 2007.

22. 'Cyprus breaks EU unity by opposing Kosovo independence', *EU Business*, 10 December 2007.

23. 'Κύπρος-Γαλλία-Συμμαχία', *Σημερίή* (*Greek-Cypriot Daily*), 4 March 2007.

24. 'China-Greece call for early settlement of the Cyprus Problem', *People's Daily Online*, 20 January 2006.

25. Archbishop's Makarios flirtations with the Soviet Regime as well as the strong role of communist AKEL in Cypriot society are indicators of this relationship. Toying with the East-West division in the Cold War era to solidify independence (from the colonial power) in a newly established state was a practice followed by many anti-colonial leaders in that era (e.g. Patrice Lumumba in Congo). In more cases than not, this practice led to greater tragedies for the newly independent country.

26. 'Cyprus President eyes visit to boost ties with Russia', *People's Daily Online*, 21 January 2006.

27. 'ΗΓεωοικονομία του πετρελαίου', *Πολτης* (*Greek-Cypriot Daily*), 4 February 2007.

28. Interview with Foreign Affairs officials, Nicosia, 2 August 2007.

29. Indicative of the historically tense relationship between the two countries was the assassination of the US Ambassador to Cyprus in August 1974, following the traumatic events in the period. There have been a wealth of studies on the role of the US and the CIA in the country's affairs since the 1960s leading up to the military invasion of Turkey in 1974 and the eventual partition of the island. See for example Rustow, D. (1967) *The Cyprus Conflict and United States Security Interests* (Santa Monica, California: Rand Corporation); Coloumbis, T. & Hicks, S. (1975) *USA Foreign Policy Toward Greece and Cyprus: The Clash of Principle and Pragmatism* (Washington, DC: Centre for Mediterranean Studies); Hitchens, C. (1997) *Hostage to History: Cyprus from the Ottomans to Kissinger* (London: Verso Books); Joseph, J. (1997) *Ethnic Conflict and International Politics: From Independence to the Threshold of the European Union* (London: Macmillan); Ivar-Andre, S. (2000) 'A Bad Show? The United States and the 1974 Cyprus Crisis', *Mediterranean Quarterly*, vol. 11 (2), pp. 96–129; Nicolet, C. (2001) *United States Policy Towards Cyprus: 1954–1974* (Mohnesee: Bibliopolis); Drousiotis, M. (2002) *EOKA B and CIA* (Nicosia, Alfadi) (in Greek); Fouskas, V. (2003) 'US Foreign Policy in the Greater Middle East During the Cold War and the Position of Cyprus' in Fouskas, V.

Richter, H. (eds) *Cyprus and Europe: The Long Way Back* (Mohnesee: Bibliopolis); Guney, A. (2004) 'The USA's Role in Mediating the Cyprus Conflict: A Story of Success or Failure?', Security *Dialogue*, vol. 35 (1), pp. 27–42; Carver, M. (2006) 'The Gordian Knot: American and British Policy Concerning the Cyprus Issue, 1952–1974', PhD Thesis, May 2006.

30. The Council of Europe report (7 June 2006) alleged that Cyprus along with another 13 EU countries 'colluded in or tolerated the secret transfer of terrorist suspects by the US'. Also, President Papadopoulos admitted that Cyprus provided its military bases in Larnaca for the transfer of 150,000 American soldiers in Iraq ('Μετις ΗΠΑ ήμετη Γαλλία', *Πολίτης* (Greek-Cypriot daily), 4 February 2007.

31. 'Cyprus President condemns US visit to occupied North', *Cyprus Mail*, 17 February 2005.

32. Circulated as an official document of the UN Security Council.

33. For more on this line of thought see Melakopides, C. (2006) *Unfair Play: Cyprus, Turkey, Greece, the UK and the EU*, Martello Papers 29 (Kingston, Ontario: Centre for International Relations, Queen's University).

34. Others argue that this stance is more rhetorical than substantial, aiming to appeal to the historical Anti-American sentiment in Cypriot society.

35. Estimates for the claimed debt range from several hundred thousand to over 1 billion euros.

36. 'Britain is our nemesis', *Cyprus Mail*, 8 February 2005.

37. 'Protests mar Straw Cyprus visit', BBC news, 25 January 2006.

38. 'Britain is our nemesis', *Cyprus Mail*, 8 February 2005.

39. The British Bases are listed as 'special Member State territories', such as the Isle of Man and the Channel Islands, and are not officially part of EU territory. The Protocol inserted in Cyprus' Accession Treaty ensured that the sovereignty of the bases is maintained and that certain EU policies such as agriculture, customs and indirect taxation will apply to the bases. It also ensured that the border between the bases and the Republic of Cyprus will not be considered as an external border of the EU, with the UK agreeing to police those borders, thus making the bases a *de facto* part of the Schengen area, if and when Cyprus implements it. The bases are also a *de facto* member of the eurozone area with their previous use of the Cypriot pound. Finally, the inhabitants living permanently in the bases have also become EU citizens, though not from their association with British citizenship (as they are only entitled to British Overseas Territories Citizenship which is not part of the Treaty of Rome) but with their association with Cypriot citizenship as most of them have also adopted the Cypriot citizenship. For more on the politics surrounding this issue and generally the presence of British Bases in the island see Constantinou C. & Richmond, O. (2005) 'The Long Mile of Empire: Power, Legitimation and the UK Bases in Cyprus', *Mediterranean Politics*, vol. 10 (1), pp. 65–84.

40. Through some commentators argued that the Cypriot diplomacy was taken by surprise by the British.

41. 'Turkey–UK Strategic Partnership 2008/9. http://www.fco.gov.uk/Files/KFile/UKTurkeyStrategicPartnership2007.pdf

42. Among the measures that Britain agreed with Turkey in regards to the TC community were: 'to promote direct commercial, economic, political and

cultural contacts between the UK, EU and the Turkish-Cypriots', 'maintain high level contacts with Turkish–Cypriot authorities' and 'uphold the right of representation of the Turkish-Cypriots in the European Parliament' (ibid).

43. 'Λύση σύντομα ειδάλλως Ταϊβαν', *Πολίτης* (Greek-Cypriot daily), 25 October 2007.

44. For more on this shift see Tsakonas, P.J. (2001) 'Post-Cold War Security Dilemmas Greece in Search of the Right Balancing Recipe' in P.J. Tsakonas & Yiallouridies, C. (eds) *Greece and Turkey after the End of the Cold War* (New York & Athens: A.D. Caratzas). One cannot underestimate the role of the US in influencing Greece to change its position towards Turkey, particularly in lifting its veto in regards to Turkey's candidacy status in the 1999 Helsinki Summit (Güney, 2004: 39).

45. For more on this issue see Demetriou, M. (1998) 'On the Long Road to Europe and the Short Path to War: Issue-Linkage Politics and the Arms Build-Up in Cyprus', *Mediterranean Politics*, vol. 3(3), pp. 38–51.

46. In fact, such was the opposition from the Greek government that it refused to send any observers. 'No State Visit can Hide our Growing Isolation', *Cyprus Mail*, 25 October 2005.

47. 'Athens Urges Cypriots to Follow UN Plan', *Southeast European Times*, 11 March 2004.

48. 'Απογαλάκτιση της Κύπρου', *Πολίτης* (*Greek-Cypriot Daily*), 25 February 2007.

49. Turkey has strongly challenged the decision of the RoC to sign an international economic agreement on a territorial and seabed issue, with important economic implications for both communities, prior to a comprehensive agreement on the Cyprus problem.

50. Government of the Republic of Cyprus, Public Information Office, 16-30 July 2006.

51. Council Regulation (EC) 'Green Line Regulation', No866/2004, 29 April 2004.

52. In the first round of elections (17/2/08), Kasoulides received 33.5 per cent, Chistofias 33.5 per cent and Papadopoulos 31.8 per cent of the vote. In the final round (24/2/08), Christofias received 53.4 per cent and Kasoulides 46.6 per cent of the vote. Turnout was significantly high (90.8 per cent of voters registered). With his election, Demetris Christofias becomes the first communist-inspired President of Cyprus and the only one who is head of state in the EU-27.

53. 'Μηνυμα φιλίας προς τους Τ/Κ έστειλε ο Δ. Χριστοφιας', *Πολίτης* (Greek-Cypriot daily), 24 February 2008.

54. 'Μάρκος Κυπριανού-Διαφωνεί με τον Τάσσο στους χειρισμούς του Κυπριακού' – *Πολίτης* (*Greek-Cypriot daily*), 18 February 2007; 'Διαφωνώ με τη τακτική', *Πολίτης* (*Greek-Cypriot daily*), 10 August 2007.

55. Ibid.

56. Interview with Foreign Affairs officials, Nicosia, 2 August, 2007.

57. See for example, the 'Berlin Plus' Agreement.

9. Justice and Home Affairs

1. Note that the Treaty of Amsterdam (1999) moved many of the provisions of the intergovernmental third pillar of Justice and Home Affairs, including

Title IV of the Schengen *acquis* (i.e. visas, asylum, immigration and other policies related to the free movement of persons) into the communitarian first pillar, with Title VI of the Schengen *acquis* (i.e. provisions on policy and judicial cooperation in criminal matters) remaining in the third pillar.

2. Supplementary Information Request at the National Entry – it is the administrative organ of the National Schengen Information System.

3. The Office is the national contact of the EU's European Agency for the Management of Operational Cooperation at the External Borders (FRONTEX).

4. 'Big-Bang enlargement for Schengen zone agreed', *EU Observer*, 8 November 2007.

5. 'Foreign Minister says Cyprus not to join Schengen before 2010', Embassy of the Republic of Cyprus in Berlin, 7 February 2008.

6. According to Eurostat (2007), Cyprus has the higher number of illegal immigrants in the EU-27 in proportion to its population.

7. 'How can Cyprus stem illegal immigration from the occupied north?', *Cyprus Mail*, 22 November 2007.

8. Foreign Minister says Cyprus not to join Schengen before 2010', Embassy of the Republic of Cyprus in Berlin, 7 February 2008.

9. According to Eurostat (2007), Cyprus claims the largest number of asylum seekers of any of the bloc's ten new Member States, and it is one of three states in the EU-27 (that is, Greece and Malta) where asylum applications are increasing.

10. Interview with Head of EU Unit, Ministry of Justice and Public Order, Republic of Cyprus, 30 August 2007.

11. Organized crime is relatively rare and overall crime is one of the lowest in Europe. The main criminal activities of local organized crime groups include narcotic drugs trafficking, illegal gambling, extortion and prostitution.

12. Cyprus is not a drug-producing country but faces significant problems in regards to drug trafficking originating from Turkey, Northern Cyprus and the Middle East.

13. Cyprus is a signatory of the European Convention for Protection of Human Rights and Fundamental Freedoms.

14. The initiative focused on a number of sensitive issues such as the automated exchange of DNA and fingerprint data, the supply of data on the basis of the principle of availability and the deployment of 'air marshals' in civil aircraft (Council, 2005). The signatory states are: France, Germany, Spain, The Netherlands, Belgium, Luxembourg and Austria.

15. Interview with Head of EU Unit, Ministry of Justice and Public Order, Republic of Cyprus, 30 August 2007.

16. Clientelism (ρουσφέτι or *rousfeti*), refers to the process whereby personal relationships are established between politicians or bureaucrats and members of the public, the basis of which is a reciprocal exchange of favours – a form of patronage. The favours which the bureaucrat or politician offers access to state resources – in the Cypriot context, employment, housing and even land. Those which members of the public offer are political support, assistance in political campaigning, and even more directly, votes. Clientelism is typically contrasted with forms of citizenship in which access to resources is based on universalistic criteria and formal equality before the law.

Corruption refers to the self-interested activities of politicians who appropriately use state resources for personal benefit or use their public position for private gain.

17. According to Transparency International's Corruption Perceptions Index (2007), Cyprus has a CPI score of 5.3/10.0 (10 is highly clean) ranking in the 39th place (1st place least corrupt) among 159 nations in the world. Among the EU-27, Cyprus is ranked 17th (1st place least corrupt). See also articles from Greek-Cypriot daily newspapers: 'Τα 'diploma' της Διαπλοκής', *Πολίτης*, 17 June 2007; 'Ρουσφέτι: Η Διαπλοκή Επωνύμων', *Πολίτης*, 18 Nov. 2006; Διεγράφει το Σκάνδαλο του ΧΑΚ, *Πολίτης*, 2 Nov. 2006; 'Καταγγελίες Μυριάνθους για Ρουσφέτι', *Φιλελεύθερος*, 24 May 2006; 'Επιταγές και υποσχέσεις', *Πολίτης*, 24 May 2006; 'Εκ των Εσω', *Φιλελεύθερος*, 13 January 2006; 'Οι ηγέτες', *Φιλελεύθερος*, 5 January 2006; 'Ενοχοι και Συνένοχοι', *Πολίτης*, 2 December 2005; 'Η Γαγγραινα του ρουσφετιού και η ομηρία της αξιοκρατίας', *Σημερινή*, 14 May 2005; 'Ανίκανοι για τη ψήφο μας', *Πολίτης*, 6 December 2005; 'Cyprus: The Champions of Nepotism', *Cyprus Mail*, 13 March 2005; 'Ο Γυάλινος Κοσμος του Ρουσφετιο και ο χρισμός τίης Πιθας', *Σημερινή*, 7 February 2003. And Georgiades, S.D. (2006) 'Favouratism as a Form of Injustice in Cyprus: Ubiquitous and Eternal?, *The Cyprus Review*, vol. 18(2), pp. 105–27.

18. Clientelism and corruption are often used as stereotypes to characterize Mediterranean politics in general (e.g. Italy, Greece, Malta), yet empirical evidence from these countries indicate that these elements are as much a stereotype as a practice. See, for example, Mitchell, J. (2002) 'Corruption and Clientelism in a 'Systemless System': The Europeanization of Maltese Political Cutlure', in *South European Society & Politics*, vol. 7 (1), pp. 43–62; Kourvetaris, G. & Dobratz, B. (1999) 'Political Clientelism in Athens, Greece: A Three Paradigm Approach', in Kourvetaris, G. (ed.) *Studies on Modern Greek Society and Politics*, Boulder: East European Monographs; Rosetti, C. (1994) 'Constitutionalism and Clientelism in Italy' in Roniger, L. & Günes-Ayata, A. (eds) *Democracy, Clientelism and Civil Society*, Boulder: Lynne Rienner.

19. According to Transparency International's Corruption Perceptions Index (2006), Cyprus has a CPI score of 5.6/10.0 (10 is highly clean) ranking in the 37th place (1st place least corrupt) among 159 nations in the world. Among the EU-27, Cyprus is ranked 17th (1st place least corrupt).

20. See above newspaper articles.

21. For example, some of the anti-corruption measures that have been implemented in the public sectors of corruption free countries such as Sweden are: the increase of public access to information about budgets, revenues and expenditure; increase the power of the Ombudsman to prosecute public officials; the disqualification of elected representatives or employees in municipality councils to deal with a matter of personal concern to the member himself and his family; the establishment of a parliamentary committee that would allow its members to raise any issue concerning a Minister's performance of his duties or the handling of cabinet business; establish a system of protection of informants to the media about corruption incidence. See also, Brinkerhoff, D. & Goldsmith, A. (2004) 'Good Governance, Clientelism, and

Old Patrimonialism: New Perspectives On Old Problems', *International Public Management Journal*, vol. 7 (2), pp. 163–85.

22. Interestingly, Cypriots trust the President, the police, the army and the Church more than these organizations. For more on civil society in Cyprus see 'An Assessment of Civil Society in Cyprus', *CIVICUS- World Alliance for Citizen Participation*, 2005; Vasilara, M. & Piaton, G. (2007) 'The Role of Civil Society in Cyprus', *The Cyprus Review*, vol. 19(2), pp. 107–21.

23. 'Cyprus and Poland agree to further cooperation to curb asylum seekers', *Financial Mirror*, 1 March 2005.

24. 'Justice Minister cautions Turkey over illegal immigrants', Embassy of the Republic of Cyprus in Washington D.C, 17 January 2006.

25. As mentioned earlier (Chapter VI: Economy), Cyprus has the third largest merchant ship fleet within the EU, with 16 per cent of the total fleet of EU-27 registered under Cyprus flag.

26. In fact, these countries were responsible for slowing down EU Council negotiations on the relevant directive and a deal was only reached (2005/35/EC) after a complex compromise package distinguishing between different degrees of gravity of the offences and leaving wide margins of discretion to the Member States as regards minimum/penalties. Yet because of the objections of this small Member State coalition, unanimity could not be reached in the Council on excluding EU vessels from the 'foreign ships' category because of the concerns of these three states that this would lead owners of EU-registered ships to switch their flags to third countries. A deal has not been reached at the point of writing.

Bibliography

Agapiou-Josephides, K. (1998) 'European Integration: Woman and Politics/ European Union Member States, Cyprus', *Greek Review of Political Science*, vol. 11, pp. 138–49.

Agh, A. (2005) *Institutional Design and Regional Capacity-Building in the Post-Accession Period* (Budapest: Hungarian Centre for Democracy Studies).

Agh, A. (2003) *Anticipatory and Adaptive Europeanization in Hungary* (Budapest: Hungarian Centre for Democracy Studies).

Agh, A. (2002) 'The Dual Challenge and the Reform of the Hungarian Socialist Party', *Communist and Post-Communist Studies*, vol. 35(3), pp. 269–88.

Aguilar Fernandez, S. (1994) 'Spanish Pollution Control Policy and the Challenge of the European Union', *Regional Politics and Policy*, vol. 4(1), pp. 102–17.

Amstrup, N. (1976) 'The Perennial Problem of Small States: A Survey of Research Efforts', *Cooperation and Conflict*, vol. 11(3), pp. 163–82.

Andonova, L. (2005) 'The Europeanization of Environmental Policy in Central and Eastern Europe' in Schimmelfennig, F. & Sedelmeier, U. (eds), *The Europeanization of Central and Eastern Europe* (Ithaca: Cornell University Press).

Andreou, E. (1996) 'The Cyprus Economy in the Last Three Decades (1960–1994): An Applied Econometric Approach', in V. Karageorghis & D. Michaelides (eds), *The Development of the Cypriot Economy: From the Prehistoric Period to the Present Day* (Nicosia: Lithiographica).

Angelides, S. (1996) 'The Cyprus Economy Under British Rule (1878–1960)', in V. Karageorghis & D. Michaelides (eds), *The Development of the Cypriot Economy: From the Prehistoric Period to the Present Day* (Nicosia: Lithiographica).

Antola, E. & Lehtimäki, M. (ed.) (2001) *Small States In the EU – Problems and Prospects of the Future* (Turku: University of Turku).

Archer, C. & Nugent, N. (2002) 'Introduction: Small States and the European Union', Special Issue, *Current Politics and Economics of Europe*, vol. 11(1), pp. 1–10.

Armstrong, H. & Read, R. (2002) 'Small States and the European Union: Issues in the Political Economy of International Integration', *Current Politics and Economics of Europe*, vol. 11(1), pp. 31–47.

Attalides, M.A. (1979) *Cyprus Nationalism and International Politics* (Edinburgh: Q Press).

Aylott, N. (2002) 'Let's Discuss This Later: Party Responses to Euro-Division in Scandinavia', *Party Politics*, vol. 8(4), pp. 441–61.

Ayres, R. (2003) 'The Economic Costs of Separation: The North–South Development Gap in Cyprus', *Ekonomia*, vol. 6(1), pp. 39–52.

Ayres, R. (1999) 'Export Growth and Diversification in a Small State: Cyprus and the European Union', *Ekonomia*, vol. 3(1), pp. 55–69.

Bache, I. (2007) *Europeanization and Multi-Level Governance* (London: Rowman & Littlefield Publishers).

Bache, I. (1998) *The Politics of European Union Regional Policy: Multi-Level Governance or Flexible Gatekeeping?* (Sheffield: Sheffield Academic Press).

Baier-Allen, S. (2004) *Exploring the Linkage between EU Accession and Conflict Resolution: The Cyprus Case* (Baden-Baden: Nomos).

Baldwin-Edwards, M. (1997) 'The Emerging European Immigration Regime: Some Reflections on the Implications for Southern Europe', *Journal of Common Market Studies*, vol. 35(4), pp. 497–519.

Bauer, M. (2001) 'A Creeping Transformation? The European Commission and the Management of Structural Funds in Germany, Library of Public Administration and Public Policy Administration (Dordrecht: Kluwer Academic Publishers).

Beetsma, R., *et al.* (2003) (eds), *European Macroeconomic Policies After Monetary Unification* (Cambridge: Cambridge University Press).

Bicak, H. (1996) 'Accession of Cyprus to the European Union', Eastern Mediterranean University, http://www.emu.edu.tr/~eric/Papers1.htm#1

Bigo, D. (2001) 'Migration and Security' in V. Guiraudon & C. Joppke (eds), *Controlling a New Migration World* (London: Routledge).

Binnema, H. (2002), 'European Integration and the Survival of Political Parties', Paper presented for the Politicologenetmaal, Noordwijkerhout, 23–24 May 2002.

Bomberg, E. & Peterson, J. (2000) 'Policy Transfer and Europeanization: Passing the Heineken Test?', *Queen's Papers on Europeanization*, no. 2, pp. 1–43.

Bomberg, E. & Peterson, J. (1999) *Decision-Making in the European Union* (Basingstoke: Palgrave Macmillan).

Börzel, T. A. (2004) 'How the European Union Interacts with Its Member States', in C. Lequesne & S. Bulmer (eds), *Member States and the European Union* (Oxford: Oxford University Press).

Börzel, T. A. (2003a) *Environmental Leaders and Laggards in Europe: Why There is (Not) a 'Southern Problem'* (Aldershot: Ashgate).

Börzel, T. A. (2003b) 'Shaping and Taking EU Policies: Member States Responses to Europeanization', *Queen's Papers on Europeanization*, n. 2., pp. 1–15.

Börzel, T. A. (2000) 'Why There Is No 'Southern Problem': On Environmental Leaders and Laggards in the European Union', *Journal of European Public Policy*, vol. 7(1), pp. 141–62.

Börzel, T. A. (1999) 'Towards Convergence in Europe?: Institutional Adaptation to Europeanization in Germany and Spain', *Journal of Common Market Studies*, vol. 39(4), pp. 573–96.

Bossaert, D. & Demmke, C. (2003) *Civil Services in the Accession States: New Trends and the Impact of the Integration Process* (Maastricht: European Institute of Public Administration).

Boswell, C. (2003) 'The External Dimension of EU Immigration and Asylum Policy', *International Affairs*, vol. 79(3), pp. 619–38.

Brey, H. (2006) 'The Cypriot Economy Under British Rule' in Faustmann, H. & Peristianis, N. (eds), *Britain in Cyprus: Colonialism and Post-Colonialism, 1878–2006* (Mohnesee: Bibliopolis).

Brewin, C. (2000) *The European Union and Cyprus* (Huntington: Eosthen Press).

Briguglio, L. (1995) 'Small Island Developing States and Their Economic Vulnerabilities', *World Development*, vol. 23(9), pp. 1615–32.

Briguglio, L. & Cordina, G. (2004) (eds), *Competitiveness Strategies for Small States* (Malta: Formatek).

Brinkerhoff, D. & Goldsmith, A. (2004) 'Good Governance, Clientelism, and Old Patrimonialism: New Perspectives On Old Problems', *International Public Management Journal*, vol. 7(2), pp. 163–85.

Brusis, M. (2002) 'Between EU Requirements, Competitive Politics, and National Traditions: Re-creating Regions in the Accession Countries of Central and Eastern Europe', *Governance*, vol. 15(4), pp. 531–59.

Bulmer, S. & Burch, M. (2001a) 'Coming to Terms with Europe: Europeanization, Whitehall and the Challenge of Devolution', *Queen's Papers on Europeanization*, no. 1, pp. 1–27.

Bulmer, S. & Burch, M. (2001b) 'The Europeanization of Central Government: the UK and Germany in Historical Institutionalist Perspective' in Schneider, G. & Aspinwall, M. (eds), *The Rules of Integration* (Manchester: Manchester University Press).

Bulmer, S. & Lequesne, C. (2002) 'New Perspectives on EU Member State Relationships', *Questions de Recherche* (Paris: Centre d'Etudes et de Recherches Internationals Sciences Po).

Buttigieg, E. (2004) 'Challenges Facing Malta as a Micro-State in an Enlarged EU', *Bank of Valletta Review*, no. 29, pp. 1–15.

Calotychos, V. (1998) 'Interdisciplinary Perspectives: Difference at the Heart of Cypriot Identity and Its Study' in Calotychos, V. (ed.), *Cyprus and Its People: Nation, Identity and Experience in an Unimaginable Community, 1955–1997* (Colorado Press).

Caporaso, J., Cowles, M.G. & Risse, T. (eds), (2001) *Transforming Europe: Europeanization and Domestic Change* (Ithaca: Cornell University Press).

Carmin, J. & VanDeveer, S. (2004) (eds), *EU Enlargement and the Environment: Institutional Change and Environmental Policy in Central and Eastern Europe, Special Issue of Environmental Politics*, vol. 13, (London: Frank Cass)

Carver, M. (2006) 'The Gordian Knot: American and British Policy Concerning the Cyprus Issue, 1952–1974', PhD Thesis, May 2006.

Castello, S., Olienyk, J. & Ozawa, T. (1997) 'Nation Size, Outward Orientation and Structural Adaptability: Small Versus Large European Economies', *Journal of Development and International Cooperation*, vol. 13, pp. 85–104.

Castles, F. (1993) 'Introduction' in idem (ed.), *Families of Nations: Patterns of Public Policy in Western Democracies* (Aldershot: Dartmouth).

Chalmers, D. (2000) 'The Positioning of EU Judicial Politics within the United Kingdom', *West European Politics*, vol. 23(4), pp. 169–210.

Checkel, J. (1999) 'Norms, Institutions and National Identity in Contemporary Europe', *International Studies Quarterly*, vol. 43(1), pp. 83–114.

Chossudovsky, M. (2006) 'Triple Alliance: The US, Turkey, Israel and the War on Lebanon', *Global Research*, 6 August.

Christiansen, T., Jorgensen, K.E. & Wiener, A. (1999) 'The Social Construction of Europe', *Journal of European Public Policy*, vol. 6(4), pp. 528–44.

Christodoulou, D. (1992) *Inside the Cyprus Miracle: The Labours of an Embattled Mini-Economy* (Minneapolis: University of Minnesota Press).

Christophorou, C. (2006) 'Party Change and Development in Cyprus (1995–2005)', *South European Society & Politics*, vol. 11(3–4), pp. 513–42.

Christophorou, C. (2003) 'A European Course with a Communist Party', *South European Society and Politics*, vol. 8(3), pp. 94–118.

Christou, G. (2004) *The European Union and Enlargement: The Case of Cyprus* (Basingstoke: Palgrave Macmillan).

Chrysostomides, K. (2000) *The Republic of Cyprus: A Study in International Law* (London: Martinus Nijhoff Publishers).

Clerides, G. (1989) *Cyprus: My Deposition*, vol. 1 (Nicosia: Alithia Publishers) (in Greek).

Closa, C. & Heywood, P.M. (2004) *Spain and the European Union* (Basingstoke: Palgrave Macmillan).

Coloumbis, T. & Hicks, S. (1975) *USA Foreign Policy Toward Greece and Cyprus: The Clash of Principle and Pragmatism* (Washington, DC: Centre for Mediterranean Studies).

Commission of the European Communities (2004) Proposal for a Council Regulation on Special Conditions for Trade with Those Areas in Which the Government of the Republic of Cyprus Does Not Exercise Effective Control, COM 2004/0466/final, 7 July 2004.

Commission of the European Communities (1999–2003) Regular Reports from the Commission on Cyprus' Progress Towards Accession, Office for the Official Publications of the European Communities, Luxembourg.

Commission of the European Communities (1998) Regular Report from the Commission on Cyprus' Progress Towards Accession, Office for the Official Publications of the European Communities, Luxembourg, 1998.

Commission of the European Communities (1997) 'Europe's Agenda 2000: Strengthening and Widening the EU', 16 July 1997.

Commission of the European Communities (1993) Opinion on Cyprus Application for Accession, Brussels, COM (93) 313, Brussels, 30 June 1993.

Conant, L. (2001) 'Europeanization and the Courts: Variable Patterns of Adaptation among National Judiciaries' in J. Caporaso, M.G. Cowles & T. Risse (eds), *Transforming Europe: Europeanization and Domestic Change* (Ithaca: Cornell University Press).

Constantinou, M. (2006) 'Reasons of State and the Constitutional Logic of Quasi-Stateness: the Post-Colonial Contradictions of Cyprus' integration in the European Confederation', *Postcolonial Studies*, vol. 9(3), pp. 295–310.

Constantinou C. & Richmond, O. (2005) 'The Long Mile of Empire: Power, Legitimation and the UK Bases in Cyprus', *Mediterranean Politics*, vol. 10(1), pp. 65–84.

Coppieters, B. *et al.* (2004) *Europeanization and Conflict Resolution: Case Studies from the European Periphery* (Genk: Academia Press).

Council of the European Union (2006) Regulation establishing an instrument of financial support for encouraging the economic development of the Turkish-Cypriot community ('Aid Regulation'), 389/2006 L65/5, 27 February 2006.

Council of the European Union (2005) 'Prüm Convention', 10900/05, Brussels, 7 July.

Council of the European Union (2004) Regulation on a regime under Article 2 of Protocol 10 on Cyprus of the Act of Accession ('Green Line' Regulation), No 866/2004, L161, 30 April 2004.

Council of the European Union (2000) Regulation on the implementation of operations in the framework of the pre-accession strategy for the Republic of Cyprus and Republic of Malta, No 555/2000 ,OJ L 68, 16 March 2000.

Crawford, J. (1979) *The Creation of States in International* Law (Oxford: Clarendon Press).

Crawshaw, N. (1986) 'Cyprus: The Political Background' in Komoulides, J.T.A. (ed.), *Cyprus in Transition: 1960–1985* (London: Trigraph).

Crowards, T. (2002) 'Defining the Category of 'Small' States', *Journal of International Development*, vol. 14, pp. 143–79.

Damijan, J. (1997) 'Main Economic Characteristics of Small Countries: Some Empirical Evidence', *Development and International Cooperation*, vol. 13, nos. 24–5, pp. 43–83.

Dell'Olio, F. (2004) *The Europeanization of Citizenship: Between the Ideology of Nationality, Immigration and European Identity* (London: Ashgate).

Delanty, G. (1995) *Inventing Europe: Idea, Identity, Reality* (London: Palgrave Macmillan).

Demetriades, P., Fethi, M.D. & Fethi, S. (2003) 'Convergence and the Cypriot Economies: Time Series Theory and Evidence, 1977–2000', *Ekonomia*, vol. 6(1), pp. 19–38.

Demetriou, M. (1998) 'On the Long Road to Europe and the Short Path to War: Issue-Linkage Politics and the Arms Build-Up in Cyprus', *Mediterranean Politics*, vol. 3(3), pp. 38–51.

De Vreese, C. & Boomgaarden, H. (2006) 'Media Effect on Public Opinion about the Enlargement of the European Union', *Journal of Common Market Studies*, vol. 44(2), pp. 419–36.

Diamandouros, N. & Gunther, R. (eds), (2001) *Parties, Politics and Democracy in the New Southern Europe* (Boulder: John's Hopkins University Press).

Diez, T. *et al.* (2006) 'The European Union and Border Conflicts: The Transformative Power of Integration', *International Organization*, vol. 60, pp. 563–93.

Diez, T. (2002) (ed.) *The European Union and the Cyprus Conflict* (Manchester: Manchester University Press).

Dimitrov, V., Goetz, K.H., Wollmann, H. (2006) *Governing After Communism: Institutions and Policy* (Lanham: Rowman & Littlefield).

Dimitrova, A. & Toshkov, D. (2007) 'The Dynamics of Domestic Coordination of EU Policy in New Member States : Impossible to Lock in?', *West European Politics*, vol. 30(5), pp. 961–86.

Dimitrova, A. (ed.) (2004) *Driven to Change: The European Union's Enlargement Viewed from the East* (Manchester: Manchester University Press).

Dimitrova, A. (2002) 'Enlargement, Institution-Building and the EU's Administrative Capacity Requirement', *West European Politics*, vol. 25(4), pp. 171–90.

Drousiotis, M. (2002) *EOKA B and CIA* (Nicosia, Alfadi) (in Greek).

Drury, A., Krieckhaus, J. & Lusztig, M. (2006) 'Corruption, Democracy and Economic Growth', *International Political Science Review*, vol. 27(2), pp. 121–36.

Dugard, J. (1987) *Recognition and the United Nations* (Cambridge: Cambridge University Press).

Duina, F. (1999) *Harmonizing Europe: Nation-States within the Common Market* (New York: State University of New York Press).

Dunphy, R. & Bale, T. (2007) 'Red Flag Still Flying?: Explaining AKEL-Cyprus's Communist Anomaly', *Party Politics*, vol. 13(3), pp. 287–304.

Duverger, M. (1994) *Europe des Hommes: Une Métamorphose Inachevée* (Paris: Editions Odile Jacob).

Dyson, K. (2007) 'Economic Policy' in Graziano, P. & Vink, M. (eds), *Europeaniza-tion: New Research Agendas* (Basingstoke: Palgrave Macmillan).

Dyson, K. (2006) (ed.) *Enlarging the Euro Area: The Euro and the Transformation of East Central Europe* (Oxford: Oxford University Press).

Dyson, K. (2002) *European States and the Euro: Europeanization, Variation and Convergence* (Oxford: Oxford University Press).

Dyson, K. & Goetz, K. (2003) 'Living with Europe: Power, Constraint and Con-testation' in K. Dyson & Goetz, K. (eds), *Germany, Europe and the Politics of Constraint* (Oxford: Oxford University Press).

Easton, D. (1965) *A Systems Analysis of Political Life* (New York: Wiley and sons, Ltd).

Economides, S. (2005) 'The Europeanization of Greek Foreign Policy', *West European Politics*, vol. 28(2), pp. 471–91.

Eder, K. (2004) 'The Two Faces of Europeanization: Synchronizing a Europe Moving at Varying Speeds', *Time & Society*, vol. 13(1), pp. 89–107.

Eichengreen, B., Faini, R., Von Hagen, J., Wyplosz, C. (2004) 'Economic Aspects of the Annan Plan for the Solution of the Cyprus', 24 February.

Eising, R. & Kohler-Koch, B. (1999) (eds), *The Transformation of Governance in the European Union* (London: Routledge).

Ekengren, M. (2002) *The Time of European Governance* (Manchester: Manchester University Press).

Emiliou, N. (2004) 'Impact of EU Accession on the National Legal Orders of New Member States: The Case of Cyprus' in De Zwaan, J. *et al.* (eds), *The European Union: An Ongoing Process of Integration* (London: Asser Press).

Eralp, D. & Beriker, N. (2005) 'Assessing the Conflict Resolution Potential of the EU: The Cyprus Conflict and Accession Negotiations', *Security Dialogue*, 36 (2), pp. 175–92.

Ertekűn, N.M. (1981) *In Search of a Negotiated Cyprus Settlement* (Nicosia: Űlűs Matbağacilik).

European Commission (2007) 'Eurobarometer: National Report for the Turkish-Cypriot Community', Spring 2007.

European Commission (2007) 'Eurobarometer: National Report for Cyprus' (areas under the control of the Cyprus Government), Spring 2007.

European Commission (2006) 'Eurobarometer: National Report for the Turkish-Cypriot Community', November 2006.

European Commission (2006) 'Eurobarometer: National Report for Cyprus' (areas under the control of the Cyprus Government), November 2006.

European Commission (2006) Progress Report on Turkey, COM (2006) 649 final, Brussels, 8 November 2006.

European Commission (2005) 'Enlargement Strategy Paper', COM 2005 (561) final, 9 November 2005.

European Commission (2003) 'Administrative Capacity Study Phare Region – Phase 2', Country Reports, March 2003.

European Council (2006) Conclusions, Brussels, 14–15 December 2006.

European Council (2003) Conclusions, Athens, 16–17 April 2003.

European Council (1999) Conclusions, Helsinki, 10–11 December 1999.

European Council (1997) Conclusions, Luxembourg, 12–13 December 1997.

European Council (1993) Conclusions on the Commission Opinion on Cyprus' Application for Accession', 4 October 1993.

European Council (1973) Association Agreement between the EEC and the Republic of Cyprus, OJEC, L 133/3, Brussels, 21 May 1973.

European Parliament (1995) Resolution on Cyprus's Membership Application to the European Union, 12 June 1995.

Falkner, G., Treib, O., Hartlapp, M. & Leiber, S. (2005) *Complying with Europe: EU Harmonization and Soft Law in the Member States of the EU* (Cambridge: Cambridge University Press).

Fanes, J. (2002) 'The Europeanization of Spanish Policy Towards Morocco', Paper Presented a Joint Workshop on 'Europeanization of Foreign Policies' (University of Birmingham & LSE).

Faustmann, H. (1998) 'Clientelism in the Greek-Cypriot Society of Cyprus under British Rule', *The Cyprus Review*, vol. 10(2), pp. 41–77.

Featherstone, K. (2001) 'Cyprus and the Onset of Europeanization: Strategic Usage, Structural Transformation and Institutional Adaptation' in Featherstone, K. & Kazamias, G. (eds), *Europeanization and the Southern Periphery*, London: Frank Cass.

Featherstone, K. & Kazamias, G. (2001) 'Introduction: Southern Europe and the Process of 'Europeanization', in K. Featherstone & G. Kazamias (eds), *Europeanization and the Southern Periphery* (London: Frank Cass).

Fink-Hafner, D. (2005) 'Europeanization of the Core Executive in the Transition from Circumstances of EU Accession to Full Membership', Paper Presented at the EUSA 9th Biennial International Conference, 31 March–2 April 2005, Austin, Texas.

Fouskas, V. (2003) 'US Foreign Policy in the Greater Middle East During the Cold War and the Position of Cyprus' in Fouskas, V. Richter, H. (eds), *Cyprus and Europe: The Long Way Back* (Mohnesee: Bibliopolis).

Gabel, M. (1998) *Interests and Integration: Market Liberalization, Public Opinion and European Union* (Michigan: University of Michigan Press).

Geddes, A. (2000) *Immigration and European Integration: Towards Fortress Europe?* (Manchester: Manchester University Press).

Georgiades, S.D. (2006) 'Favouratism as a Form of Injustice in Cyprus: Ubiquitous and Eternal?', *The Cyprus Review*, vol. 18(2), pp. 105–27.

Giddens, A. (1990) *The Consequences of Modernity: Self and Society in the Late Modern Age* (Cambridge: Polity Press).

Gilpin, R. (2001) *Global Political Economy* (Princeton: Princeton University Press).

Goetschel, L. (ed.) (1998) *Small States Inside and Outside the European Union* (Dordrecht: Kluwer Academic Publishers).

Goetz, K. & Meyer-Sahling, J (2007) 'The Europeanization of National Administrative Systems', *Living Reviews in European Governance* (forthcoming).

Goetz, K. (2006) 'Territory, Temporality and Clustered Europeanization', *Political Science Series 109* (Vienna: Institute for Advanced Studies).

Goetz, K. (2001a) 'Executive Governance in Central and Eastern Europe, *Journal of European Public Policy*, vol. 8(6), special issue.

Goetz, K. (2001b) 'Making Sense of Post-Communist Central Administration: Modernization, Europeanization or Latinization, *Journal of European Public Policy*, vol. 8(6), pp. 1032–51.

Goetz, K. (2000) 'European Integration and National Executives: A Cause in Search of an Effect?', *West European Politics*, vol. 23(4), pp. 211–31.

Goetz, K. & Hix, S. (eds), (2000) *Europeanized Politics? European Integration and National Political Systems* (London: Frank Cass).

Grabbe, H. (2003) 'Europeanization Goes East: Power and Uncertainty in the EU Accession Process' in K. Featherstone & C. Radaelli (eds), *The Politics of Europeanization* (Oxford: Oxford University Press).

Grabbe, H. (2001) 'How Does Europeanization Affect CEE Governance?: Conditionality, Diffusion and Diversity', *Journal of European Public Policy*, vol. 8(6), p. 1020.

Grabbe, H. (2000) 'The Sharp Edges of Europe: Extending Schengen Eastwards', *International Affairs*, vol. 76(3), pp. 519–36.

Graziano, P. & Vink, M. (2007) (eds), *Europeanization: New Research Agendas* (Basingstoke: Palgrave Macmillan).

Green, P. & Collins, R. (2003) *Embracing Cyprus: The Path to Unity in the New Europe* (New York: Palgrave Macmillan).

Grugel, J. (2001) *Democratization: A Critical Introduction* (Basingstoke: Palgrave Macmillan).

Gstöhl, S., Ingebritsen, C, Neumann, I. (2007) *Small States in International Relations* (Seattle: University of Washington Press).

Guillen, A. & Bruno, P. (eds), (2004) *Special Issue on 'EU Accession, Europeanization and Social Policy, Journal of European Social Policy*, vol. 14 (London: Sage).

Guney, A. (2004) 'The USA's Role in Mediating the Cyprus Conflict: A Story of Success or Failure?', *Security Dialogue*, vol. 35(1), pp. 27–42.

Guiraudon, V. (2000) 'European Integration and Migration Policy: Vertical Policy-Making as Venue Shopping', *Journal of Common Market Studies*, vol. 38(2), pp. 251–71.

Haas, E. (1975) *The Obsolescence of Regional Integration Theory* (Berkeley: University of California Press).

Haas, E. (1958) *The Uniting of Europe: Political, Social and Economic Forces, 1950–1957* (Stanford: Stanford University Press).

Hadjikyriakos, A. & Christophorou, C. (1996) *Parliamentary Elections: A Historical Analysis* (in Greek) (Nicosia: Intercollege Press).

Hadjimanolis, A & Musyck, B. (2005) 'Towards a Knowledge-Based Economy: Does the Cyprus R&D Capability Meet the Challenge?', *Science & Public Policy*, vol. 32(1), pp. 65–78.

Hadjispyrou, S. & Pashardes, P. (2003) 'The Economic Effects of the 1974 Events on the Greek-Cypriots', *Ekonomia*, vol. 6(1), pp. 72–94.

Hatzivassiliou, E. (2006) 'British Strategic Priorities and the Cyprus Question, 1954–1958' in Faustmann, H. & Peristianis, N. (eds), *Britain in Cyprus: Colonialism and Post-Colonialism, 1878–2006* (Mohnesee: Bibliopolis).

Hall, P. & Taylor, R.C. (1996) 'Political Science and the Three New Institutionalisms', *Political Studies*, vol. 44(5), pp. 936–957.

Hanf, K. & Soetendorp, B. (1998) (eds), *Adapting to European Integration: Small States and the European Union* (London: Longman).

Harvey, D. (1989) *The Conditions of Postmodernity: An Inquiry into the Conditions of Cultural Change* (Oxford: Blackwell).

Hayes-Renshaw, F., Lequesne, C. & Lopez, P. M. (1989) 'The Permanent Representations of the Member States to the European Communities', *Journal of Common Market Studies*, vol. 28(2), pp. 119–37.

Heisenberg, D. (1999) *The Mark of the Bundesbank: Germany's Role in European Monetary Cooperation* (Boulder: Lynne Rienner Publishers)

Henderson, K. (2005) 'EU Influence on Party Politics in Slovakia', 9th Biennial EUSA Conference, Austin, TX, 31 March–2 April.

Heritier, A. (2001) 'Differential Europe: The European Union Impact on National Policy-Making', in Heritier, A. *et al.* (eds), *Differential Europe: The European Union Impact on National Policy-Making* (Lanham: Rowman & Littlefiled).

Heritier, A., Knill, C. & Mingers, S. (1996) *Ringing the Changes in Europe: Regulatory Competition and the Redefinition of the State: Britain, France and Germany* (Berlin: De Gruyeter).

Herve, Y. & Holzmann, R. (1998) 'Fiscal Transfers and Economic Convergence in the EU: An Analysis of Absorption Problems and Evaluation of the Literature' (Baden-Baden: Nomos).

Hirst, P. & Thompson, G. (1996) *Globalization in Question: The International Economy and the Possibilities of Governance* (Cambridge: Polity Press).

Hitchens, C. (1997) *Hostage to History: Cyprus from the Ottomans to Kissinger* (London: Verso Books).

Hoffmann, S. (1966) 'Obstinate or Obsolete?: The Fate of the Nation State and the Case of Western Europe', *Daedalus*, vol. 95, pp. 892–908.

Holl, O. (2000) Lecture at Conference 'Does Size Matter? Challenges and Strategies in 'Small' and 'Large' EU Member States' (Maastricht: European Institute of Public Administration).

Holzhacker, R. (2007) 'Parliamentary Scrutiny' in Graziano, P. & Vink, M. (eds), *Europeanization: New Research Agendas* (Basingstoke: Palgrave Macmillan).

Horton-Kelling, G. (1990) *Countdown to Rebellion: British Policy in Cyprus 1935–1955* (Greenwood Press).

Horvat, A. & Maier, G. (2004) 'Regional Development, Absorption Problems and the EU Structural Funds: Absorption capacity in the Czech Republic, Estonia, Hungary, Slovakia and Slovenia' (Ljubljana: National Agency for Regional Development of Slovenia).

Hosli, M. (1996) 'Coalitions and Power: Effects of Qualified Majority Voting in the Council of the European Union', *Journal of Common Market Studies*, vol. 34(2), pp. 255–73.

Houghe, L. (1996) *Cohesion Policy and European Integration: Building Multi-Level Governance* (Oxford: Oxford University Press).

Howell, K. (2004) *Europeanization, European Integration and Financial Services* (London: Palgrave Macmillan).

Hudson, J.R. & Dymiotou-Jensen, M. (1989) *Modeling a Developing Country: A Case Study of Cyprus* (Aldershot, UK: Avebury).

Hughes, J., Sasse, G., Gordon, C. (2004) *Europeanization and Regionalization in the EU's Enlargement to Central and Eastern Europe: The Myth of Conditionality* (Basingstoke: Palgrave).

Huysmans, J. (2000) 'The European Union and the Securitization of Migration', *Journal of Common Market Studies*, vol. 38(5), pp. 751–77.

Ignazi, P. & Ysmal, C. (1998) *The Organization of Political Parties in Southern Europe* (Westport, CT/London: Praeger).

Ingebritsen, C. (1998) *The Nordic States and European Unity* (Ithaca: Cornell University Press).

Ioakimidis, P.C. (1999) 'The Model of Foreign Policy-Making in Greece: Personal-ities versus Institutions', in T. Couloumbis, S. Stavridis, T. Veremis & N. Waites (eds), (1999) *The Foreign Policies of the European Union's Mediterranean States and Applicant Countries in the 1990s* (London: St. Martin's/Macmillan Press).

Ivar-Andre, S. (2000) 'A Bad Show?: The United States and the 1974 Cyprus Crisis', *Mediterranean Quarterly*, vol. 11(2), pp. 96–129.

Jacoby, W. (2005) 'External Incentives and Lesson-Drawing in Regional Policy and Health Care' in Schimmelfennig, F. & Sedelmeier, U. (eds), *The Europeanization of Central and Eastern Europe* (Ithaca: Cornell University Press).

Jeffery, C. (1996) 'Farewell to the Third Level?: The German Länder and the European Policy Process', *Regional & Federal Studies*, vol. 6(2), pp. 56–75.

Jeffery, C. & Patterson, W. (2003) 'Germany and European Integration: a Shifting of Tectonic Plates', *West European Politics*, vol. 26(4), pp. 59–78.

Joseph, S. J. (1997) *Cyprus: Ethnic Conflict and International Politics: From Inde-pendence to the Threshold of the European Union* (London: Macmillan/St Martin's Press).

Kaeding, M. & Torsten, S. (2005) 'Mapping Out Political Europe: Coalition Pat-terns in EU Decision-Making', *International Political Science Review*, vol. 26(3), pp. 271–90.

Kasoulides, I. (2007) *Cyprus–EU: My Experience of Accession...* (Athens: Livanis Press) (in Greek).

Kassim, H., Menon, A., Peters, G. & Wright, V. (eds), (2001) *The National Coordination of EU Policy: The European Level* (Oxford: Oxford University Press).

Kassim, H., Peters, G. & Wright, V. (eds), (2000) *The National Coordination of EU Policy: The Domestic Level* (Oxford: Oxford University Press).

Katsourides, I. (2003) 'Europeanization and Political Parties in Accession Coun-tries: The Political Parties of Cyprus', Paper presented at the EPSNET 2003 Plenary Conference, Paris, 13–14 June.

Katzenstein, P. (1997) *Tamed Power: Germany in Europe* (Ithaca, NY: Cornell University Press).

Katzenstein, P. (1985) *Small States in World Markets: Industrial Policy in Europe* (Ithaca: Cornell University Press).

Keating, M. & Hughes, J. (eds), (2003) *The Regional Challenge in Central and Eastern Europe: Territorial Restructuring and European Integration* (Brussels: Lang).

Ker-Lindsay, J. (2005) *EU Accession and UN Peacemaking in Cyprus* (Basingstoke: Palgrave Macmillan).

Kirby, P. (2004) 'Globalization, the Celtic Tiger and Social Outcomes: Is Ireland a Model or a Mirage?', *Globalizations*, vol. 1(2), pp. 205–22.

Kizilyurek, N. (1993) *Cyprus Beyond the Nation* (Ploutis Servas) (in Turkish & Greek).

Knill, C. (2001) *The Europeanization of National Administrations: Patterns of Institutional Change and Persistence* (Cambridge: Cambridge University Press).

Knill, C. (1998) 'European Policies: The Impact of National Administrative Traditions', *Journal of European Public Policy*, vol. 18(1), pp. 1–28.

Knill, C. & Lehmkuhl, D. (1999) 'How Europe Matters: Different Mechanisms of Europeanization', *European Integration Online Papers*, 3/7, pp. 1–19.

Knill, C. & Lenschow, A. (1998) 'Coping with Europe: The Impact of British and German Administrations on the Implementation of EU Environmental Policy', *Journal of European Public Policy*, vol. 5(4), pp. 595–614.

Knudsen, O. & Clesse, A. (eds), (1996) *Small States and the Security Challenge in the New Europe* (London: Brassey's).

Kohler-Koch, B. (1996) 'Catching Up with Change: The Transformation of Governance in the European Union', *Journal of European Public Policy*, vol. 3(3), pp. 359–80.

Kourvetaris, G. & Dobratz, B. (1999) 'Political Clientelism in Athens, Greece: A Three Paradigm Approach', in Kourvetaris, G. (ed), *Studies on Modern Greek Society and Politics* (Boulder: East European Monographs).

Kramer, H. (1997), 'The Cyprus Question and European Security', *Survival*, vol. 39(3), pp. 16–32.

Kreppel, A. (1999), 'Rules, Ideology and Coalition Formation in the European Parliament: Past, Present and Future', EPRG Working Paper, No. 4, Presented at the 1999 Annual Meeting of the American Political Science Association, 2–5 September, Atlanta, Georgia.

Kyriakides, S. (1968) *Cyprus Constitutionalism and Crisis Government* (Philadelphia: University of Pennsylvania Press).

Ladrech, R. (2007) 'National Political Parties and European Governance: The Consequences of 'Missing in Action', *West European Politics*, vol. 30(5), pp. 945–960.

Ladrech, R. (2001), 'Europeanization and Political Parties: Towards a Framework of Analysis', *Queens Papers on Europeanization*, 2/2001.

Ladrech, R. (1994) 'Europeanization of Domestic Politics and Institutions: The Case of France', *Journal of Common Market Studies*, vol. 32(1), pp. 69–88.

Laffan, B. (2003) 'Managing Europe from Home: Impact of the EU on Executive Government: A Comparative Analysis', Paper for ECPR Conference, Marburg, September 2003.

Laffan, B. (2001) *Organizing for a Changing Europe: Irish Central Government and the European Union* (Dublin: Trinity Blue Paper).

Laffan, B. & Stubb, A. (2003) 'Member States' in idem (eds), *The European Union: How Does it Work?* (Oxford: Oxford University Press).

Laitin, D. (2002) 'Culture and National Identity: The 'East' and European Integration', *West European Politics*, vol. 25(2), pp. 55–80.

La Spina, A. & Sciortino, G. (1993) 'Common Agenda, Southern Rules: European Integration and Environmental Change in the Mediterranean States', in J. D. Liefferink, P.D. Lowe and A.P.J. Mol (eds), *European Integration and Environmental Policy*, (London/New York: Belhaven).

Lavenex, S. (2007) 'Asylum Policy' in Graziano, P. & Vink, M. (eds), *Europeanization: New Research Agendas* (Basingstoke: Palgrave Macmillan).

Lavenex, S. (2001a) 'Migration and the EU's New Eastern Border: Between Realism and Liberalism', *Journal of European Public Policy*, vol. 8(1), pp. 24–42.

Lavenex, S. (2001b) 'The Europeanization of Refugee Policies: Normative Challenges and Institutional Legacies', *Journal of Common Market Studies*, vol. 39(5), pp. 851–974.

Lavenex, S. & Ucarer, E. (2004) 'The External Dimension of Europeanization: The Case of Immigration Policies', *Cooperation and Conflict*, vol. 39(4), pp. 417–43.

Lavenex, S. & Ucarer, E. (2002) *Migration and the Externalities of European Integration* (Lanham: Lexington Books).

Leiber, S. (2005) 'Implementation of EU Social Policy in Poland: Is there a Different World of Compliance?', 9th Biennial EUSA Conference, Austin, TX, 31 March–2 April.

Lendvai, N. (2004) 'The Weakest Link?: EU Accession and Enlargement: Dialoguing EU and Post-Communist Social Policy', *Journal of European Social Policy*, vol. 14(3), pp. 319–333.

Lequesne, C. (1993) *Paris–Bruxelles: Comment se fait la politique européenne de la France?* (Paris: Presses de la Fondation Nationale des Sciences Politiques).

Leonardi, R. (2005) *Cohesion Policy in the European Union: The Building of Europe* (London: Palgrave Macmillan).

Lewis, P. (2005) 'Consolidation or Collapse? Impacts of EU Involvement on Party Systems in Central Europe', 9th Biennial EUSA Conference, Austin, TX, 31 March–2 April.

Lindberg, L. (1963) *The Political Dynamics of European Economic Integration* (Stanford: Stanford University Press).

Lindberg, L. & Scheingold, S. (1970) *Europe's Would-Be Polity: Patterns of Change in the European Community* (Englewood, NJ: Prentice Hall).

Lindley, D. (2001) 'Assessing the Role of UN Peace-keeping Force in Cyprus' in Richond, O. & Ker-Lindsay, J. (eds), *The Work of the UN in Cyprus* (Basingstoke: Palgrave Macmillan).

Lippert, B. & Umbach, G. (2005) *The Pressure of Europeanization: From Post-Communist State Administrations to Normal Players in the EU System* (Baden-Baden: Nomos Verlagsgesellschaft).

Lippert, B., Umbach, G., Wessels, W. (2001) 'Europeanization of CEE Executives: EU Membership Negotiations as a Shaping Power', *Journal of European Public Policy*, vol. 8(6), pp. 980–1012.

Lordos, A. (2006) 'Rational Agent or Unthinking Follower: A Survey-Based Profile Analysis of Greek-Cypriot and Turkish-Cypriot Referendum Voters', Paper presented at ECPR Joint Sessions of Workshops, Nicosia, 25–30 April.

Lucarelli, S. & Radaelli, C. (2005) 'The European Convention: A Process of Mobilization?', in S. Lucarelli and C.M. Radaelli (eds), *Mobilizing Politics and Society? The EU Convention's Impact on Southern Europe* (London: Routledge).

Luedtke, A. (2005) 'European Integration, Public Opinion and Immigration Policy: Testing the Impact of National Identity', *European Union Politics*, vol. 6(1), pp. 83–112.

Luke, H. (1969) *Cyprus Under the Turks 1571–1878* (London: Hurst) (1st edn 1921).

Luther, R. K. & Muller-Rommel, F. (2002) 'Political Parties in a Changing Europe', Keele European Parties Research Unit, Working Paper 14.

Maes, I. & Verdun, A. (2005) 'Small States and the Creation of EMU: Belgium and the Netherlands, Pace-Setters and Gate-Keepers', *Journal of Common Market Studies*, vol. 43(2), pp. 327–48.

Mavratsas, C. (1997) 'The Ideological Contest Between Greek-Cypriot Nationalism and Cypriotism, 1974–1995: Politics, Social Memory and Identity', *Ethnic and Racial Studies*, vol. 20(4), pp. 717–37.

McGrew, A. (2005) 'Globalization and Global Politics' in Baylis, J. & Smith, S. (eds), *The Globalization of World Politics* (Oxford: Oxford University Press).

McLaren, L. (2005) *Identity, Interests and Attitudes to European Integration* (Basingstoke: Palgrave Macmillan).

Mair, P. (2007) 'Political Parties and Party Systems' in Graziano, P. & Vink, M. (eds), *Europeanization: New Research Agendas* (Basingstoke: Palgrave Macmillan).

Mair, P (2000) 'The Limited Impact of Europe on National Party Systems', *West European Politics*, vol. 23(4), pp. 27–51.

Majone, G. (ed.) (1996) *Regulating Europe* (London: Routledge).

Major, C. (2005) 'Europeanization and Foreign and Security Policy – Undermining or Rescuing the Nation State?', *Politics*, vol. 25(3), pp. 175–90.

Mallinson, W. (2007) 'US Interests, British Acquiescence and the Invasion of Cyprus', *British Journal of Politics and International Relations*, vol. 9, pp. 494–508.

Mallinson, W. (2005) *Cyprus: A Modern History* (London: Tauris).

Manners, I. & Whitman, R. (2001) 'Introduction' in Manners, I. & Whitman, R. (eds), *The Foreign Policies of EU Member States* (Manchester: Manchester University Press).

Mansergh, N. (1997) *Nationalism and Independence: Selected Irish Papers* (Cork: Cork University Press).

Manzetti, L. & Wilson, C. (2007) 'Why Do Corrupt Governments Maintain Public Support?', *Comparative Political Studies*, vol. 40(8), pp. 949–70.

March, J. & Olsen, J.P. (1984) 'The New Institutionalism: Organizational Factors in Political Life', *European Union Politics*, vol. 2(1), pp. 103–21.

Markides, A. (2002) 'UN Secretary General's Plan for the Settlement of the Cyprus Problem: Comments for the Information of the National Council' (in Greek), Office of the Attorney General of the Republic of Cyprus, 12 November 2002.

Markides, K. (1977) *The Rise and Fall of the Cyprus Republic* (New Haven: Yale University).

Marks, G. & Hooghe, L. & Blank, K. (1996) 'European Integration from the 1980s: State-Centric v. Multi-Level Governance', *Journal of Common Market Studies*, vol. 34(3), pp. 341–78.

Marks, G. & Wilson J. C. (2000) 'The Past in the Present: A Cleavage Theory of Party Response to European Integration', *British Journal of Political Science*, vol. 30(1), pp. 433–59.

Martin, A. & Ross, G. (2004) (eds), *Euros and Europeans: Monetary Integration and the European Model of Society* (Cambridge: Cambridge University Press).

Mattila, M. (2004) 'Contested Decisions: Empirical Analysis Voting in the European Union Council of Ministers', *European Journal of Political Research*, vol. 43, pp. 29–50.

Maurer, A. & Wessels, W. (eds), (2001) *National Parliaments on their Ways to Europe: Losers or Latecomers?* (Baden-Baden: Nomos).

Meehan, E. (2000) 'Europeanization and Citizenship of the European Union' in Harmsen, R. & Wilson, T. (eds), *Europeanization: Institutions, Identities and Citizenship* (Amsterdam: Rodopi).

Melakopides, C. (2006) *Unfair Play: Cyprus, Turkey, Greece, the UK and the EU*, Martello Papers 29 (Kingston, Ontario: Centre for International Relations, Queen's University).

Meny, Y., Muller, P. & Quermonne, J.L (1996) (eds), *Adjusting to Europe: Impact of the European Union on National Institutions and Policies* (London: Routledge).

Meny, Y. and Wright, V. (1985) *Centre–Periphery Relations in Western Europe* (London: George Allen and Unwin).

Metcalfe, L. (1994) 'International Policy Coordination and Public Management Reform', *International Review of Administrative Sciences*, vol. 60, pp. 271–90.

Michael, M. & Zanias, G. (1999) 'Cyprus Agriculture and the Common Agricultural Policy', *Ekonomia*, vol. 3(2), pp. 125–40.

Milward, A. (2000) *The European Rescue of the Nation-States*, 2nd edn (London: Routledge).

Mitchell, J. (2002) 'Corruption and Clientelism in a 'Systemless System': The Europeanization of Maltese Political Culture', *South European Society & Politics*, vol. 7(1), pp. 43–62.

Monar, J. (2006) 'Justice and Home Affairs', Annual Review, *Journal of Common Market Studies*, vol. 44, pp. 101–17.

Monar, J. (2003) 'Justice and Home Affairs: Europeanization as a Government-Controlled Process', in Dyson, K. & Goetz, K. (eds), *Germany, Europe and the Politics of Constraint* (Oxford: Oxford University Press).

Morlino, L. (1998) *Democracy Between Consolidation and Crisis: Parties, Groups and Citizens in Southern Europe* (Oxford: Oxford University Press).

Moravscik, A. (1998) *The Choice for Europe: Social Purpose and State Power from Messina to Maastricht* (New York: Cornell University Press).

Moravcsik, A. (1993) 'Preferences and Power in the European Community: A Liberal Intergovernmentalist Approach', *Journal of Common*

Mouritzen, H. and Wivel, A. (2005) (eds), 'Constellation Theory' in idem *The Geopolitics of Euro-Atlantic Integration* (London: Routledge).

Muller, P. (1995) 'Les politiques publiques comme construction d'un rapport au monde' in A. Faure, G. Pollet and P. Warin (eds), *La construction du sens dans les politiques publiques, debates autour de la notion de referential* (Paris: L'Harmattan).

Murray, A. & Wanlin, A. (2006) *The Lisbon Scorecard: Can Europe Compete?* (London: Centre for European Reform).

Nascimbene, B. (2000) 'Immigration Legislation Reform in Italy: The International and European Community Frameworks, Revue des Affaires Européennes', *Law & European Affairs*, pp. 94–106.

Naurin, D. (2007) 'Network Capital and Cooperation Patterns in the Working Groups of the Council of the EU', RSCAS WP 2007/14 (Florence: European University Institute).

NEI (2002a) 'Key indicators for Candidate Countries to Effectively Manage the Structural Funds', *Principal Report*, Final Report, prepared by the NEI Regional and Urban Development for the EC DG REGIO/DG ENLARGEMENT, Rotterdam, February, 2002.

NEI (2002b) 'Key indicators for Candidate Countries to Effectively Manage the Structural Funds', *Country Reports*, prepared by the NEI Regional and Urban Development for the EC DG REGIO/DG ENLARGEMENT, Rotterdam, February, 2002.

NEI (2002c) 'Key indicators for Candidate Countries to Effectively Manage the Structural Funds', *Sectoral Reports*, prepared by the NEI Regional and Urban Development for the EC DG REGIO/DG ENLARGEMENT, Rotterdam, February, 2002.

Nicolet, C. (2001) *United States Policy Towards Cyprus: 1954–1974* (Mohnesee: Bibliopolis).

Norton, P (ed.) (1996) *National Parliaments and the European Union* (London: Frank Cass).

Nugent, N. (2006) 'Cyprus and the European Union: The Significance of its Smallness, Both as an Applicant and a Member', *Journal of European Integration*, vol. 28(1), pp. 51–71.

Nugent, N. (2000), 'EU Enlargement and the 'Cyprus Problem', *Journal of Common Market Studies*, vol. 38(1), pp. 131–50.

Nuttall, S. (1992) *European Political Cooperation* (Oxford: Clarendon Press).

Nyikos, S. (2007) 'Courts' in Graziano, P. & Vink, M. (eds), *Europeanization: New Research Agendas* (Basingstoke: Palgrave Macmillan).

O'Hearn, D. (2001) *The Atlantic Economy: Britain, the US and Ireland* (Manchester: Manchester University Press).

Ohrgaard, J.C. (1997) 'Less than Supranational, More than Intergovernmental: European Political Cooperation and the Dynamics of Intergovernmental Integration', *Millennium: Journal of International Studies*, vol. 26(1), pp. 1–29.

O'Malley, B. & Craig, I. (1999) *The Cyprus Conspiracy* (London: I.B. Taurus).

Olsen, J. (2002) 'The Many Faces of Europeanization', *Journal of Common Market Studies*, vol. 40(5), pp. 921–52.

Page, C. (2003) 'Europeanization and the Persistence of Administrative Systems' in J. Hayard & A. Menon (eds), *Governing Europe* (Oxford: Oxford University Press).

Pagden, A. (2002) 'Europe: Conceptualizing a Continent', in Pagden, A. (ed.) *The Idea of Europe: From Antiquity to the European Union* (Cambridge: Cambridge University Press).

Panayiotopoulos, P. (1999) 'The Emergent Post-Colonial State in Cyprus', *Commonwealth and Comparative Politics*, vol. 37(1), pp. 31–55.

Papadakis, Y. (1993) 'The Politics of Memory and Forgetting in Cyprus', *Journal of Mediterranean Studies*, vol. 3(1), pp. 139–54.

Pappas, S. (ed.) (1995) *National Administrative Procedures for the Preparation and Implementation of Community Decisions* (Maastricht: EIPA).

Peristianis, N. (2006) 'Cypriot Nationalism, Dual Identity, and Politics', in Papadakis *et al.* (eds), *Divided Cyprus: Modernity, History and an Island in Conflict* (Bloomington: Indiana University Press).

Peterson, J. (2004) 'Policy Networks' in T. Diez & A. Wiener (eds), *European Integration Theory* (Oxford: Oxford University Press).

Pierson, P. (1996) 'The Path to European Integration: A Historical Institutionalist Analysis', *Comparative European Politics*, vol. 29(2), pp. 123–63.

Pinto, A. & Teixeira, N.S. (eds), (2002) *Southern Europe and the Making of the European Union, 1945–1980s* (New York: Columbia University Press).

Poguntke, T. *et al.* (2007) 'The Europeanization of National Party Organizations: A Conceptual Analysis', *European Journal of Political Research*, vol. 46, pp. 747–71.

Pollack, M. (2004) 'The New Institutionalisms and European Integration', in T. Diez & A. Wiener (eds), *European Integration Theory* (Oxford: Oxford University Press).

Porta, D, & Caiani, M. (2006) 'The Europeanization of Public Discourse in Italy: A Top-Down Process?', *European Union Politics*, vol. 7(1), pp. 77–112.

Potter, D. (1997) 'Explaining Democratization' in Potter *et al.* (eds), *Democratization* (Cambridge: Polity Press).

Pridham, G. (2005) *Designing Democracy: EU Enlargement and Regime Change in Post-Cummunist Europe* (Basingstoke: Palgrave Macmillan).

Pridham, G. (1996) 'Environmental Policies and Problems of European Legislation in Southern Europe', *South European Society and Politics*, vol. 1(1), pp. 47–73.

Pridham, G. & Cini, M. (1994) 'Enforcing Environmental Standards in the European Union: Is There a Southern Problem?', in M. Faure, J. Vervaele & A. Waele (eds), *Environmental Standards in the EU in an Interdisciplinary Framework* (Antwerp: Maklu).

Radaelli, C. (2004) 'Europeanization: Solution or Problem?', *European Integration Online Papers*, vol. 6(16), pp. 1–26.

Radaelli, C. (2000a) 'Wither Europeanization? Concept Stretching and Substantive Change', *European Integration Online Papers*, vol. 4(8), pp. 1–25.

Radaelli, C. (2000b) 'Policy Transfer in the European Union: Institutional Isomorphism as a Source of Legitimacy', *Governance: An International Journal of Policy and Administration*, vol. 13(1), pp. 25–43.

Radaelli, C. & Bulmer, S. (2004) 'The Europeanization of National Policy?', *Queen's Papers on Europeanization*, n. 1, pp. 1–24.

Regelsberger, E. de Schoutheete, P. & Wessels, W. (eds), *Foreign Policy of the European Union: From EPC to CFSP and Beyond* (London: Lynne Rienner).

Richmond, O. (2006) 'Shared Sovereignty and the Politics of Peace: Evaluating the EU's 'Catalytic' Framework in the Eastern Mediterranean', *International Affairs*, vol. 82(1), pp. 149–167.

Richmond, O. (2001) 'UN Mediation in Cyprus, 1964–1965: Setting a Precedent for Peacemaking?' in Richmond, O. & Ker-Lindsay, J. (eds), *The Work of the UN in Cyprus* (Basingstoke: Palgrave Macmillan).

Richter, H. (2003) 'Introduction' in Richter, H. & Fouskas, V. (2003) (eds), *Cyprus and Europe: The Long Way Back* (Möhnesee: Bibliopolis).

Richter, H. & Fouskas, V. (2003) (eds), *Cyprus and Europe: The Long Way Back* (Möhnesee: Bibliopolis).

Risse, T. (2004) 'Social Constructivism and European Integration' in T. Diez & A. Wiener (eds.) *European Integration Theory* (Oxford: Oxford University Press).

Rizopoulou-Egoumenidou, E. (1996) 'The Economy of Cyprus Under Ottoman Rule' in in V. Karageorghis & D. Michaelides (eds), *The Development of the Cypriot Economy: From the Prehistoric Period to the Present Day* (Nicosia: Lithiographica).

Rohrschneider, R. & Whitefield, S. (2006) 'Political Parties, Public Opinion and European Integration in Post-Communist Countries: The State of the Art', *European Union Politics*, vol. 7(1), pp. 141–60.

Rokkan, S. (1999) *State Formation, Nation-Building, and Mass Politics in Europe: The Theory of Stein Rokkan*, edited by P Flora with S. Kuhnle and D. Urwin (Oxford: Oxford University Press).

Rokkan, S. (1980) 'Territories, Centres, and Peripheries: Toward a Geoethnic–Geoeconomic–Geopolitical Model of Differentiation Within Western Europe' in Gottmann, J. (ed.) *Centre and Periphery: Spatial Variation in Politics* (London: Sage).

Royo, S. & Manuel, P.C. (2003) 'Some Lessons from the Fifteenth Anniversary of the Accession of Portugal and Spain to the European Union', in Royo, S. & Manuel, P.C. (eds), *Spain and Portugal in the European Union: The First Fifteen Years* (London: Frank Cass).

Rose, R. (1991) 'What is Lesson Drawing?', *Journal of Public Policy*, vol. 11, pp. 3–30.

Rosetti, C. (1994) 'Constitutionalism and Clientelism in Italy' in Roniger, L. & Günes-Ayata, A. (eds.) *Democracy, Clientelism and Civil Society* (Boulder: Lynne Rienner).

Rynning-Roederer, C. (2007) 'Agricultural Policy', in Graziano, P. & Vink, M. (eds), *Europeanization: New Research Agendas* (Basingstoke: Palgrave Macmillan).

Rustow, D. (1967) *The Cyprus Conflict and United States Security Interests* (Santa Monica, California: Rand Corporation).

Sartori, G. (1970) 'Concept Misinformation in Comparative Politics', *American Political Science Review*, vol. 64(4), pp. 1033–53.

Scherpereel, J.A. (2003) 'Appreciating the Third Player: The European Union and the Politics of Civil Service Reform in East-Central Europe', Paper Presented at the Annual Meeting of the American Political Science Association, Philadelphia, August.

Schimmelfennig, F. & Sedelmeier, U. (eds), (2005) *The Europeanization of Central and Eastern Europe* (Ithaca: Cornell University Press).

Schmitter, P. (2003) 'Democracy in Europe and Europe's Democratization', *Journal of Democracy*, vol. 14(4), pp. 71–85.

Schmitter, P. (2001) 'International Context and Consolidation' in Whitehead, L. (ed.) *The International Dimensions of Democratization: Europe and the Americas* (Oxford: Oxford University Press).

Scholte, J.A. (2000) *Globalization: A Critical Introduction* (London: Macmillan).

Schuster, L. (2000) 'A Comparative Analysis of the Asylum Policy of Seven European Governments', *Journal of Refugee Studies*, vol. 13(1), pp. 118–32.

Sepos, A. (2005a) 'The National Coordination of EU Policy: Organizational Efficiency and European Outcomes', *Journal of European Integration*, vol. 27(2), pp. 169–90.

Sepos, A. (2005b) 'The Europeanization of the Cyprus Central Government Administration: The Impact of EU Membership Negotiations', *Journal of Southern Europe and the Balkans*, vol. 7(3), pp. 369–87.

Sepos, A. (2005c) 'Differentiated Integration in the EU: The Position of Small Member States', *EUI RSCAS Working Paper*, No. 2005/17 (Florence: European University Institute).

Smith, M. (2000) 'Conforming to Europe: The Domestic Impact of EU Foreign Policy Cooperation', *Journal of European Public Policy*, vol. 7(4), pp. 613–31.

Smith, M. (1998) 'Rules, Transgovernmentalism, and the Expansion of European Political Cooperation' in Stone-Sweet, A. & Sandholtz, W. (eds), *European Integration and Supranational Governance* (Oxford: Oxford University Press).

Soetendorp, B. & Hanf, K. (1998) 'Conclusion: The Nature of National Adaptation to European Integration' in K. Hanf & B. Soetendorp (eds.) *Adapting to European Integration: Small States and the European Union* (London: Longman).

Soetendorp, B. & Hosli, M. (2000) 'Negotiations in the European Union: The Hidden Influence on Council Decision-Making', *International Studies Association Conference Paper*, 14–18 March.

Sorensen, G. (1993) *Democracy and Democratization: Processes and Prospects in a Changing World* (Boulder: Westview Press).

Spence, D. (1999) 'The Coordination of European Policy by Member States', in Westlake, M. *The Council of the European Union*, (2nd edn) (London: Cartermill).

Stavridis, S. (2006) 'Towards a European Solution of the Cyprus Problem? Assessing the Views of Some (Greek) Cypriot MEPs', Working Paper (Fundacion SIP Zaragoza).

Stefanou, C. (2005) (ed.) *Cyprus and the EU: The Road to Accession* (Aldershot: Ashgate).

Stefanidis, I.D. (1999) *Isle of Discord: Nationalism, Imperialism and the Making of the Cyprus Problem* (London: Hurst & Company).

Stephens, R. (1966) *Cyprus: A Place of Arms* (London: Praeger).

Stone Sweet, A. & Sandholtz, W. (1998) 'Integration, Supranational Governance, and the Institutionalization of the European Policy' in W. Sandholtz & A. Stone

Sweet (eds), *European Integration and Supranational Governance* (Oxford: Oxford University Press).

Stone Sweet, A., W. Sandholtz, and N. Fligstein (eds), (2001) *The Institutionalization of Europe* (Oxford: Oxford University Press).

Svetlicic, M. (1997) Small Countries in the Transforming European System: Their Honeymoon or Twilight?, Paper Presented at the ECRP Workshop on Small States in the Transforming European System, Ljubljana, 2–5 May 1997.

Taggart, P. (1998) 'A Touchstone of Dissent: Euroscepticism in Contemporary Western European Party Systems', *European Journal of Political Research*, vol. 33, pp. 363–88.

Taggart, P & Szczerbiak, A. (eds.) (2004) 'Choosing the Union: The 2003 EU Accession Referendums', *West European Politics*, Special Issue, vol. 27(4).

Talmon, S. (2006) 'The European Union – Turkey controversy over Cyprus or a Tale of Two Treaty Declarations', *Chinese Journal of International Law*, vol. 5(3), pp. 579–616.

Theophanous, A. (2000) 'Prospects for Solving the Cyprus Problem and the Role of the EU', *Publius: The Journal of Federalism*, vol. 30(1), pp. 217–41.

Thomson, M. (2006) 'Migrants on the Edge of Europe: Perspectives from Malta, Cyprus and Slovenia', *Sussex Migration Working Papers*, June issue, (Sussex: Sussex Centre for Migration Research).

Thorhallsson, B. (2006) 'The Size of States in the European Union: Theoretical and Conceptual Perspectives, *Journal of European Integration*, vol. 28(1), pp. 7–31.

Thorhallsson, B. (2000) *The Role of Small States in the European Union* (Aldershot: Ashgate).

Tocci, N. (2007) *EU and Conflict Resolution: Promoting Peace in the Backyard* (London: Routledge).

Tocci, N. (2004) *EU Accession Dynamics and Conflict Resolution: Catalysing Peace or Consolidating Partition in Cyprus?* (Aldershot: Ashgate).

Tonra, B. (2001) *The Europeanization of National Foreign Policies: Dutch, Danish and Irish Foreign Policy in the European Union* (Aldershot: Ashgate).

Tonra, B. (1997) 'The Impact of Political Cooperation' in Jorgensen, K. (ed.) *Reflective Approaches to European Governance* (London: St Martin's Press).

Tornaritis, C. (1979) *State Law of the Republic of Cyprus* (in Greek).

Triandafyllidou, A. & Spohn, W. (2002) *Europeanization, National Identities and Migration: Changes in Boundary Constructions Between Western and Eastern Europe* (London: Routledge).

Trimikliniotis, N. & Demetriou, C. (2005) *Active Civic Participation of Immigrants in Cyprus*, POLITIS (Oldenburg: Universitat Oldenburg)

Tsakonas, P.J. (2001) 'Post-Cold War Security Dilemmas Greece in Search of the Right Balancing Recipe' in P.J. Tsakonas & Yiallouridies, C. (eds), *Greece and Turkey after the End of the Cold War* (New York & Athens: A.D. Caratzas).

Tsardanidis, C. (1988) *The Politics of the EEC–Cyprus Association Agreement 1972–1982* (Nicosia: Cyprus Research Centre).

Tsardanidis, C. & Ifestos, P. (1991) *The Relationship of Cyprus with the European Communities, 1972–1990* (Athens: Papazisis Publications) (in Greek).

Tsardanidis, C. & Nicolau, Y. (1999) 'Cyprus Foreign Policy: Options and Challenges', in Couloumbis, T., Stavridis, S., Veremis, T. & Waites, N. (eds), *The*

Foreign Policies of the European Union's Mediterranean States and Applicant Countries in the 1990s, London: St'Martins/Macmillan Press.

Tsoukalas, D. & Loizides, I. (1999) 'Regional Aspects of the Cyprus Economy and the Impact of the EU Structural Funds', *Ekonomia*, vol. 3(2), pp. 141–56.

Ugur, M. (2003) 'Mind the Gap: Unification, EU Membership and Regional Disparity in Cyprus, *Ekonomia*, vol. 6(1), pp. 53–71.

Ugur, M. (2000) 'Europeanization and Convergence via Incomplete Contracts? The Case of Turkey', *South European Society and Politics*, vol. 5(2), pp. 217–43.

Van de Goor, L. *et al.* (1996) (eds.) *Between Development and Destruction: An Inquiry Into the Causes of Conflict in Post-Colonial States* (London: Macmillan Press).

Vasilara, M. & Piaton, G. (2007) The Role of Civil Society in Cyprus, *The Cyprus Review*, vol. 19(2), pp. 107–21.

Vassiliou, G. (2004) *Cyprus–European Union: From the First Steps to Accession* (Athens: Katanioti) (in Greek)

Vassiliou, G. (1976) 'Trade Agreements between the EEC and Arab Countries of the Eastern Mediterranean and Cyprus' in A. Shlaim & G.N. Yannopoulos (eds), *The EEC and the Mediterranean Countries* (Cambridge: Cambridge University Press).

Venizelos, K. & Ignatiou, M. (2002) *Kissinger's Secret Files: The Decision to Dissect* (Athens: Livani Press).

Verheijen, T. (2002) 'The European Union and Public Administration Development' in Central and Eastern Europe' in R. Baker (ed.) *Transitions from Authoritarianism: The Role of Bureaucracy* (Westport CT: Praeger).

Vink, M. (2003) 'What is Europeanization? And other Questions on a New Research Agenda', *European Political Science*, vol. 3(1), pp. 63–74.

Vink, M. (2002) 'Negative and Positive Integration in European Immigration Policies', *European Integration Online Papers*, vol. 6(13).

Vink, M. (2001) 'The Limited Europeanization of Domestic Citizenship Policy', *Journal of Common Market Studies*, vol. 39(5), pp. 875–96.

Waever, O. (1995) 'Identity, Integration and Security: Solving the Sovereignty Puzzle in EU Studies', *Journal of International Affairs*, vol. 48(2), pp. 389–431.

Waever, O., B. Buzan, M. Kelstrup & P. Lemaitre (1993) *Identity, Migration and the New Security Agenda in Europe* (London: Pinter).

Wallace, H. (1996) 'Relations between the European Union and the British Administration' in Y. Meny, P. Muller & J-L. Quermonne (eds), *Adjusting to Europe* (London: Routledge).

Wallace, H. (1971) 'The Impact of the European Communities on National Policy-Making', *Government and Opposition*, vol. 6(4), pp. 520–38.

Wallace, W. (1999) 'Small European States and European Policy-Making: Strategies, Roles, Possibilities', *Arena Report*, No. 1, pp. 3–26.

Watson, M. (2006) 'Growing Together? – Prospects for Economic Convergence and Reunification in Cyprus', Paper Presented at ECPR Joint Sessions of Workshops, Nicosia, 25–30 April.

Watson, M. & Noe, W. (2005) 'Convergence and Reunification in Cyprus: Scope for a Virtuous Circle', *ECFIN Country Reports*, vol. 2(3), pp. 1–7.

Weiler, J.H. (1991) 'The Transformation of Europe', *Yale Law Journal*, vol. 108(8), pp. 2403–83.

Wessels, W. & Rometsch, D. (1996) (eds), *The European Union and Member States. Towards Institutional Fusion?* (Manchester: Manchester University Press).

White, B. (2001) *Understanding European Foreign Policy* (Basingstoke: Palgrave Macmillan).

Whitehead, L. (2002*) Democratization: Theory and Experience* (Oxford: Oxford University Press).

Wimmer, A. (1997) 'Who Owns the State? Understanding Ethnic Conflict in Post-Colonial Societies', *Nations and Nationalism*, vol. 3(4), pp. 631–66.

Wolf, D. & Zangl, B. (1996) 'The European Economic and Monetary Union: Two-Level Games and the Formation of International Institutions', *European Journal of Political Research*, vol. 2(3), pp. 355–93.

Wong, R. (2007) 'Foreign Policy' in Graziano, P. & Vink, M. (eds), *Europeanization: New Research Agendas* (Basingstoke: Palgrave Macmillan).

Wright, V. (1996) 'The National Coordination of European Policy-Making: Negotiating the Quagmire', in Richardson, J. (ed.) *European Union: Power and policy-making*, London: Routledge.

Yannopoulos, G.N. (1977) 'Trade Preference and Economic Development: An Appraisal of the Mediterranean Policy of the EEC', *Lo Spettatore Internazionale*, vol. 12(3), July–September, pp. 186–201.

Zubek, R. (2005) 'Europeanizing from the Centre: Collective Action, Core Executive and Transposition of Community Legislation in Poland', *West European Politics*, 28 (3).

Index